YOM

KIPPUR

יום כפור

THE DAY OF ATONEMENT

Rabbi Jim Appel

OlivePress
צהר זית

יום כפור The Day of Atonement
Appointed Times Series - Yom Kippur

Copyright © 2016 by Rabbi James Appel

Printed in the USA
ISBN 978-1-941173-15-2

1. Jewish Holidays 2. Messianic Judaism 3. Spiritual Growth

Published by

Olive **P**ress Messianic and Christian Publisher
www.olivepresspublisher.org
olivepressbooks@gmail.com

Our prayer at Olive Press is that we may help make the Word of Adonai fully known, that it spread rapidly and be glorified everywhere. We hope our books help open people's eyes so they will turn from darkness to Light and from the power of the adversary to God and to trust in ישוע Yeshua (Jesus). (From II Thess. 3:1; Col. 1:25; Acts 26:18,15 NRSV *New Revised Standard Version* and CJB) May this book in particular reveal more deep meaning in the Jewish roots of our faith.

Front cover image from biblepicturegallery.com and photobucket.com

I dedicate this book to

ישרע

Yeshua
who saved me.

Other books by Rabbi Jim Appel

Yom Teruah, The Day of Sounding the Shofar

Messianic Judaism Class Teacher Book
Messianic Judaism Class Student Book

CONTENTS

CONTENTS IN DETAIL

Terms and Traditions Studied in This Book:

Moadim/Moad (moh-ah-DEEM/moh-AHD), **Appointed Times/ Time**

Yom Kippur (pronounced yohm k'-POOR), **Day of Atonement**

Cohane HaGadol (koh-HANE ha-gah-DOHL), **High Priest**

Scapegoat, the goat that is sent into the wilderness, bearing the iniquities of the people

Yomim Nora'im, also spelled Yomim Norim (yoh-MEEM nor-ah-EEM), the **Ten Days of Awe**

Slikhot, also spelled Slichot (pronounced slee-KHOHT), means "forgivenesses," a forty-five minute group of prayers for forgiveness recited daily before and during the Ten Days of Awe

Erev Yom Kippur, "erev" means "eve"

Kol Nidre service and song (pronounced kohl NEE-dray), meaning "all vows"

T'Shuvah (pronounced t-SHOOV-ah), **repentance**

Al Chet (pronounced ahl-KHET), the confession of a long list of sins

Avodah service (pronounced ah-voh-DAH), when Leviticus 16 is read. It means "work."

See the Glossary for more terms.

Introduction

In the Bible, the Hebrew word used for the Biblical "holidays" is "**Moadim**." Common English translations for this word that you might have seen in your Bibles are "designated feasts" or "feasts of the Lord." But it really doesn't make sense to call them "feasts" because the one we are going to study in this book is a fast! So, if one of the holidays is a fast, how can you call all of them feasts? The *New American Standard* translation calls these days "**Appointed Times**," which is a great term for them because these are times that God has appointed. They are specific times in which He has decided we are to meet with Him. *He* has made the appointment. Here is a list of the Biblical Moadim.

The Biblical Moadim/Appointed Times:

IN THE SPRING
EARLY SPRING:
> **Pesakh** also spelled Pesach (Passover)
> **Unleavened Bread,** seven days long.
> **First Fruits** (Resurrection Day) (the Sunday during those seven days of Unleavened Bread)

LATE SPRING (50 days later):
> **Shavuot** (Feast of Weeks) also called Pentecost

IN THE FALL
THE HIGH HOLY DAYS:
> **Rosh Hashanah** (New Year),
>> Biblically it is called:
>>> Hebrew: Yom Teruah (Day of Sounding the Shofar),
>>> English: Feast of Trumpets.
> **Yomim Nora'im** (Ten Days of Awe)
> **Yom Kippur** (Day of Atonement)

FINAL BIBLICAL MOAD (Begins 4 days after Yom Kippur)
> **Sukkot** (Feast of Tabernacles), eight days long

When we make an appointment with somebody, we set the agenda. So these are days for which God has set the agenda. The **Moad** (singular for one "Appointed Time") we'll study in this book is known as **Yom Kippur** to Jewish people and in the Tanakh (Hebrew Old Testament) and as the **Day of Atonement** in English Bibles.

First of all, let me quickly summarize the first of the two Fall Feasts called the **High Holy Days**. If you've read my book, *Yom Teruah*, you know that on the first of the month called Tishrei, we celebrate **Yom Teruah—Rosh Hashanah—the Feast of Trumpets**. Remember God calls it a "shabbaton zih-kh'ron teruah," a Sabbath of remembrance with the blowing of the Shofar and the shouting for joy. And what do we remember and shout for joy about? We remember God's goodness, His might, His power, and His awesomeness. Then, it is obvious if you look on a calendar that there are ten days between that time of remembrance and this **Day of Atonement.** They are called the **Yomim Nora'im,** the **Days of Awe**, a time for repenting, and appreciating who God is and be in awe of Him, preparing ourselves for Yom Kippur, the Day of Atonement.

Yom Kippur is the most holy day of the whole year to Jewish people. It is the second and the holiest of the two **High Holy Days**. It is a very serious, somber, sacred day.

In the Bible, Yom Kippur is the day the High Priest ("Cohane HaGadol" in Hebrew) entered the Most Holy Place, also called the Holy of Holies, taking the blood of the sacrificed animals and sprinkling it on the Mercy Seat to make atonement for the sins of the people. We will study this in depth in the first chapter.

Yom Kippur is also the day, in the Bible, when the High Priest had to casts lots over two goats. One was chosen as the **scapegoat** and the other was sacrificed. I will explain this in detail in Chapter 1. We will also look at what this means for us today in several other places in this book.

After the Temple was destroyed in 70 CE (Common Era), the Yom Kippur sacrifices, including the scapegoat, could no longer be made. However, the Jewish people continued to keep this most holy of all Moadim by observing several traditions set up by the Rabbis. The first is observing the **Yomim Nora'im**, the **Ten Days of Awe** leading up to Yom Kippur. Traditionally, these ten days are for repenting and making things right with God and others. The rabbis added the tradition of the **Slikhot,** a forty-five minute group of prayers for repentance and forgiveness, to be recited daily before and during the **Ten Days of Awe.**

The second major Yom Kippur tradition is that we have always fasted on this day because the Bible says to "**afflict your souls.**" We will study what this means throughout the book. On the Hebrew calendar, a day begins in the evening, so the **fast** begins the night before, called **Erev (eve) Yom Kippur.** The service that evening, on **Erev Yom Kippur,** is called the **Kol Nidre service,** which means "All Vows." It is when the famous **Kol Nidre** song is sung, a song of confession born out of necessity in the Middle Ages when Jewish people were forced to denounce Judaism, and **vow** to be faithful Catholics, or face death. On Yom Kippur, they repented before God for these false **vows** made under extreme duress. The **Kol Nidre** song is a most beautiful, mournful song that was made famous in Barbara Streisand's movie, *Yentle.* (There are several different renditions of this touching song on YouTube.) In Chapter 10, we will look at the meaning the Kol Nidre tradition has for us today.

Other Jewish traditions for the day of Yom Kippur include: **wearing white**, spending all day at the synagogue in repentance and prayer, reading the **Al Chet** (the confession of a long list of sins), doing the **Avodah** (meaning "work") **service** in which Leviticus chapter 16 is read, and during which lying prostrate in reverence and repentance is the response when the parts about the **Cohane HaGadol**/High Priest going in and out of the Holy of Holies is read. (We will look at these traditions again in Chapter 2.)

Why We Celebrate the Moadim/Biblical Feasts

Because the New Covenant says we are no longer under the Law, some people ask, "Why should we, as New Covenant believers, celebrate the Jewish holidays? Didn't Yeshua bring in a New Covenant with a new set of rules to live by? Aren't we saved by grace, and not by keeping festivals?" Yes, we are saved by grace. But, let's look at what Yeshua said about the Law.

Matthew 5:17 *"Don't think that I have come to abolish the Torah (Law) or the Prophets. I have come not to abolish but to complete. 18 Yes indeed! I tell you that until heaven and earth pass away, not so much as a yud (Hebrew "y" which looks like an apostrophe) or a stroke will pass from the Torah—not until everything that must happen has happened. 19 So whoever disobeys the least of these mitzvot (commandments) and teaches others to do so will be called the least in the Kingdom of Heaven. But whoever obeys them and so teaches will be called great in the Kingdom of Heaven. 20 For I tell you that unless your righteousness is far greater than that of the Torah-teachers (Scribes) and P'rushim (Pharisees), you will certainly not enter the Kingdom of Heaven!"*

Yeshua spoke this to Jewish people in the context of a culture that observed the Law. Now let's look at what the Book of Acts shows us about the Law.

In Acts 21 Sha'ul (Paul) was giving a report to the leaders of the Messianic Jewish Community in Jerusalem of his work spreading the Good News among the Gentiles.

Acts 21:20 *On hearing it, they praised God; but they also said to him, "You see, brother, how many tens of thousands of believers there are among the Judeans, and they are all zealots for the Torah (Law).*

In some translations Acts 21:20 says, *"many myriads of Jews believed and were all zealous for the law"* Myriads = ten thousands. Many myriads = many ten thousands. That's a lot of people!!

Acts 21:21 *Now what they have been told about you is that you are teaching all the Jews living among the Goyim (Gentiles) to apostatize from Moshe (Moses), telling them not to have a b'rit-milah (circumcision) for their sons and not to follow the traditions.*

Before the leaders of the Messianic Jewish community in Jerusalem, Rabbi Sha'ul was accused by Messianic Jews, who kept the Law (Torah), of teaching the Jewish people who were living in the Diaspora (dispersion of the Jewish people among the nations) to forsake the Laws of Moses. But it is very clear that this was a false accusation.

Acts 21:22-24 *What, then, is to be done? They will certainly hear that you have come. 23 So do what we tell you. We have four men who are under a vow. 24 Take them with you, be purified with them, and pay the expenses connected with having their heads shaved. Then everyone will know that there is nothing to these rumors which they have heard about you; but that, on the contrary, you yourself stay in line and keep the Torah.*

The community leaders instructed Rabbi Sha'ul to participate with four other men in a traditional purification ceremony. Rabbi Sha'ul was willing to do what they asked him to do, in order to prove the accusation was untrue. So, he himself was a Torah (Law) observant Messianic Jew.

And listen to what Sha'ul said when he journeyed to Rome.

Acts 28:17 *After three days Sha'ul* (Paul) *called a meeting of the local Jewish leaders. When they had gathered, he said to them: "Brothers, although I have done nothing against either our people or the traditions of our fathers, I was made a prisoner in Yerushalayim* (Jerusalem)*and handed over to the Romans.*

Rabbi Sha'ul denied he ever broke any of the laws or even the customs of the Jewish people

Here's another story in Acts concerning the Law.

Acts 15:23-29 *...with the following letter: From: The emissaries and the elders, your brothers To: The brothers from among the Gentiles throughout Antioch, Syria and Cilicia: Greetings! 24 We have heard that some people went out from among us without our authorization, and that they have upset you with their talk, unsettling your minds. 25 So we have decided unanimously to select men and send them to you with our dear friends Bar-Nabba* (Barnabas) *and Sha'ul, 26 who have dedicated their lives to upholding the name of our Lord, Yeshua the Messiah. 27 So we have sent Y'hudah* (Judas) *and Sila* (Silas), *and they will confirm in person what we are writing. 28 For it seemed good to the Ruach HaKodesh* (Holy Spirit) *and to us not to lay any heavier burden on you than the following requirements: 29 to abstain from what has been sacrificed to idols, from blood,*

from things strangled, and from fornication. If you keep
yourselves from these, you will be doing the right thing.
Shalom (Peace)!

This council in Jerusalem declared that Gentile believers
(I'm not using the word, *Gentile*, in a derogatory way but only to
mean non-Jewish people) did not have to keep the Law, but they
didn't say that the Jewish people didn't have to!

It's important to understand that this declaration applied
only to the Jewish Laws of the Bible. These are those laws that
were given by God specifically to the Jewish people to keep us
a distinct people. They include the Moadim or Biblical Holidays,
circumcision, and the food laws. The council was not saying that
the Gerim Mishikhim (Gentile believers) did not have to obey
God's moral or spiritual laws. His moral laws concern relations
between human beings, like Exodus 20:13 *Do not murder.* His
spiritual laws concern relations between people and God, like
Exodus 20:3 *You are to have no other gods before me.* And
Proverbs 3:5-6 *Trust in ADONAI with all your heart; do not rely*
on your own understanding. In all your ways acknowledge him;
then he will level your paths.

When Rabbi Sha'ul uses the term "not under the law" in
Galatians 5:18, he means "not saved—not made right with
God—not justified—by the law." He does not mean we are no
longer subject to God's laws. We will still experience the negative consequences of breaking His laws and the blessings of
obeying His laws.

In Acts, the headquarters of the whole new Messianic faith
was in Jerusalem. Years later, all Jews, including the Y'hudim
Mishikhim (Messianic Jews) were scattered by the Romans.
The first time was after the destruction of the Temple in
70 CE. The second was after the destruction of Jerusalem in
135 CE. Many from among the believers went out and spread
the Good News to the Jewish and Gentile peoples throughout
the Roman Empire. The early congregations started and led by
these Y'hudim Mishikhim would have been much like Messianic
congregations today. It would have been Y'hudim Mishikhim
keeping the laws, traditions, and customs of Judaism with Gerim
Mishikhim (Gentile believers who join with Messianic Jews) participating in as much of these as they were led by the Ruakh
HaKodesh (Holy Spirit) to do.

With Jerusalem destroyed and Jewish people forbidden by the Roman government to re-enter the area for a hundred years, I believe the Messianics, both Jewish and Gentile, began to think that traditional non-Messianic Judaism was about to become extinct. But, what about all God's promises to Israel in the Scriptures that had not yet been fulfilled? I think they rationally concluded that the Body of Messiah would receive those promises instead of non-Messianic Jewish people whose religion seemed to be about to disappear from the face of the Earth. This rational conclusion led to the rise of Replacement Theology which holds that the Body of Messiah has replaced the Jewish people in God's plan, claiming all the wonderful promises of the Bible for Messiah's Body, while allocating all the curses to the non-Messianic Jewish people.

But, then a surprising thing happened. Rather than disappearing when Jerusalem was destroyed, non-Messianic Judaism began to thrive and grow along side Messianic Judaism in the cities of the Roman Empire. This flourishing of non-Messianic Judaism contradicted the Replacement Theology of the Messianics.

Over the early centuries, the Gerim Mishikhim (Gentile Believers) began to outnumber the Y'hudim Mishikhim (Messianic Jews) in the Body of Messiah. Because the non-Messianic Jewish people refused to acknowledge Yeshua as Messiah and were a living testimony that Replacement Theology was not correct, the theologians and leaders of the Body of Messiah began to hate them and see them as a people cursed by God.

Since Jerusalem was no longer the headquarters, the leaders all got together in the year 325 CE (Common Era) in what is called the Council of Nicea. They were convened by the Roman Emperor Constantine to unify the faith. The terrible new rules that developed following that meeting were this:

- Sunday was substituted for the seventh day Shabbat (Saturday)

- The Holy Week was substituted for the Moadim of Pesakh, Unleavened Bread, and Firstfruits

- Keeping of Shabbat and the Moadim was forbidden.

- It was now a crime to practice Jewish customs or traditions.

So, the Christian faith that had started among Jewish people who had been directed by the Ruakh Ha Kodesh not to burden Gentiles with Jewish rules, had now turned completely against Biblical, Jewish customs, and was completely unfriendly to Jewish Believers. Eventually Jewish Believers who continued the "crime" of practicing any form of Judaism were being punished with the death penalty.

*   *   *

Another question people often ask is "Why do Gentiles celebrate these Jewish holidays? Are they trying to be Jewish?" There are four answers.

First, they have an understanding that because Yeshua was Jewish and lived in the Jewish culture they can understand Him better when they understand His culture better. Understanding a culture is best accomplished by living within it. Thus, they are enriching their faith by learning to understand the Jewish roots of their faith.

Second, they have a love for the Jewish people so they love being around Y'hudim Mishikhim (Messianic Jews), worshipping with them, and celebrating with them.

Third, some of them want to distance themselves from the history of those in centuries past, who, in the name of "Christianity," persecuted the Jewish people.

Fourth, a few of them want to be treated the same way the Torah commands foreigners to be treated:

> Exodus 19:48-49 *If a foreigner staying with you wants to observe ADONAI's Pesach, all his males must be circumcised. Then he may take part and observe it; he will be like a citizen of the land. ... 49 The same teaching is to apply equally to the citizen and to the foreigner living among you.*

> Numbers 15:15 *For this community there will be the same law for you as for the foreigner living with you; this is a permanent regulation through all your generations; the foreigner is to be treated the same way before ADONAI as yourselves.*

Prayer

Let's pray and ask the Lord to reveal what He wants us to understand about His Word.

Lord, we thank you that we can study Your Word. We thank You that it is a lamp to our feet and a light to our eyes. We have Your Word in our hands, on our desks, in our bookcases, on our computers, and in our iPads and our smart phones. Thank You for this age that we live in, where there is such an abundance of Your Word, oh God. And Lord, yet, no matter how many ways in which we have it, if it isn't alive and speaking to our hearts it is really not worth anything. But Lord, we know that You want to bring it alive to us. We ask that we would have understanding as we look into it. So we pray for our hearts to receive what You have for us, oh God. Open up our minds. Open up our hearts, in the Name of Yeshua. Amen.

CHAPTER 1

THE HIGH PRIEST ON YOM KIPPUR

Yom Kippur Explained

I am really excited about what the Lord gave me to share in this book. I've been a rabbi for more than eighteen years, and every year, as we get close to a holiday, I ask God what more can I say? But there is always something new and it always amazes me and blesses me.

Yom Kippur is one of the Moadim, one of the Appointed Times of the Lord that He commanded Israel to keep. It is an "appointment" set by the Lord. When someone makes an appointment, they have a reason. If someone in my congregation makes an appointment with me, they wouldn't like it if I controlled the whole time and never asked them what they wanted to see me about. God has set the agenda for Yom Kippur, and we need to find out what it all is.

The Hebrew words, יום כפור "Yom Kippur" mean "Day of Atonement." This day is keyed on one word. The word is "atonement." "Yom" means *day* and "kippur" means *atonement*. The actual meaning of the word "kippur" is *to cover, to cleanse, to forgive, and to pardon.* We get the word **kippah** from it—the little cap that Jewish men and boys wear. I wear one. My kippah covers my head. Kippur is the covering over of sin and iniquity.

Let's look, now, in the chapter in the Bible where God's calendar is laid out and see what He designed for this Moad (singular for Moadim).

Leviticus 23:27 *Also the tenth day of this seventh month shall be the Day of Atonement. It shall be a holy convocation for you. You shall afflict your souls and offer an offering made by fire to the Lord.*

Leviticus 16:31 *It is a Sabbath of solemn rest for you, and you shall afflict your souls. It is a statute forever.*

How long is that? Forever. So this is to be done forever.

Now the way we have always interpreted this word "afflicting our souls" is as *fasting*. Jewish people all over the world fast from sundown to sundown. I really don't like fasting, yet this is my favorite holiday. Why? Because it so much shows the love of God, in that we need a covering, and He made a way for us to have this covering.

Yom Kippur was the most important day of the ancient Israelite religious year because this was the day atonement was made for the sins of the entire Nation of Israel. This did a very important thing for the nation. It enabled the presence of God to dwell in their midst. You see, God's plan for the children of Israel was that He would be there with them in a visible presence, but He cannot dwell where there is sin. (Keep reading to find out why.) So, atonement had to be made.

Yom Kippur is not a day of remembrance of an important past event, like Passover and Sukkoth (The Feast of Tabernacles) are. In Old Testament times, Passover was for remembering events surrounding the Exodus from Egypt. Today it also commemorates the sacrificial death and resurrection of Yeshua. Sukkoth, which comes four days after Yom Kippur, is when we remember the wandering in the desert and living in tents. But the Day of Atonement is not for remembering an event. For Israel, this was a day of doing business with God—the business of receiving atonement for the sins of the entire nation, which was a necessary condition for the manifest presence of God—the Shekinah glory—to dwell amongst them.

Atonement

Why exactly is atonement needed? Well, let me explain it in a slightly unusual way. God is a just God. He is a God of justice. Every sin will be punished and every good deed rewarded either in this life or in the next life. As a child I didn't think punishment was a very good idea because I was always getting into trouble and I did not like getting punished all the time. But when I became a father, I began to see the necessity of justice. If you are a parent, have you seen its necessity? I found out that if I didn't do something when my child did something wrong, they would do it again. This became even more clear to me when I had two children because often times I had to do something to stop their bad behavior or they would hurt each other.

When I was a child, I wanted justice when somebody hurt me. We all want justice when we are treated badly. We also all want justice when somebody hurts someone we love. Well, God feels the same way!

God is omniscient. He knows everything. He knows all the things that each of us do. He sees us and He loves each of us, His creations. And so when we hurt each other, this grieves His heart; and as a good father, He must carry out justice.

So, how does He carry this out? He has very high standards. *Be perfect, even as your Father in heaven is perfect* (Matt. 5:48). He calls us to standards that are exemplified in the life of Yeshua. That's our standard to live up to—Yeshua's character. Of course, God knew that none of us would be able to live up to those standards, to the laws He had set. **Therefore,** as a loving Father, way back in the time of Moses—when the Israelites came out of Egypt 3500 years ago—He gave the Jewish people the sacrificial system to deal with their sins. When we sinned, if we were sorry for our sin and repented, we could sacrifice an innocent animal from our flocks and that innocent animal would pay the price for our sins and we would be forgiven and free of guilt and shame.

So, God made ways for us to become right with Him, even if we had messed up. And those ways are recorded in the early part of Leviticus. We are instructed in how to make sacrifices for an individual sin. If I had done something, if I had lied, but was sorry for that lie and repented, I could bring an animal from my flock and offer the sacrifice and be forgiven; be made right with God again.

Now, this is such a significant part of the Law of Moses or the Torah. It's not just a couple of verses. If you want to read about it, the first nine chapters of the book of Leviticus deal with nothing else but the sacrificial system, what the sacrifices are for and how to do each of them.

But God knew in His great wisdom that even these individual sacrifices would not be sufficient. He knew, and this is so awesome about the wisdom of our God, that even if He made that provision available—that we could all bring animals to sacrifice— that there would be times when we would forget, or we wouldn't realize that we had sinned. He knew we would miss some or that we would deny some, "Oh no, I didn't really do that." He knew that we would ignore some of the things and not believe that we were guilty, even though we were, or that we even might say, "I'm not gonna do that! I don't want to give up an animal of my flock to be right with God." So, He made a day once a year when there would be a sacrifice for all the Israelites, that would cover all their sins for that year. That is what the Day of Atonement was all about and that was what allowed the Israelites to live as He told us to live—as a Holy people with God dwelling in the midst of us. He wanted to dwell with the Nation of Israel, because He wanted to be our God, so He said once a year I am going to have a sacrifice made for the whole nation so I can continue to dwell with them.

Now, the Bible teaches us that God is omnipresent. He is everywhere. Everywhere in the universe. But at times God makes Himself known in a way that we experience with our five senses, and that is called the "manifest presence" of God. Because God is holy, that is, He is separate from sin, when God comes and dwells amongst us in His manifest presence, we must be cleansed before we can be in that presence. So, this is what atonement is all about. Ancient Israel was to be a nation with their God dwelling in their midst. So something had to be done. The verse that really speaks to this is in Exodus 33. The Children of Israel had sinned against God and God said, "*Go up to the land, but I'm not going to go with you.*" In verse 3, He tells why. He says: "*Go up to the land flowing with milk and honey, for I will not go in your midst, lest I consume you on the way, for you are a stiff-necked people.*"

So, you see, it wouldn't have hurt *God* to come into the midst of an unholy people—un-atoned-for people—it would have hurt the *people*. They would have been consumed, burned up, because of His holy Presence. So, Yom Kippur is the day of making atonement for the nation so that God's manifest presence could dwell among them, first in the Tabernacle in the Wilderness and then in the Temple that Solomon built.

This is a law of the universe that most people don't understand. The presence of God cannot be in the presence of uncleanness. God's holy presence would have consumed them (Exodus 33:3). Why was it important to the people that God's manifest presence dwelt in their midst? God's presence brought protection, provision, justice and blessing to the entire nation. Now, we still have need of God's presence in our midst today and we have the same problem today. If we want to be in God's presence in a greater way, we need atonement.

Cohane HaGadol/High Priest Duties

In Leviticus chapter 16, we find some very detailed instructions for the High Priest—the "Cohane HaGadol" in Hebrew (כהן הגדול "The Great Priest"). It gives all the details of how and when and with what he is to do in the Holy of Holies where the Ark of the Covenant was and where God appeared on the Mercy Seat.

Lev. 16:6 *Aharon (Aaron) is to present the bull for the sin offering which is for himself and make atonement for himself and his household.*

So before Aaron could make atonement for the nation, he had to make atonement for himself. The book of commentary on the Torah—the Talmud—tells us that if the High Priest's heart was not right before God, he would die when he went into that

Holy Place. God had instructed them to put bells on the hem of the High Priest's blue robe—a bell then a pomegranate, a bell then a pomegranate all the way around (Ex. 28:31-34), so one might think that the ringing of the bells would have helped to ensure them he was still alive, but for Yom Kippur, God's instructions are for the High Priest to wear only white linen garments while going into the Holy of Holies (Lev. 16:4,23-24). It is said that they had a rope tied around his ankle that led to the outside of the curtain, so they could drag him out if he died.

I want you to try to imagine being the Cohane HaGadol, the High Priest. A little scary, isn't it? I had to portray the High Priest in a theater production in Rochester. It was a little scary even acting it out.

The Talmud tells us there was great fear amongst the people that the Cohane HaGadol, the High Priest would not come out. If he didn't, the sins of the people would not be covered for that year. So, there was great concern because they needed their sins to be covered for another year.

Yomim Nora'im, The Days of Awe

Now, here's the question to think about. The priest, the Cohane HaGadol, took this bull he was supposed to take and he made a sacrifice for himself with it. So if he made that sacrifice for his own sins, why would he die when he got inside? Well, because God not only looked at the sacrifice, but also at the heart. If his heart was not right, that would be the thing that would cause him to die. Pride or unbelief or other sins might cause him to not come out of the Holy of Holies.

So, now can you imagine what the Cohane HaGadol, the High Priest would have done in the days leading up to Yom Kippur? He would have been in introspection and repentance, right? "Lord, show me. Is there anything in me that you don't find pleasing before I go in there?" It would have been heavy upon him to do soul searching. This eventually became something that the people began to do too, because they began to understand that "as for the priest (the cohane), the same for the people."

Because the appointed time of Rosh Hashanah, the Feast of Trumpets [Biblically in Hebrew called Yom Teruah (the Day

THE HIGH PRIEST ON YOM KIPPUR

of Sounding of the Shofar)] occurs ten days before Yom Kippur, it became the traditional starting day for all the people to do their soul searching leading up to Yom Kippur. These ten days became known as the Yomim Nora'im, the Days of Awe.

Pharisee Revival

It was the Pharisees that helped bring about that thinking. The Pharisees get a bad rap in the New Covenant, but the Pharisaic movement was a great revival. This was a hundred or so years before Yeshua. The key of that revival was the idea that every man was like a priest and his house was like a temple and his table was his altar. The philosophy was that we all have to live like the cohanim—like the priests—and be holy like they are required to be. This is what we see in the New Covenant. So all the people would have adapted to this idea that, leading up to Yom Kippur, we need to get our hearts right before God. The Cohane HaGadol is going in for us, but he is representing us. We need to have our hearts right before God, too.

Yeshua, the Final Atonement

I am often asked, "How is Yom Kippur relevant to you, as a Messianic Jew, today? Why do you fast and pray if Yeshua has already made atonement for all time? Aren't you confident of His atonement?" Yes, I am! Those of us who believe in the Messiah, know that there has been a final atonement made. In the Book of Romans it says that we who trust in Him are justified freely by His grace, through the redemption that came by Messiah, Yeshua. (See Romans 3:24.)

God presented Yeshua as a sacrifice of atonement that through faith in His shed Blood, we are made holy. However, as we read in Leviticus 16, the Cohane HaGadol made atonement for himself and his household so that he could make sacrifices for the rest of the people. Followers of Yeshua are what the Bible calls "A Royal Priesthood," so we are cohanim (plural for cohane) and we are called to intercede for the nations—for our own nation, for the Jewish people, and for the nations around us. So we need to make sure our hearts are right before God before we go into intercession. So I take the Ten Days of Awe very seriously and ask the Lord to reveal sin in my life. And I take Yom Kippur seriously too and pray for atonement for my nation and for the Jewish people who don't know the Messiah yet.

This system of atonement went on for 1,500 years, from the time of the Tabernacle in the Desert until the year 70 CE, when the second Temple was destroyed. That's when the sacrifice of the animals ceased.

Cohane HaGadol Duties, a Closer Look

Now let's look at the High Priest's duties a little closer to see how the atonement was made. What did the Cohane actually have to do?

Leviticus 16:2 *And the Lord said to Moses, "Tell Aaron, your brother, not to come just at any time into the Holy Place, inside the veil, before the Mercy Seat, which is on the Ark, lest ye die. For I will appear in the cloud above the Mercy Seat.*

Aaron was the High Priest—the Cohane HaGadol. Here we have an admonition to Aaron not to come just any time into the Most Holy Place. The Most Holy Place was in the Temple, separated from the Holy Place by a big curtain. Inside was the Ark of the Covenant. On top of that was the Mercy Seat where God Himself would appear and bring mercy to the people. The only time the Cohane HaGadol could come in was on the tenth day of the seventh month, which is Yom Kippur.

Leviticus 16:3,6 *"Here is how Aharon* (Aaron) *is to enter the Holy Place: with a young bull as a sin offering and a ram as a burnt offering. ... Aharon is to present the bull for the sin offering which is for himself and make atonement for himself and his household.*

So, as we noted before, this particular bull was for Aaron's own sin. First, he went in and made atonement for himself and his family, by offering the blood of that bull.

Two Goats

Then he began to make atonement for the whole nation. Two goats were selected and lots were cast over the goats; one for the Lord and one for the scapegoat. Verse 9 tells us what would happen with the goat that was chosen for the Lord.

Leviticus 16:9 *"Aaron shall bring the goat on which the Lord's lot fell, and offer it as a sin offering. Then he shall kill the goat of the sin offering, which is for the people, bring its blood inside the veil, and do with that blood as he did with the blood of the bull, and sprinkle it on the Mercy Seat, and before the Mercy Seat."*

So, there were two goats. There were lots drawn for the two goats; one was chosen for a sin offering. That goat was slain in the usual manner, its blood captured in a basin and brought into the Holy of Holies and sprinkled on the Mercy Seat, for the atonement for all the people's sins.

Now, there are a few things to understand here. This goat was killed very humanely. We have to understand that the humane, kosher butchering process comes down to us from the way these animals were sacrificed. I don't want to gross anybody out, but the way they were killed was with a very sharp knife, slitting the throat. Accounts of this say that the animal lost consciousness in two seconds because all the blood quickly drained out from the brain. To a tiny degree, you may have experienced blood draining from your brain if you've ever fainted. That's why you faint—because blood leaves your brain—everything goes black and you pass out. Your body kind of shuts down immediately to protect the vital organs, including the brain. So the animal lost consciousness right away and really didn't experience any pain. And this blood was sprinkled on the Mercy Seat. Remember that this was the only day of the year that the Cohane was able to go into this place where this Mercy Seat was. So that was the atonement with the blood of one goat.

Scapegoat

Now let's read about the other goat.

Leviticus 16:21 (NKJV) *Aaron shall lay both his hands on the head of the live goat, confess over it all the iniquities...*

(Your Bible might have a different word there, but let me assure you, I looked it up, and the proper translation is "iniquities." The New King James has "iniquities." That's why I'm using that version here. There are three words in Hebrew for sin, and this is the word that is rightly translated as "iniquities" in many places.)

Leviticus 16:21b-22 (NKJV) *... of the Children of Israel and all their transgressions concerning all their sins, putting them on the head of the goat, and shall send it away into the wilderness by the hand of a suitable man. The goat shall bear on itself all their iniquities to an uninhabited land, and he shall release the goat in the wilderness.*

Now, this goat was called the scapegoat (*azazel* in Hebrew). We have a special meaning in English for "scapegoat." It is when somebody takes blame for something they didn't do; when they take the blame, either willingly or unwillingly, for something somebody else did. So, the iniquities of the people were placed upon this goat. The innocent goat was taking the blame, so to speak, for the people's shortcomings and failures. And I want you to look at the wording of this very carefully, because this goat was to bear, or carry, the iniquities of the Israelites. So what we can see here is that iniquity is atoned for by being carried away by the scapegoat, not by a sacrifice and the sprinkling of blood.

When I first read about this in the Scriptures, I thought this was the lucky goat. But that isn't the case. You have to understand that the Judean wilderness is somewhat like the United States' Death Valley.

Verse 21 says that after Aaron has thus placed all the sins, transgressions, and iniquities on the head of the scapegoat, he is to send it into the desert "*by means of someone designated for the task*" (NRSV). Have you ever noticed those words before? I always thought they just sent the goat on his way alone! But God specifically instructed that someone take him. The designated man took the goat out the East Gate to the wilderness. This would be going the direction of the Mount of Olives. On the other side of the mountain, the land is nothing but barren, rocky, sandy mountains and very deep, treacherous ravines. The Talmud records that people set up stations in the desert along the way to give this man a drink and even food if he needed it for the arduous journey. But Yom Kippur is supposed to be a day of fasting. So it is recorded that none of these men over the centuries ever took of the food. The man led the goat by a scarlet cord that was tied around its horns when it received the lot, of which a piece was cut off and later hung on the Temple door for all to see (more about that cord later).

The Bible only says to send the goat away into the desert, so they used to do that. They let the goat go there in the middle of nowhere. It is very hot and dry at this time of year, so the goat would have wandered around till it died of thirst and dehydration, which could have taken several days—and would have been a very miserable way to die.

The Scapegoat Came Back!

But here's what we learn in the Talmud. You wouldn't know this unless you studied the ancient Jewish writings because it really isn't stated in the Scriptures. One year this goat, that was supposed to carry away all the sins of the people, found his way back into the city of Jerusalem, the scarlet cord still around its horns! This was quite disturbing to the people!! Their sins had returned to haunt them!!! It was like their guilt was coming back upon their heads.

The priests decided to make sure it would never happen again. So the Talmud says that from that year on they kept the following tradition. The man led the scapegoat to the top of a very high, steep precipice, brought it to the edge, and pushed it off into the deep rocky gully to its death. It would die of the bruising from the fall. This demonstrates a very important picture for us. We need to grasp this. It is one of the key things to understand. What it demonstrates is that it took a greater sacrifice to atone for iniquity than it did for sin. Do you see that? It took a suffering sacrifice to make atonement for iniquity.

Sin and Iniquity

So now, to have an even better understanding of what the scapegoat did, we need to understand two words that are important here. What do the words "sin" and "iniquity" mean, and are they really different? I mean, when I first read the Bible I thought they were just synonyms, and you know, just for some reason the translators decided to change the wording in order to keep it from being boring, or something. But they are not synonyms. They are very different Hebrew words.

I want to give credit for this understanding to Messianic leader, David VanSlyk. We used to have his teaching on this on our web site, shemayisrael.org. (Now you can read his teaching here, http://davidvs.net/religion/concept-iniquity.shtml.) Interestingly, I got an e-mail from a minister somewhere in the West, who had come to our web site and saw David's teaching there, and he was so excited because he had never seen an explanation of this before. I forwarded the e-mail on to David. The minister even sent an offering because he was so thrilled with what he found on the web site. So this is really significant, I believe.

The word that is translated "sin" in the Old Testament is the Hebrew word "*khatahah*" (one of those spitting words). What it means is *unlawful acts: breaking of a written or spoken commandment of God.* It is something we actually do, yet do unintentionally. It is also sometimes defined as missing the mark. Like not doing something that you were trying to do, missing the mark. So that is *khatahah.* That's the word that should be translated "sin." Now, there is another word. We learned about this at our Passover one year, when Bert Schlossberg, an Israeli kept it with us. There is the word that is translated "transgression." That is actually the Hebrew word "*pesha"* which means intentional sin. That is when you know it's wrong and you do it. Bert Schlossberg called it "organized crime."' It was like when you conspire to do something and you know it's wrong and you just do it.

Now, I want you to note the difference between iniquities and sin. The first goat was for sin. The second goat, it says over and over again here, was for iniquities. Iniquities are defined as the evil inclinations of our hearts. In the New Covenant, it is called our fleshly nature, our carnal nature. What it means is, the promptings we have to do evil things—to do ungodly things, and the promptings are there even if we don't act on them. So, this goat was to atone for the iniquities of the children of Israel; not things that they had done, but just attitudes and desires that they had that were evil, even if they resisted them. Sin is an actual breaking of the law, something you do; whereas iniquity can be just an attitude of the heart.

For instance, we all know that the Ten Commandments are the commandments of God that tell us that we shouldn't do certain sins, but there is one of the Ten Commandments that has nothing at all to do with sin; it just has to do with iniquity. Do you know what that is? "You shall not covet." You see, to covet, you don't do anything wrong. It's simply something in your heart. You want something that somebody else has. Probably most of us could recognize a time when we were guilty of that iniquity. So, iniquities need to be dealt with, even if they are not acted on, in order to come into God's presence.

Notice also that the sin, the *khatahah,* was atoned for by an animal which was painlessly, humanely sacrificed. Remember, the first goat was sacrificed in the kosher way (its throat slit with a very, very sharp knife), which is very humane; it died instantly, without any suffering. So the goat that was sacrificed for sin never felt any pain; whereas, the scapegoat, as we noted above, suffered in a very awful way. It was taken out into the wilderness and pushed off a cliff causing it to die an agonizing, slow, painful death. It was a terrible way to die, but the point is very, very clear. It takes more to atone for Iniquity than for sin. **The scapegoat was "bruised and crushed" to death from the fall off the cliff. Yeshua was beaten and bruised. His suffering was for our iniquities—our tendency toward sin. Our iniquity cost our Savior a greater price than our sins did.**

Now, Leviticus 17:11 says, *It is the blood that makes atonement.* So how can bruising make atonement for our sin nature? There is no shed blood in bruising. Or is there? Think about what a bruise is. What is it that turns the wound all shades of red and purple or black and blue? Blood! Bruising is internal bleeding! So it *is* blood—painful bleeding that atones for our iniquities, **so that God's Spirit—the very presence of God can dwell IN us.**

Rejoicing for the Atonement

Now, in the Talmud, it is recorded that the High Priest, the Cohane HaGadol went in and out of the Holy of Holies three times. And each time he went in and came out, he led the people in a confession of sin: First for repentance of his own sin, then for the repentance of the priesthood, and then for the repentance of all the people. Each time the Cohane came out the people repented and prostrated themselves.

The people waited anxiously in the Temple courts for the completion of the sacrifices, because they needed to know that God had accepted their sacrifices; that their sins were forgiven; and that He would come and dwell with them for another year. And, of course, they were wondering if the Cohane HaGadol would come out because it was dangerous to go in there, into the presence of God. Remember the rope tied around his leg so he could be dragged out in case he was struck dead.

The Talmud records that in the days of the Temple, after the High Priest was finished—after he went into the Holy of Holies and out again those three times and everybody repented, and they knew that he had successfully made the sacrifice and sprinkled the blood on the altar and the Mercy Seat—after all that, the mood shifted from a very solemn mood to joyfulness. They rejoiced when he came out the third time because there was a tangible sense that atonement had actually been made. It was real. They really knew it had happened. So, Yom Kippur ended in great joy.

The Talmud also speaks of a cord tied around the doors of the Temple. When the atoning sacrifice of the scapegoat was made the Talmud tells us that the tradition was to tie a crimson or scarlet cord around the doorknobs of the Temple doors. The Talmud goes on to record that when the scapegoat died, that scarlet cord would mysteriously and miraculously turn white, and the people once again would have great joy in this further confirmation that the atonement for their iniquity had been made.

Isaiah 1:18 *Though your sins be as scarlet, they shall be white as snow. Though they are as crimson, they shall be like wool.*

CHAPTER 2

YOM KIPPUR TRADITIONS

N ow I would like to take a look at Jewish traditions for celebrating Yom Kippur. It is a very solemn, very holy day to
observant Jewish people. In fact, it is the most important, the
highest, and the holiest day of the year to nearly all Jewish people everywhere. Whether they are observant or not, the rest of
the year, most Jewish people go to synagogue on Yom Kippur.
Just as many non-church-going Christians do go on Christmas
and Easter, most non-observant Jewish people celebrate
Passover and honor Yom Kippur.

Fasting

The most prominent feature of the traditional observance of
this day is fasting. Why? Because it is repeated three times in
the passages in Leviticus that we are to "afflict our souls." In
the synagogue (and I completely agree with this) the traditional
reading for the day is Isaiah 58, which talks about what a true
fast is—that true fasting is setting prisoners free and helping the

hungry. So it brings forth that sense of social justice, if you will, as being the true fast. We will look into that Isaiah chapter in great depth later in Chapter 15.

Yomim Nora'im/Ten Days of Awe

As mentioned, there are ten days between Rosh Hashanah (Yom Teruah or the Feast of Trumpets) and Yom Kippur. These Ten Days are a time of examining yourself and your relationships and setting things right, even making restitution, if necessary. In Rabbinic tradition, it is believed that Elohim decides your fate for the next year between Rosh Hashanah and Yom Kippur, whether you will live another whole year and whether your name will be written in the Book of Life.

Rosh Hashanah is the Jewish civil new year. One of the traditional greetings on Rosh Hashanah is "L'shanah Tovah Tikkah Tevu." "L'shanah Tovah" means "to a good year." "Tikkah Tevu" means "May your name be inscribed." So, the greeting is "May your name be inscribed (in God's Book of Life) for a good year." On Yom Kippur, the greeting is "L'shanah Tovah Tikkah Tevu v'Tikkah Temu" - "May your name be inscribed *and sealed* for a good year"

Those Ten Days are called, as I told you before, "Yomim Nora'im" ("Days of Awe") because they lead up to the most holy day of the whole year, Yom Kippur. They are also called the "Aseret Yemei T'shuvah"—"Ten Days of Repentance." (There is much more on these Ten Days in later chapters and in my book, *Rosh Hashanah, Yom Teruah, Day of Sounding the Shofar.*)

In Jewish tradition, these Ten Days are set aside for soul-searching—for examining our deeds and attitudes. It's a time to turn from evil, to devote more time to Torah (Bible) study, to performance of its precepts, and to giving to charity. And also, most importantly, as mentioned, it's a time to make amends for misdeeds against others.

This time is very similar to the Christian tradition of Lent. The similarity becomes especially marked when you realize that for the whole month before Rosh Hashanah, the month of Elul, the Shofar is blown every morning to remind people of the upcoming Days of Awe, and to remind them to begin to make their hearts ready for repentance.

Slikhot

Maimonides, the great Jewish scholar from the Middle Ages who wrote the Mishna, wrote this prayer for these days:

> Awake you that are sleepy, and you that slumber awake from your slumber, and ponder your deeds, remember your Creator, and go back to Him in penitence. You who miss the truth in your hunt after vanities, and waste your years in seeking after vain things that can neither profit nor deliver, look after your own souls, and improve your ways and your deeds. Let everyone of you abandon his evil ways and thoughts and return to God that He may have mercy on you."

This prayer is part of a forty-five minute group of prayers for repentance and forgiveness, called the Slikhot, that are recited daily starting at midnight after the Shabbat before Rosh Hashanah and continuing through the Ten Days of Awe. If Rosh Hashanah falls on a Monday or a Tuesday, these prayers are started two Shabbats before Rosh Hashanah.

Wearing White

Another very prominent tradition in Orthodox congregations is wearing white. I wear a white robe, which is called a kittel. The wearing of white is a reminder of the priesthood. It is understood that the special linen tunic the Cohane HaGadol (High Priest) was to wear on Yom Kippur was white (Lev. 16:4,23). You can also read in Exodus 28:40 what the priestly garments were for the regular priests. It is understood that God instructed that they wear white.

Al Chet, Confession of Sins

As we learned, the Cohane HaGadol came in and out three times from the Holy of Holies, confessing sins and making atonement each time. So, there is repentance on Yom Kippur. Part of the repentance is reading what is called the Al Chet (pronounced Ahl Khet), which is the confession of a long list of sins. This recalls those confessions of sin in the Temple. We will be looking further into the Al Chet later in chapter 12.

Sin of the Golden Calf

Another interesting fact is that traditional Judaism believes it was on Yom Kippur that God forgave the Israelites for worshipping the golden calf at Mt. Sinai. From the Biblical account and from what the Talmud says, they have calculated it. God came down on Mt. Sinai on Shavuot—the Feast of Weeks or Pentecost, which is in late May or early June. Moses went up on the mountain immediately after that. He was up there on the mountain for forty days and nights. Then he came down and saw them worshiping the golden calf they had made. He broke the stone tablets in anger and took time to punish the people. Then he went back up on the mountain to get new tablets of stone. If you put all that together, you come up with it being actually on Yom Kippur when he pleaded on the mountain before God for forgiveness for the Israelites. And so forever this day is seen in Judaism as a day of forgiveness—forgiveness that God extended based purely on His mercy and grace, along with the forgiveness He grants after atonement is made.

After the Temple was Destroyed

Now I would like to go back in time and take a look at the historical background of this day. I want to show you what problem Rabbinic Judaism had when the Temple was destroyed and then I will tell you what they did about it. The destruction of the Temple in the year 70 AD presented a huge problem to Judaism. In fact, it could have caused the disintegration of the whole religion.

To understand the problem, we must go to Scripture. Here's a verse that you all should know.

Leviticus 17:11 *"The life of the flesh is in the blood, and I have given it to you upon the altar to make atonement for your souls. For it is the blood that makes atonement for the soul."*

So, this atonement, or this covering, this kippur, required blood—the shed blood of a sacrificed animal. It had to be blood from a perfect, blemish free, innocent animal. But, look where the sacrifices had to be made.

Leviticus 17: 8, 9 *"An Israelite, or a stranger among you, who offers a burnt offering or a sacrifice..."* (now verse 9) *"and does not bring it to the entrance to the Tent of Meeting, to sacrifice it to the Lord, that man must be cut off from his people."*

Now, do you see the problem? The atoning sacrifices were necessary for God's presence to dwell with the people, but they could only be made at the Temple. You couldn't just do it at home or in a synagogue. And after 70 AD, there was no longer a Temple. Not only was there no longer a Temple, but the Romans had also plowed the Temple Mount. They literally took the Temple down stone from stone and the Jewish people were not allowed to go back there and rebuild that Temple. So, what was to be done?

Rabbinical Judaism:
Prayer, Good Works, and Study of the Bible

Well, there was a great leader of the Jewish people, named Yochanan ben Zakkai. He gathered together the rabbis who did not believe that Yeshua was the Messiah (this was around the year 100) to a place called *Yavneh*, and they had a council there in Yavneh, and decided to declare that the decisions that they made as rabbis, that they all agreed on, would be like Law. They would be as weighty as the Scriptures; as powerful and as binding as the Scriptures upon the people. I can understand why they did this. They felt they had to do this, because the people could no longer obey what God had told them to do. There was no longer a Temple. And so, for them to continue on with their religion they had to do something, and they decided that they would come up with a declaration and a teaching that would enable the people to feel right about God, and to continue to worship God. Their decision was that from now on the atoning sacrifice was not needed—blood was not needed. They decided instead that prayer, good works, and study of the Bible were what made a person right with God.

It sounds really good, doesn't it? It sounds like a wonderful religion. I mean, if I were starting a religion, I would base it on those things, too! Maybe you would also! It is a nice, palatable religion! Unfortunately, it is not the religion of the Bible.

Because, in the Bible we just read what? The blood is what makes atonement.

So, those who followed the rabbis' teachings were, and still are, without a blood atonement. It is the Judaism that we have with us today; we call it Rabbinic Judaism, which says, as I noted above, that a person can be right before God through prayer, good works, and study of the Torah. If you come from a Jewish background, you will recognize that. You've been taught that the way in which a person can be right with God is through obedience to those rules. However, many Orthodox Jews are hoping for the Temple to be rebuilt one day. And do you know why? So they can start making the sacrifices once again. Many who are not Orthodox Jews do not understand the need for blood atonement. But the Orthodox Jews very clearly understand it. We had Gershon Salomon in our synagogue a few years ago, the head of the Temple Mount Faithful. He is zealous to rebuild that Temple. He believes God has called him to rebuild the Temple so that they can re-establish the sacrifices, so that they can have atonement once again.

Kapparot

So, what we have today in Traditional Judaism, for the past 1,946 plus years, is a religion that is based on something other than blood atonement. However, in Traditional Judaism, the result has been that people do not have confidence that their sins have been forgiven. In addition, the Ultra Orthodox have developed a tradition in which we can see this blood atonement very clearly. It is a tradition called the *Kapparot*. (Hebrew: כפרות) Kapparot is something that only very orthodox Jewish people do today. They take a live chicken and hold it over their heads and they recite this prayer: "This is in exchange for us, this is instead of us, this is ransom, Kapparot, for us. This chicken will go to its death, but we may go forward to a good life and unto peace." And then the chicken is slaughtered and given to the poor, which is very nice. But, right in there is a very clear remnant, a remembrance of the need for the blood atonement. A chicken is used because a chicken is never mentioned as one of the animals to be sacrificed. They don't want to in any way make this look like it's a sacrifice because Leviticus 17:9 said you can't make a sacrifice anywhere except at the Temple. So that is why it is a chicken.

Attending Synagogue, Fasting, Reciting Prayers

The traditional practice of Jewish people today is to go to the synagogue and spend almost the whole day in the synagogue fasting, reciting prayers, and seeking forgiveness from God and from those whom they have wronged—which are all wonderful things to do. Most Jewish people have the belief that if they go to the synagogue on Yom Kippur it makes things okay between them and God, that the tradition of fasting and reciting prayers replaces atonement.

Avodah Service

Another tradition that keeps alive this need for atonement is what is called the *Avodah* service (Hebrew: עבודה) at the synagogue. This is when they read the whole chapter of Leviticus 16 where it gives all the instructions of what the Cohane HaGadol is supposed to do. Remember we said he would go into the Holy of Holies three times. Not only was he making atonement inside at the Mercy Seat for himself, but remember he was making atonement for the Holy Place, for the courtyard, for the altar of burned incense, for the altar of burnt offerings, for the people, and for the priests; all of these things had to have atonement made for them, so the presence of God could dwell amongst them. And so, in the traditional synagogue today in the Yom Kippur Avodah service, Leviticus chapter 16 is read. When they get to the part about the Cohane HaGadol coming in and going out the people kneel and prostrate themselves all three times in remembrance and reverence. But again, there is no blood, so there is no Biblical atonement.

So, now we have a question—a very difficult question. If Yom Kippur can no longer be fulfilled, has God forsaken humanity? Heaven forbid! No! He fulfilled it another way. When Yeshua was walking the earth He said: *"Do not think that I came to destroy the Law or the Prophets. I did not come to destroy but to fulfill."* (Matthew 5:17 NKJV).

Isaiah 53:5 (NIV) *He was pierced for our transgressions* (transgressions are specific violations of the Law), *he was crushed [or bruised] for our iniquities.*

The question is, do Jewish people who don't believe in the Messiah believe their synagogue attendance and prayers, etc., on Yom Kippur have been effective? Do they believe that atonement has been made? Well, I've talked to a lot of them, and I have never found one that does. What I find is that their belief in this is not very strong. They're a little bit shaky about it, but that's what they have been told by the rabbis. Why is it shaky? Because it is against what is written in the Bible! Atonement isn't really happening, according to the Word of God. And so it cannot be justified. The traditions are just something that everybody does without really believing in them.

I've talked with many Jewish people, even on the day of Yom Kippur when they are coming out of the synagogue. I ask them "Do you know that atonement has been made and you are right with God?" They almost always answer, "Well, I hope so, nobody can be sure."

It's a sad thing.

Well, that gives you a quick picture of how traditional Judaism keeps Yom Kippur—their highest and holiest day of the year.

CHAPTER 3

SEVEN APPOINTMENTS

Yom Kippur consists of seven appointments. Let's dig deeper into the meaning of Yom Kippur for our own personal lives by looking at each appointment separately. We will learn about them from a message given by an intern of our congregation one year on Yom Kippur. At the time, this former farmer was in his forties and had five grown children.

My wife and I and two of our daughters went to Israel for the first time ever last year over Christmas. I'm the least of the least standing up here on Yom Kippur. I was raised Gentile. I'm a third year student at a Bible college, so I'm still learning. Being raised in a Christian home and in the church these days, you are mostly studying the New Testament. You don't study the Old Testament very much. So I didn't know much about Yom Kippur. I started digging into it about three weeks ago. What I found is that in the instructions for Yom Kippur there are seven appointments.

1. Appointed Purpose

There had to be a purpose for Yom Kippur. The children of Israel have been in the desert, and Moses has gone off and is getting all these laws. The Lord is telling them, "You need to do these things." There is a reason. The purpose goes all the way back to the beginning. Let me give you a quick review. God made the heaven and the earth. It was good. He created man and said that was good. The thing is, He created man with a free will. He didn't want a robot. Nobody wants a robot. No man wants a wife who is just a robot. I don't anyways. They want the person to love them with a free will. The problem is, what snuck in right away is that terrible problem called sin. We can see it right from the start. Adam and Eve sinned. Before that they did have a perfect relationship with the Lord—which is what we are looking for as believers. They had a perfect relationship, but sin took them out of that relationship with God. Because they sinned, you were born in sin. Your every day walk is affected by sin. Your worship is affected by sin. Everything you do is affected by sin now. So, the purpose of Yom Kippur is for that sin to be covered.

Leviticus 16:30 *For on this day, atonement will be made for you to purify you; you will be clean before ADONAI from all your sins.*

The purpose of Yom Kippur was to bring people back into relationship with a Holy God. A sinful people, a sinful nation is being brought back into relationship with God. To go ahead through Biblical history—Adam had children and they were born into sin. You come up to the flood and God makes this state-ment, "I am sorry that I have made man." That is how bad sin is. It causes a Holy God to say, "I'm sorry I made this creation." God is a creating God and whatever He creates, He loves. I want you to get the picture how bad sin is. For a Holy God to say to His creatures that He lovingly and carefully created, "I'm sorry I made them" is unthinkable! But because of sin, it happened.

As we continue, we have Noah. Then we have the flood. This righteous man was saved out of the flood and people began to populate the earth again. Then we get to Abraham. God called Abraham out to conceive a people that would be an example to the rest of the world. Abraham had a son and then grandchildren and God fulfilled the covenant He had with him that out of his seed the rest of the world would be blessed. The problem is, we now have a people that went into Egypt and are there for 400 years. What was in Egypt? Egypt was full of idolatry and immorality. In addition, they were slaves! As a slave, you do as you are told or you disappear. They did remember the God of their fathers, Abraham, Isaac, and Jacob in their houses, though. Finally, the four hundred years were up and God called them out to become a nation. But first He had to get them out of the sins of Egypt and the slavery mindset. So, the purpose of Yom Kippur was to bring the Hebrew nation back into fellowship with God. How do we relate to that today? Well, we are still a sinful people. Sin hasn't changed. Man hasn't changed. Sin wants us. Our nature is still sinful. So, when I started studying Yom Kippur, I thought "Wow. We still need this day today." We have a purpose for Yom Kippur, too. The purpose is to bring us back into relationship, or into a closer relationship, with God.

2. Appointed Time

Why the seventh month and the tenth day? Seven is a perfect number. It is a complete number. To tell you the truth, I don't really know that much about meaning of numbers, but being raised a farmer, this is how I look at it. The appointed timing is perfect. This time of year in New York, as a farmer, you look at your crops. The hay is in. The corn is mostly in. There might be a little bit of corn left to harvest yet. You can make an assessment on what your abundance is. Similarly, it is also the perfect time of year to make an assessment on other things, especially your spiritual life. Vacations are over—the wild summer of going here and there is over. As a farmer, we come to the place where the crops are in from the field and maybe we can relax a little bit. You are supposed to rest, at this time of year during the High Holy Days. Rosh Hashanah is a Sabbath. Yom Kippur is a Sabbath. The first and last days of Sukkot are Sabbath days. That is what the Sabbath is for, even though in America we go all the more harder. The Sabbath is for rest. This is a perfect time to sit and reflect on our spiritual life. That is my take on it. It is the perfect time to sit quiet and reflect—to dig in. To ask the Lord, "What do I need to do differently?" Back to farming, maybe I didn't get much hay this year. Maybe I need to do something different next year to get a better hay crop. It's the same with our spiritual life. We come and say, "What works and what's not going to work." I think we need to do that as individuals and as congregations and even as a nation. We need to stop, look, and reflect.

3. Appointed Place

When God gave the commandment to keep Yom Kippur, the Israelites were in the desert. The place was the Tabernacle. You have the Nation of Israel surrounding the Tabernacle, where God, once again, can meet with the people and man can be in right relationship with Him. They can have communion with Him again. So, God made a place right in the center of the people. In that center was a place called the "Holy of Holies." This is where the Lord came. This is where the Lord can meet with man and make things right again. Here they can meet the Lord and have perfect communion again. What about today? There is no Tabernacle. There is no Holy of Holies as we know it, but through Yeshua there is something better. Today we have the heart, in the center of man. Your heart is your being. Your heart says everything about you. Sin comes from the heart. In fact, the heart is the manufacturing place for sin. If we are out of relationship with the Lord, our heart just keeps putting out sin. You don't go up to Michigan, sit on the Ford line and watch Toyotas being made. It doesn't happen that way. What you see come off the Ford line are Fords. In the same way a wicked heart manufactures wicked things, not good things.

Let's read what Yeshua said about the heart.

Matthew 15:17-20 *Don't you see that anything that enters the mouth goes into the stomach and passes out into the latrine? 18 But what comes out of your mouth is actually coming from your heart, and that is what makes a person unclean. 19 For out of the heart come forth wicked thoughts, murder, adultery and other kinds of sexual immorality, theft, lies, slanders. 20 These are what really make a person unclean, but eating without doing n'tilat-yadayim* (the ceremonial handwashing) *does not make a person unclean.*

Yeshua is saying that sin begins in the heart. The heart is what reveals the true person. The redeemed heart produces good things like gentleness, meekness, and kindness. The redeemed heart is where true worship happens. But the unredeemed heart or the fallen heart produces wrong things. Yeshua's completely pure heart is full of only love for us. He does only good for us, to help us with our wicked, sin-producing hearts, which brings me to the next appointment.

4. Appointed Price

Right from the start, there was a price to pay for sin. And right from the start God showed that it took blood to cover sin when He clothed (covered) Adam and Eve with animal skins.

Leviticus 17:11 *For the life of the flesh is in the blood, and I have given it to you upon the altar to make atonement for your souls; for it is the blood that makes atonement for the soul.*

The Lord God used the blood of animals to cover sins. The price for atoning for sin is blood. Yeshua paid the ultimate price for our sin. He shed His Blood on the cross. Yeshua's Blood was the perfect price to pay for sin. God used Yeshua's Blood to wash away our sin—not just to cover, but to totally do away with our sin. I will illustrate this to you in a minute.

5. Appointed Person

The High Priest was the appointed person for Yom Kippur, and he had his work cut out for him. He had lots of things he had to do. There were the ten days before the actual day that the High Priest had to go over everything he had to do so that it would be perfect. If it wasn't perfect, that was it. Every little step he did had to be perfect, from bathing to carrying the blood in to the Mercy Seat—all the many things he had to do. The High Priest went into the Holy of Holies and here we have the number seven again, but also the number three. First of all, he went in three times. First to bring in the incense and the coals from the altar to burn incense in front of the Mercy Seat. Then to bring blood for his own sins and the sins of his family. Then he had to go back in for the people's sins. He sprinkled the blood once up, then seven times down. It doesn't say why, but God has a purpose for everything.

What about today? Who is the appointed person for Yom Kippur today? I love the scene from John 1:29-34 of John baptizing people—hundreds—a huge crowd—regular people, leaders, rabbis, Pharisees, kings—people from all different backgrounds.

Here's John the Baptist baptizing. Here comes Yeshua. John said, "Behold the Lamb of God." Now, everyone knew that John was a man of God. So when they heard John say that, they knew who Yeshua was. However, the Pharisees later came to try to trick Jesus saying, "Who are you? By what means do you do these things?" Yeshua replied with a question. "Who do you say John is? Is he from heaven or is he from man?" He knew they could not answer that because if they said John was from heaven, then they knew John was right, meaning Yeshua was the Messiah. So, they couldn't say that. But if they say he is from man, then the people would stone them because the people knew—the multitudes knew that John was a man from God. Yeshua was the person in their day. They knew it, but they didn't want to believe it. They didn't want to see it. Yeshua is still the person for us today, not just on Yom Kippur but for every day.

As I read the Old Testament, I ask "How can you not see Yeshua in all of this?" We have 66 books in the Bible written by 40 some men over a 2000 year period all saying the same thing. All pointing to the same person. It amazes me how you can read the Torah and Tenakh and not see Yeshua in everything. In 1869 we had one guy who wrote a theory and the whole world jumped on it—the theory of evolution. Why? It goes back to the heart. People don't want to believe in our Creator God and His Son, Yeshua.

6. Appointed Procedure

The appointed procedure was the sacrifice and the sprinkling of the blood in the Holy of Holies. This passage in Hebrews ties the person, price, and procedure all in one.

Hebrews 9:11-15 (NKJV) *But Christ came as High Priest of the good things to come, with the greater and more perfect tabernacle not made with hands, that is, not of this creation. 12 Not with the blood of goats and calves, but with His own blood He entered the Most Holy Place once for all, having obtained eternal redemption. 13 For if the blood of bulls and goats and the ashes of a heifer, sprinkling the unclean, sanctifies for the purifying of the flesh, 14 how much more shall the blood of Christ, who through the eternal Spirit offered Himself without spot to God, cleanse your conscience from dead works to serve the living God? 15 And for this reason He is the Mediator of the new covenant, by means of death, for the redemption of the transgressions under the first covenant, that those who are called may receive the promise of the eternal inheritance.*

When I read this Scripture, verse 11 really stands out to me. I see a Tabernacle in heaven. I see a Holy of Holies in heaven. I see the blood from the death of Yeshua being sprinkled on that altar to pay for your sins, my sins, everyone's sins, and to cover people. Remember God was sorry that He created people. Now we have the perfect sacrifice. Sheep couldn't do it.

Let me give you an example of how much better Yeshua's sacrifice is than the animal sacrifices. If I take a cloth and put it over a book, you won't be able to see the book anymore. Right? The book is covered. In the same way the blood of the animals covered the people's sins. God chose not to see their covered sins anymore. But the book is still there, even though you can't see it, just as their sin was still there even though God didn't see it. Now I will take the book away so there will be nothing under the cloth. Now not only can you not see the book, the book isn't there at all. That is the same thing Yeshua did. He took sin and removed it. It is not there anymore because of what Yeshua did on the cross. He took our sin away. He removed it completely. And that is what it means by "a perfect sacrifice."

Yeshua shed His blood and it is sprinkled up in heaven. That is one thing that I want to see. It's that altar and the heavenly Tabernacle and the heavenly Mercy Seat. It is there, folks. His blood was sprinkled there for you and me. I just want to run there and ask the Lord if I can see it. I love that picture. I can just picture it all in my mind. God the Father. The Tabernacle. Yeshua at the right hand of the Father. There is the altar. His blood on it for you and me. You can't get a more perfect sacrifice. That is the perfect sacrifice.

So your sins are gone if you have accepted Yeshua's sacrifice. If you haven't done that, this is the time. This is the day to ask Yeshua into your heart to remove the sins. We are sinful people. God was sorry for creating us. It says it in the Word. But Yeshua brought us back into a right relationship with God. Now the Lord takes pleasure in you. What the blood from sheep couldn't do, Yeshua did. Today there is a more perfect sacrifice. When you ask Yeshua into your heart, His blood cleanses you. It makes you a new person. Yes, we're far from perfect. We need to keep working on some things. We need to keep coming to the Lord. We need to "keep on keeping on." Yeshua made the more perfect sacrifice so we can keep going forward.

So up to this point, we have the appointed purpose for us to come back into a right relationship with God. There is the appointed time. "Today is the day of salvation." The appointed place is in our hearts. We don't need to run off to the Tabernacle because of what Yeshua has done. Yeshua is the appointed person. We need to go to Him. There is an appointed price. Yeshua paid the price. The appointed procedure is that Yeshua took the Blood He shed into the heavenly Tabernacle and sprinkled it there before God.

So that is the appointed purpose, appointed time, appointed place, appointed price, appointed person, appointed procedure. There is one more.

7. Appointed Response

What were people supposed to do on Yom Kippur? If I read the Scriptures right, we are supposed to fast. We are supposed to search our hearts. We are supposed to dig in. Okay Lord, where am I not right? This is what Yom Kippur is. It is a good day to take a look at ourselves. Where we came from. Where we need to be. Where we are going.

That is the required response for back then, and it is still a correct response for today, but there is another response for today.

Titus 3:3-7 (NKJV) *For we ourselves were also once foolish, disobedient, deceived, serving various lusts and pleasures, living in malice and envy, hateful and hating one another. 4 But when the kindness and the love of God our Savior toward man appeared, 5 not by works of righteousness which we have done, but according to His mercy He saved us, through the washing of regeneration and renewing of the Holy Spirit, 6 whom He poured out on us abundantly through Jesus Christ our Savior, 7 that having been justified by His grace we should become heirs according to the hope of eternal life.*

So the procedure. We didn't have to do anything. He did it all. All we have to do is give the proper response. Who would not want to give the proper response to the Son of God? The response is accepting Him into your heart, accepting the more perfect sacrifice. The more I say that, the more beautiful that sounds in my ears.

This whole study about Yom Kippur is beautiful. The more I study Biblical Judaism the more the New Testament becomes real to me. It is amazing. I just love studying this stuff. There are people that know a whole lot more about this than I do, but I could write a whole sermon on each of these seven appointments.

So today, if you look into your heart, and you realize you haven't fully accepted Yeshua the Messiah's more perfect sacrifice. If you are not allowing Him to be fully Lord of your life, ask Him in. He will change your heart. You will no longer be sitting there at a Ford plant with Toyotas running off the line. The right stuff will come out of the heart. No more manufacturing of sin. Yeshua takes away the sin.

Salvation prayer

We thank you, Yeshua, that you are our High priest, that You made atonement with Your own blood. Cleanse our hearts, especially if we have never asked this before. Cleanse our hearts from all of the sins of our lives whether they were acci- dental or intentional. We accept Your atonement. We invite You to come in through the veil into our hearts. Take up residence. We believe that because You are in our hearts, what will come out will be good things—things of love and peace and not evil. We ask You to come in and be our Lord.

CHAPTER 4

SIN AND INIQUITY

Three Different Types of Sin

Now we are going to study the three different words for sin in much more depth. So first let's do some review and then we will go deeper. In Lev. 16:21 it says Aaron is to lay his hands on the head of the live goat and confess the iniquities, transgressions, and sins of the people of Israel. To us these three things are just different terms for the same thing—sin. But in Hebrew these terms each mean different things. "Sins" means accidental sins—things we didn't mean to do, or didn't mean not to do. It means unintentional sins. "Transgressions" means our intentional sins—things we know God doesn't want us to do or not do, but we do them or don't do them anyway. "Iniquities" means our natural inclination to sin. It is because of this nature that even good people are sinful. Even good people have to guard against sinning.

Here are the three words that often get confused in the English language.

1. **Khatahah** – *falling short – missing the mark – not living up to God's standards*

2. **Pesha** – *Premeditated sin. Organized crime. Transgression - rebellion*

3. **Avone** – *not an act of sin – but a state of being - description of the character of human beings – carnal nature – inclination to evil – attitudes, ways of thinking. Passed down from generation to generation. Even inanimate things can have avone – not fitting for the presence of the living God. Of this world rather than of the Kingdom of God.*

Clearly, these are three different concepts in Hebrew, and thus in God's mind. Even though in many Bible translations you will see these words just kind of mixed or inter-changed.

During Yom Kippur meetings today, the people recite the Al Chet (pronounced Ahl Khet)("Chet" is a form of the word for sin: "Khatahah.") The Al Chet is a traditional confession together that lists all kinds of sins—sins of commission and omission (doing and not doing) and of intention and un-intention (on purpose and by accident). The list of sins is very long and VERY convicting!! As mentioned before, we will look closely at the Al Chet in Chapter 16.

However, many Jewish people today don't see themselves as sinners before God. One Jewish graduate student was asked about Yom Kippur. She talked about making things right and receiving forgiveness. Then she was asked, "Who are you asking for forgiveness from? Is it from God?" She answered, "No, it isn't from God. It is just from other people and yourself."

No Sacrifice for Iniquity

Now, we're all familiar with sin. A sin is a particular unlawful act; something that we do that is wrong. But iniquity is different. Iniquity is a state of being. It is a description of our character, a description of what we are like. Iniquity is defined as the sinfulness of the heart. In the New Covenant it is our flesh, our carnal nature. It is there even if we don't act upon it. It's why the human heart is not holy. Not set apart. Not perfect. And it is why the human heart, or the innermost being of a human being, is not fit to be a dwelling place for the Presence of God. So, iniquity does not necessarily deal with actions. Iniquity deals with attitudes, feelings, and motivations for action. So, it is not necessarily acted upon, but it is there.

The Torah speaks of a sin offering, but never of an <u>offering</u> to remove iniquity. The Torah speaks of bearing iniquity, but never "bearing" sin (except in Isaiah 53:12 where "chet" for "sin" is most likely being used to encompass sin, iniquity, and trans-gression). The scapegoat of Yom Kippur was the only provision in the Torah for iniquity (avone) to be dealt with. This atonement was carried on for about 1600 years until it stopped in 70 CE (when the Temple was destroyed).

Evil Inclination

Orthodox Judaism has a very good understanding of iniq-uity. They call it the "Yetzer Ra," the evil inclination. In Traditional Judaism today, not in Reformed or Conservative Judaism, but in Orthodox Judaism, there is much discussion (and always has been) about it. I like the term they use because it gives a beau-tiful picture (well, not beautiful, but a very appropriate picture) of what iniquity is. Their description makes me think of an inclined plane, like a hill. If I were to take something like a sled and set it on the edge of a snowy hill, what would happen? It would slide down. That's what the Orthodox Jewish concept of iniquity is all about. It is saying that we as human beings are standing on an incline. If we let ourselves go, if we don't exercise our will and our moral strength, if we don't use restraint and listen to our conscience, we will slide down the slope toward evil. If you're anything like me, you have to resist temptation in order to do good. It takes effort and discipline and strength because we have to kind of fight our way uphill to do the right thing. It's like swimming against the current. Our very nature is inclined toward evil. That's iniquity. It is not necessarily an outward action; it is an inward description of our very nature.

For example, it's easy to be lazy, while it takes effort to *not* be lazy. It is easy to be selfish. It takes effort to not be selfish. It is easy to do a lot of the things that we know are wrong. You know another thing that is really easy to do? Gossip. Have you ever noticed that? Things just kind of slip out easily, right? It takes effort to stop. And that's our evil inclination. That is our iniquity.

Effects of Iniquity

So, what is the effect of iniquity? Well, if you begin to look for it through the Bible, it is amazing how it is there over and over again, used in passages that also use the Hebrew word for sin.

Isaiah 59:2: *Your iniquities have made a separation between you and your God, and your sins have hidden His face from you, so that He does not hear.*

Isaiah uses both words here, showing they are not the same; they are two different things that Isaiah is talking about. So, what does iniquity do? What does it say there? It separates us from God. Now, iniquity and sin are both problems for us. They're problems for us coming into God's presence.

Here is another way to try to grasp what I'm talking about here. You might want to look at these verses in Leviticus and Numbers. When I realized what these verses meant, it really cleared up this whole concept for me, because it just made so much sense.

Leviticus 16:32 *And the Cohen, who was anointed and consecrated to minister as Cohen in his father's place, shall make atonement and put on the linen clothes, the holy garments, and then he shall make atonement for the holy sanctuary, and he shall make atonement for the tabernacle of meeting, and for the altar, and he shall make atonement for the Cohens* [for the priests] *and for all the people of the assembly.*

When I read this passage, it made me ask a few questions. Why would the Holy of Holies, the Tabernacle, and the altar, need atonement? They hadn't sinned, right!? I mean, an altar can't sin. Inanimate objects can't commit wrongdoing. So, why did they need cleansing?

Numbers 18:1 (NKJV) *Then the Lord said to Aaron: "You and your sons and your father's house with you shall bear the iniquity related to the sanctuary, and you and your sons with you shall bear the iniquity associated with your priesthood."*

I read that at another time and I said, "Now, wait a minute," I thought iniquity was an evil inclination, how can the sanctuary have an evil inclination? What does this mean? Why would they need to bear the iniquity of an inanimate object? Well, as I prayed about this, and thought about it, I began to see that what this is talking about is that the sanctuary, as something made out of the materials of this earth, is not fit to hold the Presence of our Glorious God. Something had to be done to enable the Presence of God to come into a physical thing, or else it would be consumed. Does that help you to see what iniquity is like?

So, even material things had to have their iniquity atoned for in order for the Presence of God to dwell within them. That helps us understand iniquity. Even if we don't do anything wrong we need atonement for our iniquity. We are just not worthy of the presence of the Holy God to dwell amongst us. No matter how good we try to be; we'll never be that good.

Now, the Torah mentions sin about three times more often than it mentions iniquity. And that is because in the Torah, laws are being put forth, and the laws deal primarily with actions. But the prophets mention iniquity slightly more often than sin. And that is because the prophets are mostly trying to turn our hearts back to God. They are not dealing with our actions; they are dealing with the attitudes of our hearts. So, back to Yom Kippur, atonement for sin was made by sprinkling the blood of the sacrificed goat on the Mercy Seat on that day, and atonement for iniquity was made by laying the iniquity on the head of the scapegoat, and having it borne away.

God's Solution for Our Iniquity

"But," you might say, "Why do we need Yom Kippur today? We don't have God coming down here in a manifest presence, like a pillar of fire." (We wish we did, but we don't.) Well, the Scripture tells us that God wants to dwell where? In us. So, do we need atonement? Oh my! Do we ever! We have the Spirit of God dwelling right within us. And we talk about coming into God's presence. We say we want to be in His presence. We say we want to see God move; we want to see signs and won-ders—physical manifestations of His presence. So, we need atonement. It wouldn't be that *God* would be hurt if He came down to dwell in us, *we* would! We would be consumed. We would explode. We would blow up if that happened.

Well, if our iniquity keeps us separated from God, and we all have this iniquity, this inclination to evil, and if there is no longer a Temple or a Cohane HaGadol, a High Priest to send the scapegoat into the wilderness, how can we come into God's presence? Well, God gave us the most wonderful solution for that. He, Himself took on the form of a man whose Name is Yeshua (Jesus) the Messiah, and we know that He died on a cross, pouring out His blood for our sins.

In the Book of Matthew, Yeshua said: *"Don't think I've come to abolish the Torah or the Prophets, I have come not to abolish, but to fulfill."* This making of atonement; this is the crux of the Law—the Torah. It is the most important part of the Torah, and it was fulfilled by Yeshua. The fulfillment was predicted, and again I want to show you the words in here. It is so amazing when you see the way the prophet Isaiah used exactly the right words, because he knew exactly what he was talking about. Take a look again at this passage and you will see them.

Isaiah 53:5-6 (NKJV) *But He was wounded for our trans-gressions, He was bruised for our iniquities; The chastisement for our peace was upon Him, And by His stripes we are healed. 6 All we like sheep have gone astray; We have turned, every one, to his own way; And the Lord has laid on Him the iniquity of us all.*

There's that word "iniquity" again. We see it three times in Isaiah 53. Isaiah 53:5-6 talks about atonement for the different types of sins.

"But He was wounded for our transgressions (that's intentional sin), *He was bruised for our iniquities* (that's our evil inclination). ... *All we, like sheep, have gone astray* (that is missing the mark, we've strayed off the mark)*; every one to his own way.* In other words we have all done our own thing, we have all disobeyed and just done things that we wanted to do and not what the Lord wants. That sounds like rebellion (transgression). *And the Lord has laid on Him the iniquity of us all.* There's that word "iniquity" again.

Wounded and Bruised

Now look at the choice of other words there.

*He was **wounded** for our transgressions, **crushed*** (or **bruised**) *for our iniquities* and verse 6 *...the Lord has **laid** on Him the iniquity of us all.* The Hebrew word for "wounded" is "helall" means *to cut, to be pierced through to where blood would flow.* What were the woundings? The nails. For what? For our transgressions, our sins, our actions, both intentional and unintentional. This is also the word describing the way they slit the goat's throat that is sacrificed that I mentioned before. It is the kosher way all sacrificial animals were killed, minimizing pain. It is the method of shedding blood. Yeshua was made to bleed for our transgressions like which goat?. The sacrificed goat. Right! For sin. Not the scapegoat; the sacrificed goat, for our specific violations of God's law.

The word for "crushed" or "bruised" is "dukah" which is referring to a severe beating. Yeshua was bruised for what? *Bruised for our iniquities.* By what? By the beatings, the whippings. I don't know if any of you ever wondered this, but after reading the Gospels and understanding how Yeshua died such an agonizing death, and then reading in the Tanakh, the Old Covenant, about the sacrificed animals, and I began to understand that they died this humane death, I asked, "Why did He have to die such a terrible death?" The death that He died was the most agonizing death that has ever been invented by human beings. This came so much home to me in the Passion of Christ movie.

And I know you might be thinking back to that movie right now, too, if you've seen it. That was just incredible, the amount of time it took to get from the whipping post to the cross. That was just horrific how long that went on if that was anywhere near true. It was almost unbearable just to watch. So now, what we are seeing here, and I pray that you catch this, if you've never caught it before, this explains why the Messiah had to suffer an agonizingly painful death the way He did. It suddenly became clear to me one day. (I touched on it in the first chapter.) Look at the parallel here. His death on the cross was like that scape-goat that was pushed off the cliff and was bruised and beaten by hitting the ground! Slow and agonizing. Those whippings and the beatings were for our iniquities. *He was bruised for our iniquities.*

Instead of dying in a painless way like the sacrificed goat died. And not only the sacrificed goat, by the way, but all the offerings of Israel, all through the year—every offering for sin was always humane. This was the only one where the animal actually suffered. So, instead of dying a humane death, Yeshua willingly suffered agonizing pain in order to bear our iniquities. He also died outside the city—away from the Temple—as the scapegoat was led outside of the Temple and outside the city. What an amazing parallel to the Yom Kippur scapegoat! Remember, He said He came to fulfill.

Matthew 5:17, *Do not think that I have come to abolish the Law or the Prophets. I have not come to abolish them, but to fulfill them.*

The Greek Word for Sin

Now, this understanding clears up a bunch of things in the New Covenant that I want to share with you, because there is much confusion in the New Covenant. The reason is this: There has been a blurring of sin and iniquity because of the Greek language. The Greek language uses the word *hamartia* to mean both "sin" and "iniquity." One word. It is not differenti-ated. *Hamartia* is always translated "sin" and never "iniquity" in many translations, even though its context, if you look for it, is sometimes clearly speaking of iniquity. But it is translated as sin. (Greek does have the word *"anomea"* that the King James

Version translates as "iniquity," but the actual Greek meaning is "*without law*" which is not the same as "avone" at all. It is used only a couple times with the same sense of meaning as the Hebrew word for iniquity. Other times it is just means "sin" or "transgression." A few Bible versions rightly translate the Greek word *"parabasis" as "transgression."* But that Greek word is used only seven times in the New Covenant while "**hamartia**" is used 172 times indiscriminately.) This gives some added weight to the belief that I and many others have that the New Covenant was actually written in Hebrew first, and then was translated into Greek, and only had one word for sin, they just translated both of those Hebrew words into the one word.

Original Sin

So, let me share with you three other areas of confusion this blurring of sin, transgression, and iniquity causes. The first one is the area of original sin. Are you familiar with that? The original sin belief basically says that babies are born with sin. Now with the distinction between sin and iniquity, this suddenly makes sense. It doesn't make any sense for someone to be born sinful, when sin is the violation of a commandment, an action. How can a baby in the womb commit a sin? How can a baby, when it first comes out, be guilty of a sin? But, people are born with a large dose of iniquity.

Children never need to be taught to do what is wrong. Am I not correct? They need to be taught to share, and to speak nicely, etc. They never need to be taught to hit. They never need to be taught to say no and to be rebellious. None of those things! You see, that's the iniquity that we are all born with; that inclination to evil. What it means is that people are not naturally fit for God's presence to dwell in them. It does not mean that people are evil. Sometimes people make that understanding from it. It does not mean that people deserve punishment, or that newborns have broken some commandment. In fact, in the Book of Jonah, God says that there are people who don't know their right hand from their left hand, and that they are innocent; that they are not old enough yet to make decisions about right and wrong. It simply means that people are born with the tendency toward sin. They are not born holy and righteous.

Infant Baptism

Here's another part of this confusion. Back in the Middle Ages, people began baptizing their infants as soon as they were born. In fact, I heard that infant baptism was one of the largest causes of death in the Middle Ages. Really! I don't know for sure that it's true. But they would take these infants and stick them in cold water and, you know what would happen. They would get sick. But why would they do that? It's because their understanding was that the babies were born with sin, and so they had to be baptized or they wouldn't go to heaven. But that's not what the truth is. The truth is that they are born with iniquity. They hadn't done anything that was sin. So understanding the difference between iniquity and sin helps us understand this. Children are born with iniquity not in sin.

Number One Sinner

Okay, the second confusion is the question: Are we still sinners after we have come to know the Lord? Some say yes. Some say no. This is big! Here's what Rabbi Shaul (or Paul) said:

I Timothy 1:15 *Here is a statement you can trust, one that fully deserves to be accepted, the Messiah came into the world to save sinners; I'm the number one sinner!*

Well, that's pretty clear. Right? He doesn't say he WAS the number one sinner; he says I AM the number one sinner. Now, let me ask you this: Does this mean that Paul was constantly breaking the laws of God? Does it mean that he was lying, stealing, committing adultery, more than any other person on earth? What do you think? No, it doesn't mean that. Let's see what else the Bible says about Paul. This is other people talking to him, and telling him to do some things that will show that he is not always sinning.

Acts 21:24 *"Everyone will know that there is nothing to these rumors* [that he was a lawbreaker] *that they have heard about you, but that on the contrary you, yourself, stay in line and keep the Torah."*

So, what are we seeing here? It's like the Bible is contradicting itself. In the one place Paul is saying he is a sinner, and in another place he is saying he keeps all the laws. Well, it is clear, if you understand iniquity. Why does he call himself the number one sinner? It is the other meaning of **hamartia**. He was really calling himself the number one iniquitous person. (I'm coining a new word there). Why? Well, I can explain this, because I experience it. The longer I walk with the Lord the more I am able to see my own iniquity, my own inclination to evil. Are you at that place?

The higher the standard seems to get, the more you begin to catch yourself. Things that, when you were a brand new believer, you thought were just the way you were made. You thought it was just part of your personality. But after ten or twenty years you start to realize, "No, no, I can't get away with thinking like that." "I can't get away with that attitude."

So, over time we see more of our iniquity. I believe it is because of what this verse says.

Hebrews 4:12 *The word of God is alive. It is at work and is sharper than a double-edged sword, and it cuts right through to where the soul meets the spirit and the joints meet the marrow, and it is quick to judge the inner reflections and attitudes of the heart.*

So, the longer we walk with the Lord, and the more of the Word that gets into us, (and remember the Word, the Living Word, is who? Yeshua!) the more He is in us, the more we can see the difference between what is of our spirit and what is of our soul. And that which is of our soul is iniquitous. That's the flesh. That's iniquity. And the longer I walk with the Lord, the more I see this. Now, hopefully, I'm also learning how to stand against it, crucify it, and keep it in control and in check, and not walk in the flesh, but walk in the spirit.

So, I believe we all know our own iniquitous nature better than anybody else. We can see our own iniquitous nature, but we cannot see anyone else's. Aren't you glad I can't see your iniquitous nature? I'm glad you can't see mine! But, you know, God can see both of ours. So, as with Paul, I would say I'm the number one iniquitous person, because I know my iniquity more than I know any of yours. So, this explains what that contradiction was. It shows what Paul was saying there.

Saved By Grace

Now, here's another way this plays out in the way you hear people speak. Some people would say, "I'm not a sinner!" Well, that directly contradicts what Paul just said, right? But you say, "I was a sinner, I was saved by grace. Now I'm the righteousness of God in Him, according to II Corinthians 5:21." It's true. I'm not continuing to act in a way contrary to the Law, so I'm not a sinner, but it doesn't mean that I don't still struggle with iniquity. See, if we ignore the iniquity part of that, then when the Spirit begins to deal with our motivations and our attitudes and our feelings, we have a hard heart. We say, "Oh no, I don't need to change, because I'm not a sinner!" Or, we go into denial. "No, no, I don't really have those bad feelings. That's just the devil!" "I don't really do things for those wrong motivations." "I don't really have those attitudes." And that is an un-contrite attitude of the heart. Or we get into doubt, and this is really bad. "I must not have really been saved! I mean, if I have these feelings come up and these kinds of attitudes, I must not really be saved."

If we understand iniquity, we just add in a phrase, "Now I'm not a sinner any more, but I still struggle with iniquity, with the evil inclination, with the flesh." See, it's very clear. And that iniquity, that flesh was laid on Yeshua, and He has borne it away. But I still need to repent when the Spirit shows me my iniquity, so I can still have a contrite heart. (For an explanation of a contrite heart see Chapter 13)

If We Claim We Have No Sin

Now, what about the other side? I am a sinner. That is the other extreme. It is Scriptural. Paul said it. In I John 1:10, it says, *if we claim we have not been sinning we are making Him out to be a liar, and His word is not in us.* We are all sinners, present tense, saved by grace. But here, again, John is using the Greek word **hamartia** and I believe he means "iniquity." We are all iniquitous. It doesn't mean we are all going out breaking the Law all the time. I hope!

So if we can understand this, it helps a lot. If we don't under-stand this, what happens is when the Spirit of God calls us to come into God's presence, we say, "How can I come into God's presence, I'm a sinner?" We don't feel worthy. Or when the Spirit of God calls us to stand against the enemy, we're weak. "Oh no, no, I'm sinning all the time, I can't stand against ha-satan." We are incapable of standing against the enemy when we have this wrong idea of who we are. But if we understand iniquity and change the wording: *if we claim we have no iniquity, we make Him out to be a liar, and the Word is not in us.* We all struggle with the flesh. We're not going to be done with our struggle with the flesh until we go to be with the Lord. With this understanding we should feel worthy to come into God's presence, and we should feel strong enough to stand against ha-satan because our sin and iniquity was laid on Yeshua. And now we are the righteousness of God in Him, but we still have the flesh. We must crucify the flesh daily.

In this book I will use the Hebrew word "ha-satan" for our adversary, the devil. We think of the word satan as a name for the devil. But in Hebrew that's not what it is. In Hebrew it's a description. It's actually ha-satan, the adversary. And it's never used like we do in the English. "Christ" is also not a name. It's really a title, meaning "Messiah." But there are many people who think that "Christ" is the last name of Yeshua; I thought that. I thought his parents were Joseph and Mary Christ. [When I said this in a sermon, people started laughing! So I asked, "How about the Jewish people here? How many of you thought that?" Many raised their hands. Then I said, "See? Look around!"] But back in the days of Yeshua, Jewish people didn't even have last names. So, it's actually Yeshua, the Messiah; Jesus, the Christ. It's a title. In the same way, it's not satan, it's *ha-satan*, the adversary.

Romans 7

Now, here is another confusion that if we clear it up, it will help us. Who can understand the end of Romans 7? Everybody struggles with the end of Romans 7. Let's read it and understand that Rabbi Sha'ul is talking about iniquity here and suddenly it will make sense to you.

Romans 7:21 *So I find this to be the rule, a kind of a perverse law (or Torah) that although I want to do what is good, evil is right there with me.*

What is he describing? He's describing his flesh. His old nature. The iniquity of his old nature.

Romans 7:22-23 *For in my inner self I completely agree with God's Torah,* [With His Law. My born-from-above spirit, my heart, my innermost being, wants to do God's will.] *23 but in my various parts,* [in my members, in my body], *I see a different "torah"* [law], *one that battles with the Torah in my mind and makes me a prisoner of sin's "torah," which is operating in my various parts.*

In other words, my flesh, my carnal nature, my iniquitous nature continues to rebel against God's Law, continues to want to be lazy, to want to eat too much, to want to drink too much, to want to lust; all these things.

Romans 7:24 *What a miserable creature I am! Who will rescue me from this body bound for death?*

And then that wonderful verse:

Romans 7:25 *Thanks be to God [, he will]! — through Yeshua, the Messiah, our Lord! To sum up: with my mind, I am a slave of God's Torah; but with my old nature, I am a slave of sin's "Torah."*

See now, it means our iniquitous flesh is warring with our "inner self," our "inner being." But people have misunderstood this. I have heard people teach on this. They say this was Paul talking about what he was like before he came to believe. No. This is what he is talking about when he did come to believe. But why is he falling so much? Well, see, he's talking about his flesh. And we all still struggle with that flesh. Well, maybe it's just me. No? You struggle with the flesh, too? I thought so.

Some Sins Fell Off Easily

Now, when I became a believer, the desire of my inner self, my heart, was to obey God. And I don't know about you, but for me it was relatively easy to stop the acts of disobedience. One of the big ones for me was swearing and cussing. You too? It was just shut off like a switch for me. It was amazing how easy that was. It just stopped. It was the same for lying. I just couldn't do it anymore. Cheating, couldn't do that either. But you know what, I have walked with the Lord for 38 years, and I still struggle with ungodly attitudes. Am I judging that person now, Lord? Am I thinking I'm better than that person because of what I see him doing? It's feelings, too. Am I avoiding that person because he hurt me last week? I'm going by my feelings. I'm not showing them the love of God. It includes motivations. This is a tough one. Am I doing this to look good in the eyes of other people? Or am I doing it to serve You, Lord? Anybody else struggle with those? Those are big. Right? See, that's that iniquitous nature (using my new phrase again). Those are the attitudes of the heart.

Victory

And so, we go back to what Paul said in Romans 7:25, *Who will rescue me from this body bound for death? Thanks be to God [,he will]!* — *through Yeshua, the Messiah, our Lord!* So, it is possible to overcome our iniquitous nature. How? Through relationship with the Messiah, through connection to the vine, through being in Yeshua, and having Him in us. It's through all those things: Walking in the Spirit. Walking in alignment with the Word of God. Not fulfilling the lusts of the flesh. But you can't do it unless you spend time with Him. You need to spend time in the Word. You need to make that a high priority in your life because we're going to struggle with that all of our lives. We will never get away from it. And it's so important to understand the difference between iniquity and sin. And the wonderful thing is that Yom Kippur is where we get this understanding. This is where it all comes from, because this is the first place in the Scriptures where God begins to differentiate between iniquity and sin and deals with them in two different ways.

So, let me try to summarize all this. Understanding how atonement was made on Yom Kippur gives us insight into the controversy over original sin. It also gives us insight into who we are and our need to have contrite hearts. In other words, to be people who are open to saying, "Yes, I'm convicted of my iniquity. I need to repent." It gives us the ability to come into God's presence, in other words, to say, "But my iniquity has been borne. I am the righteousness of God."

It gives us the ability to stand against the devil who will accuse us and say, "You can't stand against me. Look at what you're thinking. Look at what you just thought last week. Look at the attitude of your heart."

And this last revelation—if you get anything out of this, get this: that this should touch your heart in gratitude. It gives us insight into why Yeshua had to suffer so. He suffered like that because of our iniquity, and we still have that iniquity. You see, when we came to the Lord and He cleaned up our acts, a lot of our sins fell away. We don't deal with them every day. But our iniquity is still there. He suffered for what we are struggling with right now. And He suffered so terribly for it.

This should bring in us just a fresh sense of gratitude, a restoring of that joy of our salvation, that overwhelming appreciation that says, "Look what You did for me, Lord!" I think of that woman who came and fell down at His feet and cried and wet His feet with her tears and wiped His feet with her hair, and you know what He said about her? He said: "I tell you this, her sins, which are many, have been forgiven. The evidence of it is that she is loving much. But someone who has been forgiven for a little only loves a little." So, once you grasp how much you've been forgiven of, it's not the occasional time that you told a white lie. It's not the occasional time that you maybe had an outburst of anger. It is the everyday things that you struggle with, the attitudes and the motivations and the feelings. That's why He had to suffer in the incredible ways that we saw in that movie, and that we read about in the Gospels. That's why He had to die that most horrible death.

So let's pray

Father, thank you for Yom Kippur. Thank you for it revealing the meaning of iniquity to us. I pray right now for any of us who are still confused, that all confusion about who we are would clear up, Lord, that we would come to believe that we are the righteousness of God in Yeshua. But also to understand that we still struggle with the flesh and that we need to have contrite hearts, because You are dealing with our flesh and You are going to be dealing with it all the days of our lives. Help us to be able to stand against ha-satan, that he would not be able to accuse us and say that we are not holy enough, to have authority over him, because of the things, the attitudes of our hearts and the things that we think. But that we would be able to have faith, oh Lord, that You have borne these things.

So, we thank you for Yom Kippur, Lord. And as we go through this day may our gratitude increase, and Lord, most of all we thank You for being willing, not just to die, not just to shed Your blood, but to suffer so incredibly for us, oh God. So terribly through those 39 stripes and through the beatings with the hands and the carrying of the cross, and the plucking of the beard; all the ways in which You suffered, oh God, to bear our iniquity and fulfill the role of the scapegoat. And Father, I pray that You would reveal our iniquity to us more and more, every day, because if we don't see it, we can't deal with it. We need to want to see it, even though it is hard. We need to want to see those wrong attitudes, so that we can bring them before you and ask you to deal with them.

And Father, I pray that You would give us a new sense of thanksgiving for Your great sacrifice and your terrible suffering, and that even the joy of our salvation would be returned to us, as we contemplate this. And Lord, I just pray even that You would draw us to Your Word to read about that in this day, about Your great suffering on the way to that cross, and on the cross, how You hung there for hours in terrible pain, bearing the iniquity.

And finally, Lord, we ask that You would help us to walk in the Spirit, walk in alignment, following the leading of the brand new spirit that You have placed within us, that You brought to life, that we might not act on our iniquity, that we might have victory over it, that we might partake of the divine nature and that our inner nature would become more and more like You, oh Lord. More and more like You and the iniquity would become less and less. That we would walk more and more in the Spirit and less and less in the flesh. And we ask these things in the mighty Name of Him who suffered and died for us, Yeshua HaMeshiakh. Amen. Thank you, Lord. Thank you, Lord.

CHAPTER 5

INGRAINED INIQUITY
AND
A GUILTY CONSCIENCE

Now let's look a little deeper at how even more amazing Yeshua's atonement is in bearing our iniquities. We will do that by looking at how bad and how ingrained and entrenched some of our iniquities are—so entrenched that we don't even realize we have some of them in us. We think they are just a part of our personality, or that they aren't even wrong. Or when we do realize, we won't admit we are guilty of them.

As Messianic Jews and those who are with us who are not Jewish—we call you "Gerim Mishikhim" (Messianic Gentiles), we still keep Yom Kippur because it is a very powerful day of soul searching and making sure our hearts are right with God who sees everything in our hearts. He sees all of it, no matter how secret or how entrenched.

Psalm 90:8 *You have placed our faults before you, our secret sins in the full light of your presence.*

There are secret sins—secret, ingrained iniquities—that we can't see in ourselves. We can very easily see the ways we are missing the mark, or our intentional violations, but there are so many iniquities that we ***can't*** see. Why can't we?

First of all, it's because of our ignorance of the Word. We don't know they are against God's commandments. We are doing things, and we are just not aware that God says not to do them. It is surprising how much there is of that.

The second reason is denial. "I don't want to hear about that because I like doing that and I've always done that. It's part of my life."

The third reason we don't know about these things is because of deception by our enemy. Ha-satan's ways are ways of deception. He works overtime to make it so that we don't see the things we are doing that are displeasing to God, so that we won't deal with them.

I had a recent revelation which I think is very important to me. The reason God established the Ten Days of Awe and Yom Kippur was actually to deal with secret and entrenched iniquity. Because it is so hard to uncover them, we need ten days for it. When you think about it—the sins we know about—we don't need ten days to figure those out. We know we do those things. So why do we have those ten days of soul searching culminated by a day of fasting? I believe it is so that we uncover the things that we're not aware of, or don't believe are a problem.

Why is it important to deal with secret, embedded iniquity? Our walk with the Lord is held back by these things. We will progress when we understand them and deal with them. We don't bear the fruit that we should for others to be brought into the Kingdom if there are things that are holding us back.

Galatians 6:7-8 (NKJV) *Do not be deceived, God is not mocked; for whatever a man sows, that he will also reap. 8 For he who sows to his flesh will of the flesh reap corruption, but he who sows to the Spirit will of the Spirit reap everlasting life.*

That corruption of our flesh can be sickness in our bodies or it can be other problems we have because we are living with our iniquity. We are continuing to sow to the flesh.

What is an example of this kind of secret, deep-rooted iniquity? I'll give you several examples.

Fear Not!

Many people don't know that this first example is a type of iniquity. Many will deny that they have it, partially because our culture doesn't call it what it is. They give it all kinds of other names. I'm talking about fear. The Bible commands us to "Fear Not" in many many places. If you look at all the places that it says that, you will see they are in the imperative. It says, "Fear Not!" It doesn't say, "Please try not to be afraid." So what do you think? When it is said like that, isn't it a command of God? Yet our society uses words for it like "anxiety" and "worry" and "stress," and they say these things are normal. What are they really? They are all aspects of fear—different levels of fear. So, if I am anxious or stressed, I am disobeying the Word of God.

It is not easy to stop fearing. The first thing is to realize that it is there. We need to realize that if I am walking in anxiety, it means I am walking in fear. Doctors have known for many, many years that there is a connection between fears and our health. I'm sure you know it, too. What is the connection between stress and anxiety and some very common diseases? High blood pressure. Ulcers. Heart conditions. You can see why it is important to get rid of these things. Maybe you just had something uncovered here today. You didn't know fear was against the Word of God, and you didn't really realize that you've been walking in anxiety and stress.

It's going to take a little work to stop doing that. At least now you know that this is a problem.

The Spirit of God's direction to me has been that there is healing power in these Appointed Times, including in the Days of Awe—spiritual, emotional, and physical healing and the power to keep us in health. God appointed them to deal with our secret iniquity which is so often the cause of many of our ailments and other dysfunctions. When we bring our secret iniquities out into the open for cleansing, healing often comes too.

Root of Bitterness

On Rosh Hashanah one year, the Lord directed me to start dealing with one of our secret iniquities. It is called "Bitterness." Many people accept that bitterness is their normal state of being because, "Look what somebody did to me!" "Look what I had to live through." Many of you have had those thoughts and feelings. What does the Bible say about bitterness? Is it something God wants us to live in?

Hebrews 12:15 *See to it that no one misses out on God's grace, that no root of bitterness springing up causes trouble and thus contaminates many.*

There is a lot in this verse. If there is bitterness, you are missing out on God's grace. Bitterness is like a root. This is very interesting because it grows in us like a root. It is not the root of a beautiful flower. It is a root of a thorn bush or the root of a weed. I want to carry this root analogy a bit further because I believe the Holy Spirit wants us to see this. Where are roots? Where do you find roots? Under the ground. Do you see roots? No. They are hidden. Bitterness is often hidden. It's hard to see it in ourselves. You can see it in other people. Right? How many of you know somebody who is bitter? You can spot it right away. But can you see it in yourself? This is why it is called a secret iniquity.

Here's another point about a root. Is it easy to get a root out? Generally some of those weed roots are really tough to pull out. You have to dig out around it to get the whole root out, because what happens if you just take part of the root? The weed just pops right back up again. Bitterness needs to be completely removed, or else, what happens? It sprouts other stalks of iniquity. It also says in the verse that it will contaminate many. This is interesting because it doesn't just affect us. It affects other people, too.

Many people misunderstand this and think bitterness is a feeling. But it's not and it's not an emotion. It is an attitude that has been taught to us by a spiritual force assigned against us by the enemy called "the spirit of bitterness."

That force will try to get us to be bitter and get us to the point where we accept it. It will deceive us and train us to be bitter. Let me talk for a minute about how this works.

Discern Our Thoughts

In the kingdom of the enemy there are spirits that have different ranks. Bitterness is a high-ranking spirit. It brings with it others that try to destroy us. How do these spirits influence us? We are spirits living in bodies and having souls which is our mind and our emotions and our will.

Proverbs 20:27 *The human spirit is a lamp of ADONAI; it searches one's inmost being.*

God speaks to us through our spirit, not to our souls or our bodies. God is a spirit and He speaks to us spirit to spirit. Who else is a spirit? Ha-satan and all of his helpers are spirits. They also communicate to us through our human spirit. We experience these communications from our spirit as thoughts popping into our minds. "Oh, that's an interesting thought—where did that come from?" We have our own thoughts. We have thoughts come from things we pick up from other people—something somebody says to us, or what we read or what we see in a video or on TV. But sometimes there are other thoughts—I know they come to me and I'm sure they come to you too—sometimes we get this thought and we say, "Where did that come from?" Did you ever have that happen? They either come from God or they come from the enemy.

Part of the challenge of maturing as a follower of Yeshua is to have discernment. Which of those thoughts are from the enemy and which of those are from the Lord? We want to keep the ones from the Lord and we want to reject the ones from the enemy. When we choose to take hold of thoughts that come from God and begin to live by them, that is called obedience. What happens when we obey? We're blessed. When we choose to take hold of thoughts that come from ha-satan—when we entertain them and begin to live by them—let them become our habitual ways of thinking, what is that called? Disobedience to God. What is the result of disobedience? The Curse! When we give way to temptation from these spirits they actually gain power over us. People talk about people having a demon. I don't like to use that phrase. I like to think more like—the spirit has us—we're had. They've got us because we are following in their ways and listening to them. We may be thinking that it is us or God, but we are following them and we are being deceived. Praise God, by the power of the Holy Spirit and the Name of Yeshua, that spirit can be removed. When we hear a voice and we discern that it is the evil one, what can we do? We can command it to shut up! It will shut up and it will be removed.

Unforgiveness

In ha-satan's organizational chart, I believe there are seven spirits related to bitterness. Each one is more dangerous than the one that proceeds it and harder to deal with. I will give only a few here. Bitterness starts out with something that we are all very subject to. It is unforgiveness. That is the beginning of bitterness. And then as it grows, it goes to resentment, retaliation, anger, hatred, and finally violence and murder. You may be thinking, "I'm not going to be taking a gun to anybody," but hatred, violence, and murder don't require a gun. They can be done with the tongue. You can murder people with your tongue.

Unforgiveness is the first spirit that ha-satan sends to bring us under the control of bitterness. Unforgiveness comes when we are offended and we don't forgive immediately. If unforgiveness has grown sprouts in you, you may not recognize it any more. You may think that it is just an innocent feeling. "No, I don't have unforgiveness, I just resent them." Or "It's not that I have to forgive them or anything, I just can't stand them." The root of any of those thoughts or feelings is unforgiveness. To get rid of these other things, we have to start with forgiveness.

Mark 11:25, 26 *And when you stand praying, if you have anything against anyone, forgive him; so that your Father in heaven may also forgive your offenses. But if you do not forgive, your Father in heaven will not forgive your offenses.*

This passage immediately follows Yeshua's foundational teaching on prayer. I have taken that to mean that if we want the Lord to hear and answer our prayers, we have to forgive.

Matthew 18:21-22 *Then Kefa (Peter) came up and said to him, "Rabbi, how often can my brother sin against me and I have to forgive him? As many as seven times?" "No, not seven times,"* answered Yeshua, *"but seventy times seven!*

If you do the math, that's 490 times—which basically means forever—or infinite.

What do we do when someone has hurt us or wronged us? What I have found very helpful is that we must separate the person from their sin. We have the right to hate the sin, but 99 out of 100 times, I have found that when somebody does something that hurts me, it is because they were deceived. The enemy deceived them so that they did it. It wasn't done because they just wanted to hurt me. It was done because they thought they were doing something right or good, but the enemy deceived them. When we can separate that person from that sin, it's much easier to forgive.

If you've been severely hurt, wounded, or assaulted by friends, family, or brethren, we have Yeshua as our example and our inspiration of the ability to forgive them. Remember when He was hanging on that cross? What did He say? "Father, forgive them—the very people that put me here— [and why?] —because they don't know what they are doing." It is because He was separating the sin from the people who actually did it. He knew they were deceived by the enemy into doing what they were doing.

Here is Yeshua's prescription for the person that has done something against you.

Matthew 18:15-17 *Moreover, if your brother commits a sin against you, go and show him his fault -- but privately, just between the two of you. If he listens to you, you have won back your brother. 16 If he doesn't listen, take one or two others with you so that every accusation can be supported by the testimony of two or three witnesses. 17 If he refuses to hear them, tell the congregation; and if he refuses to listen even to the congregation, treat him as you would a pagan or a tax-collector.*

Bitter About Our Circumstances

There are two aspects of forgiveness that we often don't think about. Many people have unforgiveness toward God. Bitterness toward God. They blame Him for the hard things that they have experienced in life. It's not like they are thinking, "I will not forgive God." They are just bitter against God. If they were born into a poor family, a single-parent family, or a dysfunctional family, they may say, "I didn't have the upbringing I should have had." Or if they were abused or neglected—sexually, physically, or emotionally, as a child, they may say, "Look what happened to me. God allowed this to happen to me." This includes if they suffer heart-break or have a disability or some sickness, or some great loss, or a great injustice; if they've been rejected, or have failed. It includes even if they don't like their looks or stature or mental abilities or even their personality. All of these things are things for which we can have bitterness toward God. We ask things like, "Why did You make me this way?" or "Why did You put me in these circumstances?"

The Bible teaches us that God created each one of us the way He wants us to be—our looks, our talents, and our personalities. He created us that way. So if we are angry with Him for how He made us, what is that? We're really saying that we know better than He does. Right? We know better how things should have been than He does. And what is that? We are exalting our own wisdom over His wisdom. Do you see that? What is that? That is idolatry. That is saying, "I am above God." It is self idolatry.

The Bible also teaches us that God knows that we live in a fallen world. His Son came into our fallen world in the form of a man. He knew we'd experience many, many hardships, as all people do. The Word says that if we will come to Him and obey Him, He will help us overcome every possible hardship in our lives and bear much fruit.

I believe there is a spirit of unforgiveness that combines with what is called an unloving spirit that together deceive us into believing that God doesn't love us. Then we are deceived by a spirit of rejection that God doesn't accept us. A spirit of fear can tell us that God won't care for us. Another spirit can cause us to not see all that God has done for us! So, we remain in this place where we are just bitter about life's circumstances.

Of course, there is always that old spirit of self-pity. "Woe is me! I've got it so bad!" Yet God has given us life—the very life that we have. In the prayer we use around the holidays we say, "He has given us life and sustained us and brought us to this season." He created us for a purpose. He revealed Himself to us. He suffered to pay the price for our sin. He gave us the Holy Spirit! We should be thankful. We should be grateful for how He has made us. He's given us the power to overcome all the things that we have to deal with. He has made us just the way we are supposed to be. However, we don't want to give thanks because this spirit has deceived us. It is a spirit. We can't war against it in the flesh. But we can break this power over us simply by taking responsibility for it, repenting of it, and removing that spirit of unforgiveness and that spirit of bitterness by the authority of the Name of Yeshua and in the power of His shed blood.

Bitter Toward Ourselves

The second area of unforgiveness is also very interesting. There are many people who have unforgiveness toward themselves. Can you believe that? Why is that? They haven't forgiven themselves for their sins. This becomes very, very critical because I am talking about believers. They have asked the Lord to forgive them in the name of Yeshua, and He has forgiven them. But yet, they haven't forgiven themselves. What do they carry around? It is a very common word. It is called shame. They carry around shame. Shame and remorse that are still there after being forgiven by God! Shame is a form of iniquity. God says, "I forgive you," yet they still carry it around. Their iniquity was carried away by Yeshua as the scapegoat carried away the iniquity of the people of Israel, yet they are still down on themselves. They're still ashamed of those things.

Done Away

The book of Hebrews tells us some amazing things about this. First of all, it tells us that Yeshua's sacrifice did something much more than the animal sacrifices on Yom Kippur. I first understood something about this in the "Tashlikh" ceremony a few years ago. This is a time on Rosh HaShanah afternoon when the congregation goes out to a stream and tosses bread-crumbs in the water. The breadcrumbs represent our sins. We watch how they are carried down the stream and eventually carried into the ocean. The Tashlikh ceremony was inspired by the prophet Micah.

Micah 7:19 *He will again have compassion on us, he will subdue our iniquities. You will throw all their sins into the depths of the sea.*

The word "tashlikh" means "to throw." The word "kippur" meaning, to cover, is not used. Throwing our sins into depths of the sea is taking them away, far away. It is speaking of some-thing more than covering sins.

Psalm 103:12 *He has removed our sins from us as far as the east is from the west.*

I always thought of these verses as describing what animal sacrifices did, but, in preparing for Tashlikh that year, I read a verse that surprised me.

Hebrews 10:4 *For it is impossible that the blood of bulls and goats should take away sins.*

Animal sacrifices were a kippur, a covering for sin. Sin was covered so God could dwell among a sinful people. But then I realized that Micah & Psalm 103 were prophesying a time in the future when sins would not just be covered, but would be taken away, enabling God not to dwell only in the Tabernacle, or the Temple, but to dwell where? In us—because our sins would be taken away, not just covered. How would this taking away be accomplished? Back to the book of Hebrews where it shows Yeshua fulfilling these prophecies.

Hebrews 9:26-28 ... *But as it is, he has appeared once at the end of the ages in order to do away with sin through the sacrifice of himself. 27 Just as human beings have to die once, but after this comes judgment, 28 so also the Messiah, having* *been offered once <u>to bear</u> the sins of many, will appear a second time, not to deal with sin, but to deliver those who are eagerly waiting for him.*

What is the difference between the sins being done away with and being covered? The B'rit Hadashah (New Covenant) tells us that those who made the animal sacrifices were forgiven and made right with God. The Torah agrees with this

Leviticus 16:30 *… you will be clean before ADONAI from all your sins.*

What so surprised me was that I began to understand that there was still something missing in power of the animal sacrifice system, besides that they had to do them over and over.

Our Guilty Conscience

Hebrews 10:1-2 *For the Torah has in it a shadow of the good things to come, but not the actual manifestation of the originals. Therefore, it can never, by means of the same sacrifices repeated endlessly year after year, bring to the goal those who approach the Holy Place to offer them. 2 Otherwise, wouldn't the offering of those sacrifices have ceased? For if the people performing the service had been cleansed once and for all, they would no longer have sins on their conscience.*

Let us break this down a little bit. The "people performing the service" and "those who approach the Holy Place" are the people making animal sacrifices, referring both to the cohanim making the Yom Kippur and other sacrifices and to ordinary people making sacrifices for sin at any time.

In verse 1 it uses the phrase "bring them to the goal." What is the goal? It tells us what it is in verse 2. It is a clean conscience. It is our consciences being cleansed. They would no longer have sins on their conscience. *Syneidēsis* pronounced *soon-i'-day-sis* is the Greek for conscience.

What is our conscience? I believe our conscience is part of our soul. God has given it to us. It knows right from wrong. Maybe it is part of the Spirit. I would have to have further revelation on that. It continually confronts us when we do something wrong. It is a really important thing that we have. It makes us feel guilty and ashamed for things we've done wrong to bring us to repentance. However, if we don't believe that we are forgiven, it can torment us. It can drive us crazy, in fact. Some people try to silence their consciences by keeping very busy and working very hard to be successful. Other people "sear" their conscience by indulging in evil consistently until it is overwhelmed. They say, "Oh well, if it's going to bother me about that, I'll just do this too!" Other people try to drown out their conscience with things like drugs and alcohol. They just cover it over so they won't hear from it. Some people just try to ignore it.

However, consciences have a way of being heard. They can pop up in our dreams. They can pop up with random thoughts, making you wonder, "Why did I think that?"

Suddenly I had a striking revelation. Those offering animal sacrifices for their sin according to Laws of Moshe were still left with sins on their consciences. See that in Hebrews? They still had remorse, sorrow, and shame for what they had done that was wrong. They still carried around a load of guilt, regrets, and blame even though they had done the sacrifices and were cleansed and forgiven by God but their consciences were not cleared. That is a big problem. It was a problem back then and it still is today. Many people are tormented and burdened by guilty consciences even today, because they do not have clear consciences.

After I got this far in studying this, I thought, "This is weird. Am I making this up?" Can I find something in the Bible that would actually say that this is what happened in the days before Yeshua? I prayed and asked the Lord, "Show me if there is something like that." Immediately, I was sent to Psalm 51. In this Psalm David was telling a bit of his life story. For those of you who don't know it. David had committed adultery and murder. He was attempting to cover it all up. God sent his friend and prophet, Nathan, to him, who confronted David. And David repented! He admitted he had done it and he repented. Immediately God told Nathan to tell David, "I have forgiven him because he repented. I saw his heart." Psalm 51 was written about this. It was written after he repented. There is a verse in this Psalm that is very amazing. Listen to what David says after he has repented and been forgiven of God.

Psalm 51:3 *For I know my crimes, my sin confronts me all the time.*

What do you think is happening here? Has his conscience been cleansed? No. He's still carrying around that load. True, he had a lot of reason to be guilty. He did terrible things. Clearly, even though he repented, he still had a guilty conscience. It was still confronting him and tormenting him.

Cleansing Our Conscience

Hebrews 10 isn't the only place that the author of Hebrews declares the power of Yeshua's sacrifice to cleanse our consciences.

Hebrews 9:14 *Then how much more the blood of the Messiah, who, through the eternal Spirit, offered himself to God as a sacrifice without blemish, will purify our conscience from works that lead to death, so that we can serve the living God!*

I never noticed this before I got into this study. So, when we confess our sins and ask His forgiveness, ask Him by the power of Yeshua's sacrifice to take away our sins, His sacrifice fulfills the prophecies of Micah and of Psalm 103. "*He casts them into the depths of the sea*" and "*He removes them as far as he East is from the West.*" This means He cleanses our guilty consciences. He sets us free from the shame of the wrong things we've done. We should be able to go on with our lives, not blocking out the memory that we did those things, but knowing that "it's been dealt with." The blood of Messiah has cleansed me of those things. "Shame, you can't come on me anymore. You can't have me. You can't convince me that I have to live a life of guilt." No longer do we have to live with shame, fear of judgment, remorse, guilt, and sorrow.

When I turned to the Lord I repented of many things I had done; that I was sorry for and ashamed of. When memories or dreams of those things came up, I was led by the Ruakh HaKodesh (the Holy Spirit) to ask the Lord to cover them with Yeshua's blood, which helped. But my conscience wasn't completely cleansed. It wasn't until I learned this lesson I'm giving you now that I understood that having our consciences cleansed is part of the heritage of those who enter into the B'rit Hadashah—the New Covenant. It is part of what Yeshua paid for when He made His atoning sacrifice. Just as healing, deliverance, peace, and eternal life are part of what He purchased for us, so is a clear, cleansed conscience.

Why?

What kinds of things cause us to have guilty consciences? Why do people carry around guilt and shame even after they have received the Messiah? Some people have a good reason. It is because they can't make restitution for what they did. Here are some examples. If somebody killed someone, even if it was manslaughter—accidental—maybe they were driving drunk or careless and they killed someone, they can't bring the person back. That is really, really heavy. Or perhaps they permanently injured a person—physically or emotionally or relationally. If they abused someone, that person is scarred for life. How can you change that? You can apologize, but you can't take it back. How about ruined relationships? Perhaps we know that we are the reason the relationship was destroyed and we know it can never be restored. Or if we've done something to someone that we want to apologize for, but that person has already died. We can never go back and make it right.

So what happens when someone has done something like this? They become a believer in the Lord—they repent—their sins are taken away, but they are still struggling in their conscience over these things. This is what I think is happening. The spirit of unforgiveness combines with the spirit of shame to deceive us into believing that we should live our lives in shame for what we did in the past. You might think, "What does forgiveness have to do with this?" Well, see, you haven't forgiven yourself. God has forgiven you, but you haven't forgiven yourself. That is the spirit of unforgiveness. "I can forgive everybody else, but I can't forgive myself." But, wait a minute! God forgave me, and what am I doing? I'm exalting myself over the Lord by having that unforgiveness. It is a spirit that has deceived us into believing, "You have done something terrible! Now you have to live your life in shame! That's your lot!" However, if you receive what the author of Hebrews is saying, and you have anything that you are still ashamed of, today can be a day of freedom for you. You have to make restitution whenever and wherever you can, but what you also need to do is receive the power of Yeshua's atoning sacrifice to cleanse your conscience of shame and guilt and remorse.

How?

So how do we do this? How do our consciences get cleansed? We're going to find out right now, and then we are going to do it. We have the power in the Name of Yeshua to get rid of those spirits that have tempted us into doing this. We have to break the power of this shame over us. We do it by taking responsibility and repenting and removing a spirit of unforgiveness toward ourselves and this spirit of shame. Then we will rejoice, because if you are carrying around shame this is the greatest thing that can happen to you.

To get rid of shame, we need to understand what happened when we allowed shame to take residence in us. There is a scientific fact that I have learned. When we think a thought, or recall a memory for a long time, psychologists understand now that what happens is that thought passes from short term memory into long term memory. When it goes into our long-term memory, it actually gets encoded into our brain cells. So, in a sense, it becomes part of us. The way this fits into our Bible teaching on this is that it becomes part of our flesh. It is stored in there. What I have come to believe is that our carnal nature is the ungodly thoughts that the enemy has taught us to think that have become part of our habitual way of thinking. It becomes a habit. We believe it's part of our brain. We think, "This is who I am. I'm just a bitter person. I've been thinking these thoughts for years." Or we say, "I'm a person filled with shame. I've been thinking these thoughts of shame for years even though I bind the spirit and command it to leave." So what is happening is that it is not our spirit anymore, it is our flesh, our iniquity. It is part of us. This is a little bit harder to deal with. Have you tried to break a bad habit? Does it happen overnight? Some scientists tell us it takes 28 days to break a bad habit.

The Prescription

We have bad thought habits too. Are you aware you have habitual ways you think? Yes, we all have them. So, if we have a thought habit that has been placed there by the enemy and we've accepted it and think this is us and this is how we think, we will continue to think that way, even when the enemy is gone, because now it's part of our flesh. That is what we need to deal with. How do we deal with this? We have to replace that negative, evil thought with good thought habits.

Philippians 4:8 *In conclusion, brothers, focus your thoughts on what is true, noble, righteous, pure, lovable or admirable, on some virtue or on something praiseworthy..*

That's the prescription. When you catch yourself falling into shame or unforgiveness, stop and replace it with a pure, noble Biblical truth. Catch yourself. Say, "I'm going to think thoughts that are true.... I have overcome." Here's ways to do it. Memorize those words. Put Philippians 4:8 into your brain cells. Memorize it! Make it part of you! It's amazing how many descriptions Paul uses there for the kind of thoughts that we should have. Each one of them could be a sermon. These are the words that we are supposed to put back in there. Another way is to meditate on the Word of God. Roll it around in your mind. Keep meditating on it. The third way, which I find to be very very useful, is to sing the Scriptures. Many worship songs that you hear on the radio; many worship songs that we use in our worship services; many worship songs on CDs are simply Scripture put to music. It is the easiest way that has ever been devised to memorize something. That is why we Jewish people, if you've ever heard the Torah being read, you know this, we chant it because that helps us to memorize it. Sing Scripture songs and they will become part of your long-term memory. They will be part of your flesh instead of the bitterness and shame. And when those negative things come up—just start singing! Pretty soon the good thoughts will replace all the bad thoughts.

Let's pray

Father, thank You for the Days of Awe and Yom Kippur to reveal to us hidden iniquities. Thank you for the blood atonement, and the shedding of the blood, and coming as a man to bring us atonement. We confess to You today that we have broken Your commandments. In Yeshua's name we ask you to forgive us for anything we've done, said, or thought that is against Your will. We look to Yeshua's sacrifice, the sacrifice of the Son of God, to pay the price for our sin.

Right now, in the authority of Yeshua's Name, I bind the spirit of bitterness. I bind its power over every person reading this. We bind the power of the spirit of bitterness. We repent and take responsibility for any bitterness toward God, any unforgiveness toward God, any blaming of God. We also repent of any bitterness or unforgiveness toward ourselves or toward others. We repent of this. We take responsibility for any resentment or retaliation or anger or hatred or violence or thoughts of murder or injurious thoughts toward others or ourselves or toward God. Father, I pray that if there is any reader that needs to make restitution to someone, that needs to go to apologize or pay back something, that You would show them what that is.

Now Father, we come with thanksgiving that You came as a man, not just to cover our sins, but to remove them as far as the east is from the west. I break the power of the spirit of unforgiveness over every person reading this. I remove this spirit and I command it to go to the dry places. I break the power of the spirit of shame over every reader. I remove it and command it to go to its dry places. I break the power of the spirits of resentment and retaliation, anger, hatred, violence, murder, over every person.

For those who have carried a load of guilt or shame or remorse, I pray, O God, that You will fulfill Your promise to take that away and set each person free from that conscience. Cleanse their conscience by Your blood, as Your Word says in the book of Hebrews. We receive right now, that atoning sacrifice to cleanse our sins, our transgressions, our iniquities, and our consciences. I break the power of the spirit of bitterness over every person reading this. It must leave in the name of Yeshua and must go to its dry places. I pray now, Holy Spirit, to come and help us to resist these spirits as they try to get back in or tempt us to be bitter or walk in that unforgiveness again. I also pray for the power of your Spirit to remove those habits of thinking that have been programmed into us by bitterness and to replace those patterns of thinking with true thoughts, noble thoughts, righteous thoughts, loveable thoughts, admirable thoughts, virtuous thoughts, praiseworthy thoughts. We thank You, Lord, that You are capable of this and we rejoice in Your deliverance. Hallelujah!! Thank You, Lord!!!!

CHAPTER 6

לא אזכר עוד
LO EZKHAR OD
REMEMBER NO MORE

Something Greater is Needed

It is the B'rit Hadashah—the New Covenant—that brings Yeshua's wonderful, amazing sacrifice. It is in the New Covenant, that His amazing sacrifice makes atonement for our sins and iniquities—even, as we have noted, our secret, deeply entrenched things like fear and bitterness—and besides all that, also clears our conscience. So, let's look closer at this New Covenant.

About five or six hundred years before Yeshua, a thousand years after Moses gave the commandments from God about Yom Kippur, there was a man named Jeremiah, or in Hebrew *Yirmiyahu*, who wrote and spoke and prophesied. He wrote a passage that to me is one of the most important passages in the entire Bible. You are probably familiar with it. It is where he speaks of the New Covenant. So, let's look at that passage now.

Jeremiah 31: 31-32 (NKJV) *Behold, the days are coming, says the Lord, when I will make a New Covenant (a B'rit Hadasha) with the House of Israel and with the House of Judah. Not according to the covenant that I made with their fathers in the day that I took them by the hand to lead them out of the land of Egypt. My covenant, which they broke, though I was a husband to them, says the Lord.*

Now, this is a new covenant. It's newer than the covenant with Moses. Keep in mind that if you talk to Jewish people, they won't agree with this. I've never met a Jewish person who says we have a covenant after Moses. They just believe this New Covenant hasn't happened yet. I don't know what they believe in regards to when it will happen.

The covenant with Moses, made as the people came out of Egypt, referred to in these verses, is the covenant that contained the commandments concerning Yom Kippur. That is the covenant that explained how they could have God dwelling in their midst, through the sacrifices.

Jeremiah 31:33 *But this is the covenant that I will make with the House of Israel after those days, says the Lord, I will put my Law in their minds and I will write it on their hearts, and I will be their God and they will be my people.*

So, what do these things mean, the Law in our minds? It's pretty obvious. It means we will remember it. It means we will understand it. It will be clear to us. But what about putting the Law in our hearts? Well, the heart is the place of love. It means we will love the Law. It means we will want to obey God. That was really the biggest change in my life when I turned to the Lord. I went from **not wanting** to obey God to **wanting** to obey God. It was as simple as that. Many of you experienced that kind of a change, too. To obey God became the most important thing in my life. The Law was written in my heart, so I desired and wanted to obey.

Jeremiah 31:34 *No more shall every man teach his neighbor and every man his brother saying "know the Lord," for they*

*shall all know me, from the least of them to the greatest of them,
says the Lord.*

Now, the Tanakh, the Old Testament, records that there were
people who knew the Lord before the time of Yeshua. Moses
certainly knew the Lord. It says that God spoke to him as a
friend, face to face. Joshua had a visitation of the Captain of the
Lord of Hosts. Abraham certainly knew the Lord. Samuel knew
the Lord, and called Him by name. If you read the Psalms, it
is obvious that David knew the Lord. He had a wonderful relationship with Him. But they were all leaders and prophets and
kings. Not all the people knew the Lord. But this New Covenant
that is promised says not just the leaders and the prophets and
the kings, but all the people will know the Lord.

So, how could this be possible? Well, I believe it is only possible because something greater than the Mosaic Covenant was
needed, to make this happen. And that was something that was
given in this New Covenant, that Jeremiah speaks about here.
Something greater than the presence of God in that Temple was
needed. Because, remember what we read, that God's presence was there, but only one person could come in only once a
year and be in His presence. Right?

So something greater was needed. There is a song, it's a
Don Potter song called "Seek Your Face." It's on Paul Wilbur's
2001 CD. It has two lines in it that I want you to see. It says
this, "David knew there was something more than the Ark of
Your presence. In a manger Messiah was born, among kings
and peasants." So, what was that something more? It was that,
just as God's presence was in this Ark, in this box, Messiah was
going to be born in a manger, a similarly shaped container. A
baby was going to be born, and it would be "something more."

Now, how are we all going to know God? Here's the way I
see it. His presence, His manifest presence could not be behind
a curtain in the Temple if we are all to know Him. The New
Covenant promises that His presence will be in us.

I Corinthians 6:19 *Don't you know that your body is a temple for the Ruach HaKodesh* [Holy Spirit] *who lives inside you,
whom you received from God?*

So, let's get this picture. In the time of the Temple, the presence of God was behind the curtain. But in the time of the New Covenant, so that we can all know Him, the presence of God is going to be in each one of us because we are each a temple. We are each a temple of the Holy Spirit.

Remember No More

So, in the Temple a Day of Atonement was needed for the Spirit of God to dwell in that Temple. What was necessary to enable the Spirit of God to dwell in us? Something was needed. Something huge was needed—a really big sacrifice. And it's right there in the last part of that verse in Jeremiah 31. Take a look at verse 34 because I stopped in the middle of the verse where it said they shall all know me, from the least of them to the greatest, and then it gives the reason they shall all know Him:

Jeremiah 31:34 *For I will forgive their iniquity and their sin I will remember no more.*

Now, I took a look at the Hebrew in this, and actually I don't think that's the way it should be translated, because it sounds like He's going to forgive iniquity and He is going to remember sin no more. Right? Two separate things. According to the Hebrew, it would be correct to read: "I will forgive their iniquity and their sin, and I will remember them no more." In other words, the remembering no more and the forgiving deal with both iniquity and sin. So, I want to focus in now on this little phrase, 'remember no more.' Because it is very specific in the Hebrew. It does not say 'forget.' It says: Remember no more. And when you think about that, forgetting is an unconscious act. Right? It just sort of happens, and the older you get the more it happens! Right?

But, remembering no more is a conscious act. The memory can't come back if you decide to remember it no more. It's like erasing a file from your computer. You erase everything, and you erase all the back-ups, and then it can't come back. It's not there anymore. Or, if it is paper, you burn them, and they're gone forever. Now, think about human relationships for a minute. Let's talk about relationships.

Let's take the example that we do something that offends someone or hurts them, and we go to ask their forgiveness. Have you ever had to go do that? Yeah, I think we all have had to do that. Hopefully, the person will forgive us. Right? But do they forget? No. Sometimes they do forget, but because it is an unconscious act, it can come back. They might suddenly remember it again. We are not even capable, as human beings, of doing what is described here. Do you know anyone who can decide to remember something no more? In other words, can you just say, "I'm going to block that right out of my memory; it's gone, and I'll never remember it." People with dementia can. But they don't do it consciously. They don't decide to do that. It tragically happens to them.

I want you to grasp this. This is a supernatural thing, and it is very important to understand, that only God can do this. In other words, He is saying, "I'm going to erase this from the divine memory banks." And, of course, He's God, so He can do it. But it's not something He has given you the ability to do. We can't do it. So, He's going to intentionally erase the remembrance of our sin and our iniquity.

Now, I had an interesting experience with this, when I first came to this understanding years ago. I did something wrong, and I repented of it and asked the Lord to forgive me. Then, you know, I went on my way, and a while later, it came back to me in the form of a fear that I would do that wrong thing again. That fear was holding me back from doing something I was supposed to do. I went back to God, and I said, "Lord, please forgive me of this." And He said, "What are you talking about? You didn't do that!" And I said, "But, Lord, I know I did that." He said, "I don't remember it!" He didn't remember it!

See, I was afraid that I was going to face that temptation again, and I would fall. But God was saying, "I don't even remember you doing it. I'm going to trust you to face that temptation again." And He did! So, here is the understanding. For all the people to know Him personally, an atonement that was greater than what happened in the Temple had to be made. And that atonement was so great that God would remember our sin and our iniquity no more. He wouldn't just forget it, wouldn't just put it aside, He would remember it no more. Hebrew: *Lo ezkhar od.* לֹא אֶזְכָּר עוֹד Remember no more.

Greater Atonement

And this greater atonement is why, in the book of Hebrews, it says that this shows how much better the covenant is of which Yeshua has become the guarantor. The New Covenant, it is saying, is better because this atonement is greater. So, what was the greater atonement that came with the New Covenant, that enables God's presence to dwell in the Temple, and so that He would remember our sin and our iniquity no more? I want to give you several ways in which the atonement was greater.

Well, we've already seen that Yeshua's sacrifice is greater because it takes away our sins rather than just covering them, that it thus gives us a clean conscience, and that He voluntarily died the most agonizing death that has ever been invented by human beings so He could carry our iniquities away. But there are even more ways in which His atonement is greater. I'm going to give you six of them.

First of all, Yeshua, whom the Scriptures speak of as God, Himself, come as a man—a man without sin—and gave Himself as an atoning sacrifice to shed His blood to make atonement. So, you've got a goat, and you've got God, Himself, as a man; there is a little difference in the blood, wouldn't you say—a huge, astronomical difference!

Second: Where was the sacrificed goat's blood sprinkled? It was sprinkled on the Mercy Seat. And what was significant about the Mercy Seat? That was where the presence of God was. Now, where was Yeshua's blood sprinkled? On earth, while He was being crucified, where was it dripping? Onto the cross. And if Yeshua was God, Himself, who was on the cross? God, Himself. So, you see the parallel here? The blood was sprinkled on the place where the presence of God was. Just like the Mercy Seat. Do you see that? But it was the Blood of God, Himself, come as a man. In chapter 7, we will look at where else He sprinkled His blood.

We have already mentioned the third thing for which it is greater. It was done once and for all! Whereas the goat sacrifice was done how often? Every year.

Hebrews 10:3-5 ... *in these sacrifices is a reminder of sins, year after year. 4 For it is impossible that the blood of bulls and goats should take away sins. 5 This is why, on coming into the world, he says, "It has not been your will to have an animal sacrifice and a meal offering; rather, you have prepared for me a body* [to take away sin].

We have studied in detail the fourth way it is greater: that Yeshua suffered more than the scapegoat. Yeshua's death, as we said, was by the most terrible means of execution that has ever been devised by humankind. Crucifixion was a horrific, diabolical way of killing someone.

So, we have a goat that had suffered and died a terrible, painful death, and then we have the Son of God, God, Himself, come as a man, who voluntarily allowed Himself to be nailed to this cross and spend several hours there in agony after having been beaten and whipped. He was bleeding and bruised and in terrible, terrible pain and agony. How much greater was the price that He paid? The goat was pushed off the cliff and that was it. It wasn't beaten and flogged over and over, to the point of death before he was pushed off the cliff. Yeshua's sacrifice was infinitely greater.

The fifth way is the "*'eretz gezera;*" that's Hebrew for "the land uninhabited." Remember, that the scapegoat carried the iniquities to an uninhabited land. He bore them. And his body, the body of that goat, was left there in the wilderness to symbolize very clearly that the people's iniquities were left in the wilderness. Do you see that? They were taken far away. So, the question is, where did Yeshua bear our iniquities? Yes, outside the city where He was crucified, but after He died, where did He take them?

Ephesians 4:9 *What can it mean if not that He first went down into the lowest parts, that is the earth?*

So, Yeshua was buried in that tomb, but we understand that He went into the depths of hell. Not into the wilderness, but into the depths of the earth, to a land uninhabited by the living. Our iniquities are not just carried a few miles away. They were carried into another dimension, if you will, because I don't think we can get to that place in these bodies. I don't think we want to get to that place. But we cannot go there. They are so far away. The iniquities were carried so far away that they could never be found. So that is the fifth way in which this atonement was greater.

The sixth way has to do with the "*parokhet.*" The "*parokhet*" is the curtain—the very thick and very tall curtain in the Temple that separated the Holy Place from the Most Holy Place as described in Exodus 26:31-33. And remember, we read that the High Priest could only go through that curtain once per year, lest he die. In Matthew 27, and in two of the other Gospels, it speaks of the curtain at the moment of Yeshua's death.

Matthew 27:50-51 *Yeshua again, crying out in a loud voice, yielded up His Spirit.* [He died.] *At that moment the parokhet in the Temple was ripped in two from top to bottom; and there was an earthquake, with rocks splitting apart.*

Why was it ripped in two?

Hebrews 10:19-20 *So, brethren, we have confidence to use the way into the Holiest Place, opened by the blood of Yeshua. He inaugurated it for us as a new and living way through the parokhet, by means of his flesh.*

So, He opened the curtain.

Now, the curtain was opened from top to bottom, signifying that no man did that, but that God did it. And what it was signifying was that people could come into the presence of God, all the people could now come into the presence of God. Not just the Cohane HaGadol, the High Priest, but everyone who wants to can enter into the presence of God. Everyone who enters into the New Covenant, which Jeremiah 31:32-34 talked about would enter into the presence of God. Not just once a year on Yom Kippur, but whenever we need to go in there. And that's the greater atonement that brought about the New Covenant, and that's what makes it possible for God to remember our sins no more, because the atonement was so great. This once and for all atonement that has been made is what makes it possible for Him to dwell within us.

So, let's pray

Father, we thank You for what Yom Kippur teaches us. We see our need for atonement, to have You dwell in our midst, to come into Your presence. We see our need to have both our sins and our iniquities atoned for. We thank You for that time, those 1,500 years that the Temple stood, when these atoning sacrifices were made and so many of Your people experienced that yearly atonement. And we also thank You, Father, for Yeshua, for Him fulfilling the Yom Kippur atonement, for shedding His blood, the blood of Your only Son, of You Yourself come as a man, to wash away our sin, our *khatahah,* for bearing our iniquity, our *avone* as the scapegoat. For bearing our iniquity, not just out into the Judean wilderness, or into that tomb, even, but to the very depths of the earth. And we thank You for tearing the *parokhet,* the veil, that we could enter into Your presence. And most of all, Lord, we thank You for remembering our sins no more. *Lo ezkhar od.* For erasing our sins and transgressions. We thank You for this wonderful New Covenant.

Father, we just thank You for what You've shown us here in Your Word. We thank You for shedding Your blood for us. We pray, Father, that You would make these things real to us, that these would not just be concepts that we walk away from here and forget, but that we would have a new appreciation of how great Your atonement is. A new appreciation of Your blood, of Your bearing of our iniquity, suffering in that terrible way for our iniquities, of You ripping the veil, and that we would understand that You remember our sins no more. That you removed them as far as the east is from the west. And we invite, once again, Your presence, oh Lord, Your Spirit, to come and dwell within us. Thank you, Lord. In Yeshua's Name. Amen.

Now I would just like to offer that if you would like to experience the fulfillment of Yom Kippur and enter into that New Covenant, the *B'rit Hadashah*, and have Yeshua's blood cover your sins, and have Yeshua, Himself, bear your iniquities to the depths of the earth, so that you could come into the presence of God, right inside the Holy Place, to the very throne. The Scriptures speak of coming before His throne boldly and the other promise of that New Covenant, to experience this "remembering no more" of your sins, so that God can dwell in you, so that you can know Him. If you would like to enter into that New Covenant, it's simple: you need to believe in Him, trust in Him, rely on Him, follow Him, trust in His atoning work, and make Him your Lord. I just want to give you a chance, if you've never done that. Now is your time, this Yom Kippur is your day to experience that greater atonement, a greater atonement than was available in the Temple. Shalom to you.

Just bow your head right now and tell the Lord that you want to become His.

Entering the New Covenant Prayer

Father, Yeshua, I confess I have broken Your command-ments. In Yeshua's name forgive me for my sins and my iniquity. Forgive me for all the things I've done that have been against Your will. Forgive me for transgressing—for rebelling against You. I look to Your sacrifice, Yeshua, of Your life when You came as a man to pay the price for my sin. I receive Your atoning sac-rifice for my sins. I give You control of my life. I commit myself to following Your direction for the rest of my life. Thank You for the New Covenant. Thank You for making the way for me to be cleansed and redeemed and made white as snow before You. Thank You that You will not remember any of my sins any-more! Thank You that they are erased forever! Thank You that I can now enter through the torn curtain into Your presence. In Yeshua's Name I pray. Amen.

Now, lift your hands and begin to thank Him and praise Him for what He has done for you and for what He is doing inside of you right now. Allow His joy to enter your soul and His Holy Spirit to fill you to overflowing!

Isn't Yom Kippur a wonderful Appointed Time?!

Chapter 7

MYSTERIOUS SIGNS

The Curtain

The thick, tall curtain, the parokhet, separating the Holy Place from the Most Holy Place, as we have learned, is very significant. Let's take a deeper look at the parokhet. Turn back to the book of Hebrews again. This passage in Hebrews is talking all about the Yom Kippur atonement.

Hebrews 9:11 *But when Messiah appeared, as Cohen Gadol of the good things that are already happening.*

The author of the book of Hebrews is speaking of Messiah being the Cohane HaGadol, the great High Priest. He took that role. That was one of His roles. He has many roles. He is also our King.

Hebrews 9:11b-12 *Then, through the greater and more perfect tent, which is not man-made, that is, which is not created of this world, He entered the Holiest Place once and for all.*

What tent, or tabernacle, is being described here? Does anybody know? In Jerusalem? No. Where? What Temple is being described here? The Temple in heaven. Yes, the one not created by man. He entered the Holiest Place once and for all. And remember, the Tabernacle was a model of this. And it goes on to say that He entered not by means of the blood of goats and of calves, but by the means of His own blood, thus setting people free forever. So, what did He bring with Him into that Holy of Holies in heaven? His own blood! He carried His own blood. Just try to imagine that scene. This happened sometime after He died on the cross. He entered into this Holiest Place in heaven, offering His own blood.

Hebrews 9:12 (NKJV) *Not with the blood of goats and calves, but with His own blood He entered the Most Holy Place once for all.*

I'm curious; what did He look like? Did He look like a lamb, as John saw him? Or did He look like a human being at this point in time? Was He still bleeding? Is that how He sprinkled the blood? Did it just come from his hands? Or did He carry it somehow in some kind of container, as the High Priest would have done in the earthly Tabernacle? We don't know. Maybe when we get to heaven, we will see these things.

He sprinkled His own blood on the Mercy Seat, or the Throne, in that heavenly Tabernacle. Go ahead a little bit to Hebrews chapter 10. We're going to dig into this a little bit.

Hebrews 10:19 *So, brothers, we have confidence to use the way into the Holiest Place opened by the blood of Yeshua.*

So we have been given access to the Most Holy Place, the Holy of Holies, to the presence of God, because of Yeshua's blood, as we said before, making a way. He opened the way with His blood.

Hebrews 10:20 (NIV) *By a new and living way opened for us through the curtain, that is, His body.*

Now, the curtain mentioned here, in the Tabernacle and the Temple on earth, separated the people from the Most Holy Place. It separated even the priests. Only one priest, and only once a year, could go into that Most Holy Place. And the author of Hebrews is saying that Yeshua made a way for us to come through the curtain so that we could have confidence to enter the Most Holy Place and be in the presence of God.

This is so foundational, so much a key to what Messiah has done. It is the whole reason that we can come in; not because of what we have done, but because He made a way for us. That is why the New Covenant, in Jeremiah, says: *They will all know me, from the least of them to the greatest.*

"The Curtain, that is His Body"

But I want to just focus on verse 20 for a minute here, because there is a very interesting phrase at the end of verse 20 that has always struck me. Take a look at it in your Bible. I'm not sure it will say it the same way in your translation. Take a look at it again here.

Hebrews 10:20 (NIV) *By a new and living way, opened for us through the curtain, that is, His body.*

What does that mean, "that is His body?" *The curtain that is His body.* I think there are three possible answers to it. And I think they are all valid. They are all wonderful.

The first explanation is His body refers to the corporate body of believers. We can only come into the presence of the Living God because we are part of His body, here on earth. We know that we don't have a relationship with the Father in a vacuum. 1 John 4:21 tells us *this is the command we have from him: whoever loves God must love his brother too.* So, perhaps the curtain that is His body means us, His body. We can come through His curtain because we are part of His body. Does that makes sense? That's number one.

The second explanation: *"That is His body"* refers to the way through the curtain. In other words (let's read it again): *The new and living way opened for us through the curtain, that is, His* *body.* In other words, the "that is" refers back, not to the curtain, but to the way. Do you see what I'm saying there? All of you English majors? The clause, "that is His body" refers back to the way. His body is the way, in other words. Now, David Stern, in the Jewish New Testament, supports this. He says it through the curtain by means of His flesh, or his body. So that gives it a little bit of a different meaning. By offering His body, He opened the way through the curtain for us, just as the High Priest went through the curtain in the earthly Temple, His resurrected body, or whatever form His body was in at this time, went through the curtain in the heavenly Temple, and when His body passed through there, something else happened. An amazing thing happened on earth. Remember what it was? In the Temple on earth, the curtain was torn.

Mark 15:37-38 *Yeshua let out a loud cry and gave up His spirit, and the curtain in the Temple was torn in two, from the top to the bottom.*

What did this tearing of the Temple curtain signify? The way into the presence of God was open! Praise the Lord!

And I believe it happened at that same moment when He entered through the curtain in the heavenly Temple. And remember why it ripped from top to bottom? Because it was God doing it! It wasn't man. If you could see a picture that was to scale, you would see how high that curtain was. You would have to get a big ladder to get up there and rip that curtain from the top to the bottom. (You would also have to be very strong because that curtain was thick. It was woven of three different kinds of yarn and was embroidered.) So that's the second way this can be interpreted, His body is the way through the curtain.

The third explanation, which I find the most interesting, is that the phrase, "*that is, His body*" refers to the curtain, itself. Now, this is a little deep, so I want to say it again so everybody catches this: What I am saying is that the third way of interpreting it is that His body is the actual curtain.

So let me read verse 20 again, and make sure you hear it this way: *By a new and living way, opened for us through the curtain that is His body.*

His body is the curtain. Well, what does that mean? In what way was Yeshua's body a curtain?

Colossians1:19 *For in Him dwells all the fullness of the Godhead, bodily.*

So the fullness of the Glory of God dwelt in the body of Yeshua when He walked this earth. Now, that's hard to comprehend. I mean, because God was still making the universe run while His fullness dwelt within the Messiah, which is hard to comprehend. But, His body, His flesh, if you will, concealed the fullness of the Godhead dwelling within Him. The manifest presence of God was in Him, like the manifest presence of God was on that Mercy Seat, but the body was like a curtain, concealing it. Do you see that? It concealed the glory. And so, if His body was the curtain, how was a new and living way opened through the curtain? Well, Isaiah tells us He was wounded for our transgressions. The Hebrew word there for wounded "chalal," means a break in the skin, like a cutting. So, His body, the curtain, that concealed His divine nature, was torn by the whip, by the crown of thorns, by the nails, and finally by the spear that was thrust into Him. His body was torn, just as the Temple curtain was torn.
But there's an even deeper meaning here. If His body, His physical body, is the curtain, how do we enter through His body into that throne room of God? Well, I want to go back to Mark. I want you to look at a description of what happened just after the curtain was ripped in two.

Mark 15:37-39 *But Yeshua let out a loud cry and gave up his spirit. 38 And the parokhet in the Temple was torn in two from top to bottom. 39 When the Roman officer who stood facing him saw the way he gave up his spirit, he said, "This man really was the son of God!"*

So, what happened to this Roman officer when he heard Yeshua's cry and saw Him die? He became sure that Yeshua was the Son of God, the Messiah, Emmanuel, God Himself, come as a man. And in seeing this he saw the manifestation of the presence of God in that torn and dead body.

In John 14:9, Yeshua says, "*Anyone who has seen me has seen the Father.*" And that Roman centurion saw through Yeshua's human form to the Truth, that within that human form was contained the Living God, that Yeshua and the Father were one. And so, that Roman officer entered in. You see that? He entered in by perceiving that the body of Yeshua was just a curtain. It was only covering over the glory of God. And he was able to enter into the presence of God.

Now, let me ask you this. What happened to you and me when we came to know the Lord? We trusted in Yeshua's sacrificial death as an atonement, and we believed that Yeshua was God, Himself, come as a man because no human could make that kind of atoning, sacrificial death. And we saw that His human body was like a curtain, and we saw through that to the manifest presence of God within. So, we all came through His body. Through that living curtain that was His body, we came into His presence. That's how we received the atonement. Like the Roman officer, we could see the Truth, that He was really God. And I don't know about you, but that was the most important day of my life, when I had that revelation that this man was really God, Himself, come to lay down His life for my sin and my iniquity, for my redemption from curses, for my healing, for all of those things. That's awesome, isn't it? But there is more.

Actually, there are two more awesome things that I need to share. We need to go back to a verse we are now familiar with.

I Corinthians 3:16 *Don't you know that you people are the Temple, and that God's Spirit lives in you?*

Do you know that? You are the Temple. God's Spirit lives in you. The Holy Spirit, the *Ruakh HaKodesh* lives in you. However, we have a body. We have a flesh. We have a carnal nature, an old man. And you know what? That carnal nature conceals the glory of God living within us from others. You know what I am talking about here? When we act out of our carnal nature what do people see? Do they see the glory of God in us? No! They see our carnal nature. Right. Our actions, our fleshly actions, and our words, can keep others from seeing the Spirit of God, the presence of God within us. So, it's like that curtain.

So, we're going to pray in just a minute that God would tear that curtain so that others would see Him in us.

But first here is one more awesome thing. This is even more astounding.

The Veil of the Corporate Body

The Spirit of God, the Ruakh HaKodesh, dwells in us individually, but He also dwells in us corporately, doesn't He? He calls us the body of Messiah, doesn't He? So, let's just carry this further. The ungodly behavior of His body is like what? It's like a curtain. It keeps people from seeing the Glory of God. Do you see that? Now, maybe you're not aware that there has been some ungodly behavior of His body. If you are not, you need to know the history of the Jewish people. Because there have been two millennia of ungodly behavior toward the Jewish people, by those who claim to be His body. They may not have been His true body, but they claimed they were, and so to Jewish people today there is still a curtain.

Speaking of the Jewish people, Rabbi Sha'ul says:

II Corinthians 3:14-15. *What is more, their minds were made stone-like, for to this day the same veil remains over them when they read the Old Covenant. It has not been taken away because only by the Messiah is the veil taken away. Yes, still today, when Moses is read, a veil lies over their hearts.*

The veil mentioned here is the curtain that keeps people from seeing the Glory of God. And in the case of us corporately, it represents the centuries of the church's actions against Jewish people that have kept us, have kept my people, kept your people, from seeing the Glory of God in the Messiah. (We will go into more detail about that later.) So, we're going to pray today that God would tear that curtain, so that the Jewish people would see Him, even in spite of His body. That His body would be torn, that we could see through.

A Major Sign to the Cohanim

Now, the curtain being torn in two was an outward, physical sign to the Jewish leaders of what Yeshua's sacrifice meant.

Can you imagine what that was like for them—seeing that huge, very thick curtain being ripped by unseen hands right before their eyes? This would have happened while the cohanim were in the Holy Place doing their twice-daily Torah duties. Every morning and every evening, they had to offer incense on the altar of incense. They also had to trim the wicks on the Menorah and fill the seven lamps with oil. They most likely would have been doing this at the very same time that the curtain tore in two. I think the one or ones who witnessed it would have immediately run to tell the rest of the cohanim and the Cohane HaGadol. Of course, some of them might have been just leaving the scene of the crucifixion. But you would think they would have come right away to see this latest news event of the torn curtain.

What do you think went through their minds? They had to know it was a sign from God! The timing of it should have given them the idea that it had something to do with Yeshua's death. Of all people, they should have been able to figure out that it had something to do with the Messiah opening the way to God's presence.

Think about this too. They would have had to repair the tear! Maybe they even had to make a whole new curtain! Yet somehow, shockingly, they chose to ignore this sign that God so graciously gave them. Some of them did eventually get it, though, because it says in Acts 6:7 that *a large crowd of cohanim were becoming obedient to the faith.*

More Signs in the Talmud

Yom Kippur is so important that, as we have seen, there is plenty of Scripture explaining how to obey the command to keep it. There's Leviticus 23:26-32 and Numbers 29:7-11. And, as you know, the whole chapter of Leviticus 16 is about the many sacrifices the High Priest had to make including the two special goats. There are even B'rit Hadashah Scriptures about this Day of Atonement. In fact, a major part of the book of Hebrews talks about it! That's how pivotal Yeshua's fulfillment of this Moad/Appointed Time is!

Well, in studying the Talmud, I have discovered some things about the history of this Moad which actually help prove, along with the curtain being torn, that Yeshua is the Messiah, and that

His sacrifice really was the final atoning sacrifice. These are mysterious signs that point to Yeshua. Keep in mind that these signs are not made up by Messianic rabbis. They are recorded in the Talmud, written over a thousand years ago by non-believing rabbis, recording what had been oral tradition from the time of Yeshua. Let me repeat. The Talmud is written by Jewish rabbis who do NOT believe in Yeshua. The last thing they would want to do is prove the things about Yeshua are True!!

Lot in the Right Hand

The first of these mysterious signs concerns the lots. Remember, Leviticus 16:8 tells us that the Cohane HaGadol— the High Priest—had to cast lots on the two goats to determine which would be the sacrificial one "for the Lord" and which the "azazel" or scapegoat.

This is how it was done. They had two wooden, oval plaques that fit easily into the palms of the Cohane HaGadol's hands. The face of each was covered with a special metal that was inscribed. Each also had a hinged cover so the Cohane HaGadol could not see the inscriptions. With the goats facing him, one on the right and one on the left, he would reach both hands into the special box containing the lots and would quickly remove them both simultaneously, one in each hand.

It was traditionally considered a sign of God's favor if the Cohane drew the one that said "For the Lord" in his right hand. Thus the goat to his right would be the one sacrificed on the altar to the Lord. For all the years recorded, according to the Talmud, this lot was drawn in the right hand. But for each of the last forty years before the Temple was destroyed, again according to the Talmud, it was drawn in the left hand—every time!! .

They considered it to be a bad omen. Can you imagine that happening for forty straight years? Do you know what the odds are of that, of drawing lots and you always get the same one in the same hand? Well, I guess it was also extraordinary odds that it was always drawn in the right hand for the 1500 previous years! But just think about it. For forty straight years this went on. After more than a century of having the good sign, now this bad omen happened year after year, every year until the Temple was destroyed in the year 70. Did they connect this to what happened at the hill called Golgotha? No, they chose not to.

The Scarlet Cord

I mentioned earlier that the Talmud also talks of a crimson cord or sash, most likely made of wool, being tied around the horns of the scapegoat, and that a portion of that sash was also attached to the doors of the Temple. So while the man was taking the scapegoat away, the people in the Temple would be watching the scarlet cord tied to the door. According to the Talmud, when the goat was pushed off the cliff in the wilderness, when he was thus killed, the piece of woolen sash that was tied around the doors turned from crimson to white. The Talmud says it always turned white. The people took this as a sign that their iniquity was atoned for, for another year. This must be why Isaiah says, *Though your sins be as scarlet, they shall be as white as snow; though they be red like crimson, they shall be as wool* (Isaiah 1:18 KJV). (It makes you think of the red cord in Rahab's window too, doesn't it?)

Again, the Talmud (Yoma 39b) records that for the last forty years before the Temple was destroyed, the sash stopped turning white!!! It stayed red every year for those four decades! Why? Because Yeshua had already borne our iniquities forever! It was another sign for the Jewish leaders. But again they chose not to connect it to Yeshua at all.

Two Other Mysterious Signs

So those are three signs that help prove Yeshua is the Messiah: the curtain being torn, the goat "for the Lord" being drawn in the left hand, and the scarlet cord not turning white. Here are two more mysterious signs that are recorded in the traditional Jewish historical records.

The first one is about the Temple doors. One day shortly before the Temple was destroyed the doors to the Temple flew open. The Jews took this to mean destruction was coming soon. They based it on this prophecy.

Ezekiel 26:2   *"Son of man, because Tyre has said of Jerusalem, 'Aha! The gate to the nations is broken, and its doors have swung open to me; now that she lies in ruins I will prosper.*

Yes, sudden, terrible destruction did come to the Temple and Jerusalem shortly after the Temple doors flew open. The Romans came and destroyed both. So the rabbis were correct in their interpretation. But they missed the significance of the timing of this event and the symbolism of it.

Yeshua said in John 10:7, "*I am the door for the sheep.*"

The last mysterious sign has to do with a lamp in the Temple court for women—the one where all the people always gathered at special times—on the Sabbath and at Appointed Times. The western most torch-light of this Temple court was the one the servants always used to light all the other lights. For some mysterious reason it always stayed lit. It miraculously never went out all through the centuries. However for the last forty years, it would not burn at all! It was a mystery to the rabbis—another omen. But it makes perfect sense to us believers because Yeshua said:

"*I am the Light of the world*" (John 8:12).

So, again, what happened forty years before the destruction of the Temple, around the year 30? Well, let's figure it out. Yeshua died at age 33. We won't go into all the detail, but our Gregorian calendar is not completely accurate plus it has no year zero. Year 1 is supposed to be the year Yeshua was born, but they got it a little off. He was actually born four years BCE (Before Common Era). So the year 30 is actually when He died.

The Scriptures tell us that the sign of the Temple curtain being split in two definitely signifies that there was a new atonement that had been made that opened the way for everyone to come into the presence of God. That sign is recorded in the Bible. It is so amazing that these other signs are in the Talmud. I am stunned that they would be recorded there to tell us of these other signals God gave His people so they would believe in Yeshua's greater atonement.

Let's Pray

Lord, we have so much to be thankful for. Thank You for dying and shedding Your blood for the forgiveness of our sins. Thank You for dying on a cross to redeem us from the curses of the Law. Thank You for bearing those stripes that we could be physically healed. Thank You for bearing that chastisement for our peace, our shalom. And today, Lord, we just want to thank You for dying a slow agonizing death as the scapegoat, as that goat in the wilderness, with our iniquities laid upon You, bearing our iniquities, oh God. Give us a fresh revelation, Lord God, of our iniquitous nature. Give us a fresh revelation of how much we need Your forgiveness, of how unworthy we are of coming into Your presence. Give us a fresh revelation, Lord, that those iniquities were placed upon You. That as You hung upon that cross all the iniquities and all the sins of all time were placed upon You and, oh, how You suffered for all that. What an awful price to pay. And Lord, may that revelation give us a joyful confidence in Your completed work on the cross.

And, Lord, we thank You today that You passed through that curtain in heaven, and that You tore the one on earth. And we thank You, Lord, that by tearing that curtain on earth You made a way for us to come into Your Holy of Holies, into Your presence. Thank You, Lord, that there was no way that we could get there by ourselves, but You made a way. And we thank You, Lord, that You took on the form of a man and that while You walked this earth the Glory of God was concealed by Your flesh, and yet it dwelt within You, the fullness dwelt within You, bodily. And we thank You, Lord, those of us who have come to know You, we thank You that You opened our eyes and You removed the veil and that we could see through that curtain to the Glory that was inside. To the Glory of the Living God, the Shekinah Glory. May this revelation, again, lead us to a joyful confidence that we can come into Your presence, that the way has been made to come into Your throne room, and to intercede there, to be intercessors, Lord God.

And Lord, we also thank You for this revelation that we are like a curtain. Our bodies, our actions, our carnal natures; that these cover the Glory of God within us. Lord, we want that Glory to shine out! We want it to be like a light, like You say it is to be, but we know so many times we get in the way; what we do and what we say get in the way. And so, Father, we pray that You would, especially for our loved ones, just tear that curtain. Let them not see our flesh, Lord God, and our carnal nature, but let them see Your Glory within us. Let them see Your Glory, Father.

Father, our hearts are so heavy knowing the terrible history of persecution and the letter of the law and deadness and power and ego trips, of torture, of burnings at the stake, all kinds of horrible things, against both Jews and against true believers; all done in Your name. And, Lord, we know that this history is a curtain that keeps so many people from seeing Your Glory in Your body. And so we pray, Lord, that You would tear that curtain, especially over our Jewish people, that You would tear the curtain, Lord God, that they would see through all the terrible things that have been done in Your Name, and they would see through it all to the Glory that You are. Lord, I know You did that for me, because somehow, when You opened my eyes, seeing You was more important than all of those other things. And so we pray for the tearing of that curtain.

We pray that all Jews everywhere who are looking for their Messiah, who are feeling the lack of atonement in their life will receive a special revelation of You as the fulfillment of the sacrificial goat and the scapegoat—that you bore all their sins, transgressions and iniquities and have turned their sins from scarlet to white as snow. May they walk through the Door you have opened for them and be flooded with Your Light. In Yeshua's Name. Amen.

CHAPTER 8

MYSTERY OF THE BLOOD: CLEANSING THE LAND

Thirty Messianic Rabbis at Ground Zero

In the year 2005 near Yom Kippur, I went down to Ground Zero. There were two reasons for going. One was to be there for the commemoration of 9-11. The other was to pray with other Messianic Rabbis from the Northeast of the United States for the revival of the New York Metropolitan area.

I hope you understand the burden of prayer for this area of the country that is huge on my heart, and I hope it is on yours too, because there are three million Jewish people in the New York Metropolitan area. That is the largest collection of Jewish people outside of Israel in the world. And it took a little while for Israel to get to the point that there were more Jewish people in Israel than there were in New York City. It's wonderful that there are so many Jewish people there. The problem is that there are almost no Messianic Jewish congregations in that region.

There's one in Queens and one out in New Jersey. Two of the rabbis that were there were just starting works in Manhattan. The congregation in Queens was just starting a Friday night meeting in Manhattan. Another rabbi had recently moved to Manhattan from Kazakhstan after five years of reaching out to the community in Kazakhstan. He was moving into Manhattan where he thinks it's a harder field than in Kazakhstan!

So the purpose was to pray for these works. We gathered at Beth Yisrael in Garfield, NJ. It's a huge congregation of about 1200 people. We had about 30 Messianic rabbis and their wives there, and we had a great time. First we had a ceremony to commemorate 9-11. The most touching part for me was the fireman who was actually in the collapse of the towers. He still had injuries and he was still grieving. He tried to speak and couldn't get the words out because of what he had experienced four years earlier. So we spent some time praying for the grieving and the injured.

The rabbi of Beth Israel gave a message explaining what we were going to do after the service. It was about his understanding that the gate of America, the place where most people came into America, is the mouth of the Hudson River. Most of the immigrants came up to the docks there where the ships landed for Ellis Island. Of course this was before air travel. That gate actually stands from Manhattan across the river to New Jersey. If you can visualize—I don't know if you know the geography of New York City—but Manhattan is an Island and on the west side of Manhattan is the Hudson River and just across the river is New Jersey.

The World Trade Center is down at the lower, southern end of Manhattan. And right across from the World Trade Center is Jersey City. The hotel at which we chose to have the Northeast Regional Messianic Conference that year is right on the water, directly across from the World Trade Center. So what the rabbi was seeing was this gate that extends across the river, one end at the World Trade Center and the other end at the hotel. What he had planned for us to do was to go pray at the gate. The prayer was that the Spirit of God would come in through that gate because obviously with three million Jewish people there and no one to reach out to them, we need a miracle to happen!! We need the Spirit of God to begin to move in that area. We need that gate to be closed to evil and opened to God's Spirit.

So we proceeded from the service down to the World Trade Center. There were about sixty of us, and, we prayed right there at the fence around Ground Zero. Then we went back across the Hudson to the Hyatt Hotel where there's a pier right on the water and we had a powerful time of prayer looking at the Jersey sky-line. Then we went and prayed looking across at the Manhattan skyline. So, we were praying on both sides of the gate, as was the idea. There were many confirmations on each side that the Lord was in this. There were actually a couple people who got saved while we were there! Also there was an unexpected TV interview. Reporters from a local TV station showed up and interviewed the rabbi.

Redeeming the Land

At Ground Zero, I was led to share a passage that I have been praying about for a long time—about redeeming the land. It was actually from the Parasha of the preceding week, Deuteronomy 21. I was led to share about redeeming the land because, as you know, there were several thousand innocent people murdered on that site. The people who committed the murders were also killed on the site, but not those who planned and continue to plan actions like that.

So read along with me as we look at these instructions here concerning redeeming the land.

Deuteronomy 21:1-4 (NAS) *If a slain person is found lying in the open country in the land which the LORD your God gives you to possess, and it is not known who has struck him,*

[In other words, for unsolved murders]

then your elders and your judges shall go out and measure the distance to the cities which are around the slain one.

[In other words, they should figure out which city should take responsibility for this murder.]

It shall be that the city which is nearest to the slain man, that is, the elders of that city, shall take a heifer of the herd, which has not been worked and which has not pulled in a yoke; 4 and the elders of that city shall bring the heifer down to a valley with running water, which has not been plowed or sown, and shall break the heifer's neck there in the valley.

Now, this phrase "breaking the heifer's neck" has always confused me so I did a little study on it. I discovered that another translation could be "to cut off the heifer's head." I believe that is the correct translation because they were making a blood sacrifice there. And they were doing it in the stream so that the water would carry the blood. I believe that was the whole point of this because the land had been defiled from this murder.

Deuteronomy 21:5-7 (NAS) *Then the priests, the sons of Levi, shall come near, for the LORD your God has chosen them to serve Him and to bless in the name of the LORD; and every dispute and every assault shall be settled by them. 6 All the elders of that city which is nearest to the slain man shall wash their hands over the heifer whose neck was broken in the valley;*

This is where, in my understanding, that the blood from the heifer would have been flowing in the stream and they would have been washing their hands in the bloody water over that heifer. We understand that believers of the New Covenant, according to Scripture are a nation of cohanim, priests. So this group of Messianic rabbis, as New Covenant cohanim, was gathered at Ground Zero. (We did not go to an unsown valley and cut off the head of a cow. You probably couldn't find an unsown valley in that region of the world, and we probably would've gotten in trouble if we had tried to cut off the head of a cow out there.) But what we did was we declared the verses that follow and took responsibility for that innocent blood that had been shed.

Deuteronomy 21:7-9 (NIV) *And they shall answer and say, "Our hands did not shed this blood, nor did our eyes see it. Forgive Your people Israel whom You have redeemed, O LORD, and do not place the guilt of innocent blood in the midst of Your people Israel." And the blood guiltiness shall be forgiven them. So you shall remove the guilt of innocent blood from your midst, when you do what is right in the eyes of the LORD.*

NKJV: *Then they shall answer and say, "Our hands have not shed this blood, nor have our eyes seen it. 8 Provide atonement, O Lord, for Your people Israel, whom You have redeemed, and do not lay innocent blood to the charge of Your people Israel." And atonement shall be provided on their behalf for the blood. 9 So you shall put away the guilt of innocent blood from among you when you do what is right in the sight of the Lord.*

CJB: *Then they are to speak up and say, "This blood was not shed by our hands, nor have we seen who did it. 8 ADONAI, forgive your people Isra'el, whom you redeemed; do not allow innocent blood to be shed among your people Isra'el." And they will be forgiven this bloodshed. 9 Thus you will banish the shedding of innocent blood from among you, by doing what ADONAI sees as right.*

So, this group, particularly about a dozen of the rabbis that are the most closely connected there, declared this at Ground Zero. That was an amazing thing to me because I had come across this passage three and a half years earlier and I had written in my notes, "Does this need to be done for New York City?" Then I had tried to organize something. I had talked to a few people, but it never got off the ground. So, I just waited on the Lord. Then suddenly I got the invitation, "Come down to the metropolitan area. We're going to go to Ground Zero with a bunch of Messianic rabbis and we're going to pray at Ground Zero." And I just went, "Wow! This is the fulfillment of what God was showing me!" So, I was really blessed to be able to share. And I would like to have you agree with me in prayer later because I think there is more and more power in having more and more people agree in prayer in that.

The Blood Cries Out

So, now I'd like to take you on a little study about this mysterious material called the Blood and how it has a spiritual meaning, and what that spiritual meaning is. If you would follow me here, we're going to start with the first appearance of blood in the Bible. It actually starts with the story of Cain and Abel. When Cain murdered his brother, Abel, and the Lord confronted him, this is what God said.

Genesis 4:10 *The voice of your brother's blood is crying out to me from the ground!*

Now, sometimes, we just think He's just speaking figuratively here. But as we go through, we'll see that He's not speaking figuratively. He's speaking spiritually. There is something about the blood that cries out to God when there's a murder. Somehow God can hear the blood crying out from the ground. And that's what's been crying out to Him from Ground Zero for more than a decade.

The next place where the blood is mentioned in a significant way is in what we call the "Noahide Covenant."

Genesis 9:4 *Only flesh with its life, which is its blood, you are not to eat.*

I want to point out that this prohibition against eating flesh with the blood in it is not just for Jewish people because this is the Noahide Covenant which is for all nations. Also this verse connects life with the blood. We'll see this as a theme that is spoken about the blood all through Scriptures.

Genesis 9:5   *... I will certainly demand an accounting for the blood of your lives: ... Whoever sheds human blood, by a human being will his own blood be shed;*

Now what in our legal system do we get from those Scriptures? Capital punishment! And notice it's not just for Israel. This is the covenant with Noah. And notice also that in the earlier verse, God places the responsibility on man. He clearly said, "*... by the hand of man must the murderer's blood be shed*" (NIV) Then He gives the reason for it in the next verse.

Genesis 9: 6 *for God made human beings in his image.*

This is, I think, one of the most powerful phrases in the entire Scripture. This is the greatest incentive for us to treat other human beings as holy beings! Every human being is made in the image of God.

Now, we get some further understanding about the blood in Leviticus 17.

Leviticus 17:10   *When someone from the community of Isra'el or one of the foreigners living with you eats any kind of blood, I will set myself against that person who eats blood and cut him off from his people.*

Now, we need to understand that at that time and possibly today, there were groups that participated in idolatrous worship, eating the blood of their sacrifice. So, it was specifically dealing with that—prohibiting it in Israel and anyone living amongst the Jewish people.

Then in verse 11, He says this amazing thing.

Leviticus 17:11 *For the life of a creature is in the blood.*

Now, for anyone who has taken basic biology, if you just think about this a little bit, biologically this is true because the blood carries the oxygen and the nutrients throughout the body of every animal. So, the life is in the blood. When the blood stops flowing, the life ends. Without the blood, there would be no life. But, there's also a spiritual mystery that's in this verse that I think is just amazing. It amazingly points to how the Bible is the inspired Word of God because how could anyone know this back then?

Genesis 2:7   ... *breathed into his nostrils the breath of life*

That is "nifshma Khaim." "Khaim" is life and "nifshma" is "breath."

Genesis 2:7 *and man became a living being.*

"Nefish khayah" is "living being." So, when you think about this, God breathed life into man. It was like His breath of life "nifshma khaim" and He breathed it right into Adam's nostrils, it says. Now, we know today that Adam's blood carried oxygen and therefore carried God's breath to every part of Adam's body. Do you see the incredible spiritual significance of that? In other words, it wasn't just that it's oxygen. It's life itself that the Scripture was saying was breathed into Adam and then carried throughout his body by his blood. This is why it says that the life of the flesh is in the blood—biologically, yes, but spiritually also—that "life" is the breath of God.

And this breath of life, incredibly, is passed on through our ability to reproduce because when we have offspring, they, too, have the breath of life. So, because the life of the flesh is in the blood, blood has a spiritual power. It's more than just a liquid. It has a spiritual power because look in the rest of the verse there.

Leviticus 17:11b (NIV) ... *I have given ... for it is the blood that makes atonement for the soul.*

Now, this is referring to the Mosaic Law where the blood of sacrificed animals was sprinkled on the altar making atonement.

Let me just refresh your memory. The Hebrew word for "atonement" is "kippur." It is the same word we get "kippah" from and it means "*to cover*" or to "*expiate, to appease, to cleanse, to forgive, to pardon, to purge, to reconcile.*" So "kippur" the "atonement" means all of that. And in this verse we'll see that the blood and only the blood can make a kippur. It's only through the blood.

Leviticus 17:12-14 (NKJV) *Therefore I said to the children of Israel, 'No one among you shall eat blood, nor shall any stranger who dwells among you eat blood.' 13 Whatever man of the children of Israel, or of the strangers who dwell among you, who hunts and catches any animal or bird that may be eaten, he shall pour out its blood and cover it with dust; 14 for it is the life of all flesh. Its blood sustains its life. Therefore I said to the children of Israel, 'You shall not eat the blood of any flesh, for the life of all flesh is its blood. Whoever eats it shall be cut off.'*

Leviticus 17:12-14 (CJB) *This is why I told the people of Isra'el, "None of you is to eat blood, nor is any foreigner living with you to eat blood." 13 When someone from the community of Isra'el or one of the foreigners living with you hunts and catches game, whether animal or bird that may be eaten, he is to pour out its blood and cover it with earth. 14 For the life of every creature—its blood is its life. Therefore I said to the people of Isra'el, "You are not to eat the blood of any creature, because the life of every creature is its blood. Whoever eats it will be cut off."*

So, not only does man's blood carry the "nifshma khaim" but the blood of every animal carries this breath of life. "The blood is the life of all flesh." This is an amazing biological revelation, if you imagine back to 3500 years ago and what they knew biologically. We know that it was only in the last hundred years that people figured out about germs. They were draining people's blood to heal them just a couple hundred years ago. So, there was so much ignorance about what the blood really did. And here, 3500 years ago, Moses knew all about it. Astounding! Amazing confirmation, I believe, that this book—the Bible—is definitely, divinely inspired.

Another proof of its divine inspiration is circumcision. It is commanded that a baby boy be circumcised on the eighth day, and scientists have discovered that on the eighth day the clotting ability of human blood maximizes. It increases until the eighth day and then it goes back down again. So, how would they have known that if they just made up this book? God knew it.

[This passage, by the way, is the basis for kosher butchering. What we have in kosher butchering, which is really the way almost all of our butchering is done today, is the blood is always drained out of the animal so that we eat the minimal amount of blood. Of course, Orthodox people go to great lengths to make sure they get all the blood out. They salt the meat. They boil the meat. They pound the meat to get every last little bit of blood out of the meat. But most of the meat that we buy in our stores today has the blood drained from it because if the blood wasn't drained, it would spoil quicker. So, there's a very clear economic reason for doing that.]

Murder Defiles the Land

Now, we are going to look at another passage that speaks about the power of the blood. This is Moses speaking to the children of Israel.

Numbers 35:33 *In this way you will not defile the land in which you are living. For blood defiles the land,*

Now this is talking about murder—blood of innocent victims.

Numbers 35: 33b (NIV) *And no atonement can be made for the land for the blood that was shed on it except by the blood of him who shed it.*
CJB: *and in this land no atonement can be made for the blood shed in it except the blood of him who shed it.*

Once again, this is another one of the verses from which we get capital punishment. The blood of the perpetrator is the one that can atone for the land.

Now, I want to turn our focus a little bit to this idea of atoning for land. Atonement to us is about atoning for people because people have committed sins and atonement gets them back right with God. This is what it's all about—being forgiven of your sins. But here it's talking about atonement for the land. It's a little bit hard for us to understand that. It says in verse 34, *"Do not defile the land that you inhabit in the midst of which I dwell for I the Lord dwell among the children of Israel"*(NIV). So that verse helps us to understand what this means. Why would you make atonement for the land?

Blood Atonement for Things?

Let me back up and say this. The universe and everything in it can be divided into two parts. There's God and there's His creation. Okay? Agree with me? Now, God, according to the Hebrew, is kadosh, meaning He is separate from the created universe. But the creation is not kadosh. The creation is what God is separated from. But God at times chooses to make part of the creation kadosh. He chooses to bring part of that creation to Him, or He chooses to dwell IN that part of the creation. So, what He's saying here is that I chose to dwell in the land of Israel. That was the whole point of bringing us out of the land of Egypt to the land of Israel. God was going to dwell amongst us! So, He's saying, "I cannot dwell there unless the land has been atoned for—unless I bring the land into what is called kadosh—into the part of the universe where I can dwell. If the land has been defiled by innocent blood, I cannot dwell there anymore unless atonement is made for the land. Follow that so far?

So, this is the case in Israel when we were in the wilderness. Aaron was instructed to make atonement for the sanctuary. And again, the sanctuary never committed any sin. But God's presence was going to dwell there. So the Yom Kippur offerings made atonement for the whole nation and included atonement for the Tabernacle so that God could dwell amongst the people of Israel. Many years later when we find the conquest by Babylon and the exile of our people into Babylonian captivity, the presence of God left the Temple. We find it recorded that the reason God left was because innocent blood was shed.

II Kings 24:3-4 NKJV *Surely at the commandment of the Lord this came upon Judah, to remove them from His sight because of the sins of Manasseh, according to all that he had done, 4 and also because of the innocent blood that he had shed; for he had filled Jerusalem with innocent blood, which the Lord would not pardon.*

CJB *Yes, it was at ADONAI's order that this happened to Y'hudah, in order to remove them from his sight because of the sins of M'nasheh and all he had done, 4 and also because of the innocent blood he had shed - for he had flooded Yerushalayim with innocent blood, and ADONAI was unwilling to forgive.*

M'nasheh (Manasseh) was one of the last kings of Israel. If you've read the book of Ezekiel, you will remember that Ezekiel saw the glory of God departing from the Temple around this time. There was much shedding of innocent blood in the land of Israel prior to the birth of Yeshua. There were terrible times—the times of the Maccabees and the times of the Hasmonian's—brother fighting against brother—all kinds of uprisings. But

I believe that God's presence returned to the Temple when Yeshua came there. We understand in the Talmud that in the year 70, when the Temple was destroyed again, remember there were two Temples—both destroyed on the same day of the year, as a matter of fact, on Tisha B'Av—it says the Second Temple was destroyed for the same reason—for the shedding of innocent blood. And, of course, we could say that could have been Yeshua's blood because He was killed as a sinless, righteous man 37 years before. But there were many others that were killed also because there was much turmoil, much anarchy going on in Israel during those years. There were also all the people martyred for the Gospel: James, Stephen, later on Peter, etc.

So, where does God dwell now? There's no Temple. Does He dwell in the land of Israel? Possibly. But the New Covenant Scriptures say that God dwells IN His people. We need to understand—this is important to understand—that He can't dwell in us unless atonement is made for us because we are not kadosh. We are of this creation. So, how is atonement made for us so that He can dwell in us? I'd like to read here without too much comment what is discussed in the book of Hebrews.

Hebrews 9:11   *But when the Messiah appeared as cohen gadol of the good things that are happening already, then, through the greater and more perfect Tent which is not man-made (that is, it is not of this created world),*

This tent or Tabernacle he is speaking of is God's throne room in heaven.

Hebrews 9:12 *he entered the Holiest Place once and for all. And he entered not by means of the blood of goats and calves, but by means of his own blood, thus setting people free forever. 13 For if sprinkling ceremonially unclean persons with the blood of goats and bulls and the ashes of a heifer restores their outward purity;*

That was how it was done under the Mosaic covenant.

Hebrews 9:14   *then how much more the blood of the Messiah, who, through the eternal Spirit, offered himself to God as a sacrifice without blemish, will purify our conscience from works that lead to death, so that we can serve the living God!*

How much more purifying than the blood of animals is the blood of the Messiah who as we understand was God Himself come as a man? So this is the blood of God Himself being shed. And this phrase here, "purifying our conscience" other translations say "our moral consciousness" means purifying our minds and our ability to make moral decisions.

Hebrews 9:18-21 *This is why the first covenant too was inaugurated with blood. 19 After Moshe had proclaimed every command of the Torah to all the people, he took the blood of the calves with some water and used scarlet wool and hyssop to sprinkle both the scroll itself and all the people; 20 and he said, "This is the blood of the covenant which God has ordained for you." 21 Likewise, he sprinkled with the blood both the Tent and all the things used in its ceremonies.*

Here we see that atonement for **things**—sprinkling them so God's presence can dwell among them—purifying them with blood. The writer of Hebrews is quoting Moses in Exodus 24:7-8.

Hebrews 9:22 *In fact, according to the Torah, almost everything is purified with blood; indeed, without the shedding of blood there is no forgiveness of sins.*

Now, this is a restating of what we read in Leviticus 17:11. But also notice that it interprets it a little bit because in Leviticus 17:11 it says that the blood is given for atonement, but here it says that without the blood there is NO atonement. So it makes it even stronger.

Hebrews 9:23 *Now this is how the copies of the heavenly things had to be purified, but the heavenly things themselves require better sacrifices than these.*

Better Than the Blood of Animals.

Hebrews 9:24-26 *For the Messiah has entered a Holiest Place which is not man-made and merely a copy of the true one, but into heaven itself, in order to appear now on our behalf in the very presence of God. 25 Further, he did not enter heaven to offer himself over and over again, like the cohen hagadol who enters the Holiest Place year after year with blood that is not his own; 26 for then he would have had to suffer death many times - from the founding of the universe on. But as it is, he has appeared once at the end of the ages in order to do away with sin through the sacrifice of himself.*

Can you say amen? All that is an amazing passage! I hope you understand—this explains how the Spirit of God can dwell in us unholy human beings. It's only because His blood has made atonement for us.

Now, did this really happen? Or is this author of Hebrews just kind of making this up? Well, I believe the greatest confirmation that this actually happened is history. What the author of Hebrews is describing happened around the year 33 CE. That's when Yeshua was crucified and died. What we know from history is that the Temple where the animal sacrifices could be made was destroyed 37 years later in the year 70. And it was not destroyed by followers of Yeshua. We had nothing to do with it. It was destroyed by the Romans.

Leviticus 17:8-9 (NKJV) *Also you shall say to them: "Whatever man of the house of Israel, or of the strangers who dwell among you, who offers a burnt offering or sacrifice, 9 and does not bring it to the door of the tabernacle of meeting, to offer it to the Lord, that man shall be cut off from among his people."*

Leviticus 17:8-9 (CJB) *Also tell them, "When someone from the community of Isra'el or one of the foreigners living with you offers a burnt offering or sacrifice 9 without bringing it to the entrance of the tent of meeting to sacrifice it to ADONAI, that person is to be cut off from his people."*

So, these verses prohibit sacrifices being made anywhere except at the Temple. Do you see that? So when the Temple was destroyed the religious leaders of Israel could no longer make the Temple sacrifices. They had to stop those sacrifices. What we find also 65 years later, with the complete destruction of Jerusalem by the Romans, Israel didn't have a land anymore either. The people were scattered at that time. Obviously, God's presence was no longer there because the Romans drove everybody out.

As we pointed out, the Jewish leaders got together and decreed that, from then on, a person could find atonement by praying, by repenting, by studying the Torah, and by doing good works. Well, that is a great idea. However, there was something missing. What was missing? The blood!

Well, what happened to Messianic Judaism? Messianic Jews trusted that the Messiah's Blood atonement was the thing! It was what enabled the Spirit to dwell within us—not in the Temple built with hands—but in our hearts. In the New Covenant this is what is stated that we are the temple of the living God.

II Corinthians 6:16 *For we are the temple of the living God.*

It is so important to understand, though, that we are not the temple of the living God just because we decided to be or just because we asked for it. No! We are only the temple of the living God because God made a way for Him to dwell within us by making atonement for us with His Blood.

So, the Blood of Messiah has several functions. We see at Passover how it saves us from eternal death, just as the blood of the Passover lamb saved our forefathers from the tenth plague coming out of Egypt. But Messiah's Blood also has a cleansing and a purifying power over our bodies, souls, and spirits. It protects us from demonic invasion.

S'udat Adonai/Communion

The equivalent in the New Covenant to the Passover is the ceremony that the Lord gave us to remember Him by. We, in the Messianic congregations call it the S'udat Adonai which means "The Lord's Supper." In churches, it is called the Communion. The S'udat Adonai focuses on the renewing power of the Blood of the Messiah. Understand that this is the covenant meal of the New Covenant. So, it is a very, important, serious time. You should only partake of it if you have embraced the Covenant. That means that you are trusting in the Messiah for your atonement and that you have made Him Lord—the One that you follow in your life.

I Corinthians 11:26 *For as often as you eat this bread and drink the cup, you proclaim the death of the Lord, until he comes.*

I saw something new in this passage in 2005. When we take the cup and the Matzah, it's a visual way of proclaiming His sacrifice. Therefore we are proclaiming His blood and His body. I had an opportunity to visit Ground Zero and I was thinking we would actually do this at Ground Zero. I had actually bought some Matzah and some grape juice, but the Lord said, "No, this is not the place to do it." But we did it later in our congregation. The Spirit knows no distance.

I Corinthians 11: 27 *Therefore, whoever eats the Lord's bread or drinks the Lord's cup in an unworthy manner will be guilty of desecrating the body and blood of the Lord!*

So, we see in these verses the healing power of the body and the blood. There is healing power in partaking of this. And we also see healing in self-examination. Really, it's not just **self**-examination. It's being open to the Spirit of God revealing anything that we need to repent of, that we need to change, that we need to turn back to the Lord.

So, we're going to pray those things. We're going to proclaim the power of the Lord's Blood. I saw communion for the first time as a weapon of spiritual warfare. I never saw it like that before. But it is. It's a weapon of spiritual warfare for the cleansing of the land, for the cleansing of ourselves, for dealing with the powers of darkness. And then we're going to recite those words in Deuteronomy 21 that we recited down at Ground Zero in agreement for the redeeming of that land and the redeeming of other lands.

So, if you have entered into the New Covenant you can partake of the S'udat Adonai as you pray the prayer below. If you have not entered into the New Covenant you should not partake, unless you want to enter in at this time. If so, partaking in this S'udat Adonai can be your means of entering into the New Covenant. So, you can just read along if you're not ready to partake or you can get some Matzah (or other unleavened bread) and some grape juice and partake as you pray. If you're going to partake, hold the Matzah and cup in your hand.

Praying and Declaring before Partaking

So, Father, we come to You today. We ask, first of all, that Your Spirit, Your Ruakh, would speak to us. Reveal to us any ways in which we need to change—anything we need to repent of—anyone that we need to go and apologize to—anyone, a wrong that we need to correct—to forgive. We pray that if there's any root of bitterness, any resentment, any unforgiveness, any unwarranted anger, reveal to us any judgmental attitudes, O God, any pride. Lord, we repent of these things. We confess of falling short of Your standards. We ask Your forgiveness based upon Your sacrifice.

According to Your instructions, we recognize this cup and this Matzah as representing Your body and Your blood, we recognize the great sacrifice that You made for us. So, we hold up the Matzah and the cup and we proclaim Your death to the powers of darkness in this world and in the spirit world. We proclaim Your death and resurrection. We proclaim the power of Your Blood, that this is not just grape juice, but it is spiritually a powerful instrument of righteousness.

Let's recite the words of the priests and the elders for Ground Zero and for Israel and for wherever you live.

"Our hands have not shed this Blood, nor have our eyes seen it. Provide atonement, O Lord, for Your people in Israel and for America and for my city—Your people whom you have redeemed. Do not lay innocent blood to the charge of Your people."

We're going to believe in faith now, as we recite the rest of this together.

"An atonement shall be provided on their behalf for the blood."

" So You shall put away the guilt of innocent blood among you when you do what is right in the sight of the Lord." Amen.

So, Father, we thank You for what is transpiring in the Spirit right now at Ground Zero, in my city, across America, and in Israel, all these places, that Your presence might dwell in these places in an ever greater way. We agree now that the gates would be opened and the Spirit of God would come into this country and especially into the metropolitan area of New York City, in a way in which has not been seen in the past—the fullness of the power of Your Spirit—and that we would see revival in that place, that we would see the three million Jewish people in that area touched by Your Spirit, that we would see Messianic congregations spring up in all those boroughs and suburbs, that we would see testimonies of those who have been transformed, those that have turned from ungodliness to Godliness. Thank You, Lord.

And Father, we want to turn our attention to the power in these things that You've given us for ourselves. Your Word talks about the power of healing in these. So we ask today that there would be a power in what we put into our bodies today. There would be a power of healing, a power for strengthening. We know there are many reading this who have physical ailments. We pray, O Lord, that this would have that power.

If you need healing, this is for you.

Father, we thank You for the power of Your Blood and of Your body. I am in need of Your touch upon my body. I pray, Father, that as these simple elements enter my body, they would enter with a spiritual power of Your Blood, O God, and Your body, and that there would be an impartation of Your healing power to me, and impartation of Your strengthening. I need Your strength, O God. Thank You, Lord.

The Lord said as He was celebrating Passover with His disciples, He took the Matzah and He blessed it. Let's recite the blessing on it.

"Baruch ata Adonai Elohenu Melekh ha olam, ha motzi lekhem min ha aretz."

"Blessed are You, Lord our God, King of the Universe, who brings forth bread from the earth."

Amen

Then He said the most astounding words, "This is My body broken for you. Take and eat."

You may eat the bread.

Then He took the cup and recited the blessing.

"Baruch ata Adonai Elohenu Melekh ha olam, bore' pri ha gaafan.

Blessed are You, Lord our God, King of the Universe, who creates the fruit of the vine. Amen

And He said, "This is the Blood of the New Covenant poured out for the forgiveness of sins. Take and drink."

You may drink the wine (or grape juice).

Let's Pray

Father, we don't understand the fullness of the power of Your Blood. But we agree together that the fullness of that power would work in every individual that is praying this today, that it would bring the power of Your Spirit into their lives to bring healing, restoration, wholeness, strength, and complete health into their whole body. In the Name of Yeshua, Amen. Amen. Amen.

Chapter 9

MYSTERY OF THE BLOOD: THE COVENANT SYMBOL

N ow, we are going to look further into the Word into more about the Mystery of the Blood. We are going to do a second part to what we just studied. Here's what we've learned so far.

The life is in the blood.

It's only in the blood that atonement is made.

The blood is more than a physical thing.

The blood of those who have been innocently killed cries out from the earth.

Yeshua went into the Holy Place of heaven, the very throne of God and offered His own Blood and made atonement once and for all.

I'd like now to start from that last point. I'd like to just get you thinking about what that moment was like because I believe that was a pivotal moment in the world's history. The moment that He made that atonement, the world changed. In fact, we have our

Jewish calendar that has been around for thousands of years, but if you look at our modern calendar, it dates from that time. That's what it's all about. In fact, I think of the word "history." Did you ever think about how that word is constructed? His – story. Whose story? Well, it's God's story. It's Yeshua's story. It's His story. So, the world changed at that moment.

In our Beit club (the sequel to the Alef club where seekers can learn more about God and Scripture) we were talking about how we can deal with sin. We talked about how sin is not allowed in the presence of the Holy God. God's most definable characteristic in the Bible is that He is kadosh. He is holy. It means that He is separate from sin, and that sin cannot be in His presence. So, in the Beit club we were talking about this and were saying that somehow for a person to come into God's presence something needs to be done with their sins. They need to be taken away. One person who comes to the club said, "Where did they all go? What happens to all those sins?"

Well, that moment when Yeshua sprinkled His Blood on the altar, not on the earth, but in heaven, was the moment at which atonement was made for all sin, for all time, past, present, and future. It was His Blood sprinkled on that altar in the throne room of God in heaven that made that happen. That was the pivot point, if you will, of world history because the world changed. Before that atonement was *not* made; after that atonement *was* made.

Defeating the Adversary

So, now I'd like to talk a little more about the Blood. There are a couple things we are going to do. We are going to talk about the power of the Blood and relate it to the Tanakh—the Old Testament. But we are also going to talk about a passage that has always been a mystery to me, and I suspect it's been a mystery to you also. We're going to get there in a few minutes. But first let's go to Revelation. This is speaking about ha-satan, the adversary. It's actually speaking about a time in the future, I believe. The word "they" in this context is talking about the followers of Yeshua. The word "him" is understood to be ha-satan.

Revelation 12:11 *They defeated him because of the Lamb's blood and because of the message of their witness. Even when facing death they did not cling to life.*

NKJV: *And they overcame him by the blood of the Lamb and by the word of their testimony, and they did not love their lives to the death.*

So this speaks of the defeat of ha-satan, his ultimate defeat. And, as we see in this verse, it's going to be caused by three things. What are those three things? The Blood of the Lamb, the word of our testimony, and our willingness to lay down our lives—the willingness to sacrifice our lives. We are going to come back to this passage a little later, but that's the context of what we are going to be talking about because what we see from this is that the Blood of the Lamb is a spiritual weapon. Do you see that? It is part of what defeats ha-satan, the adversary.

You are probably familiar with this verse.

II Corinthians 10:4 NKJV *For the weapons of our warfare are not carnal but mighty in God for pulling down strongholds,*

CJB: *because the weapons we use to wage war are not worldly. On the contrary, they have God's power for demolishing strongholds.*

So, the Blood is one of the mighty weapons of God that we can use in the spirit world. So I'd like to take you to some verses now that show some things here—the power of the blood in the Tanakh, first of all—the blood of the sacrificed animals and how that's connected to the Blood of the Messiah.

The Cleansing of the Blood

The first thing we are going to look at is the cleansing of the blood. In the Torah—the books of Moses—in the book of Leviticus, there are passages dealing with Yom Kippur. Back in the time when the Temple still stood, when people were making animal sacrifices, there were instructions as to what was to go on in the Temple on Yom Kippur. These were instructions to the Cohane HaGadol, the High Priest who at that time was Aaron, the brother of Moses.

Leviticus 16:15 *Next, he is to slaughter the goat of the sin offering which is for the people, bring its blood inside the curtain and do with its blood as he did with the bull's blood, sprinkling it on the ark-cover and in front of the ark-cover.*

NKJV *Then he shall kill the goat of the sin offering, which is for the people, bring its blood inside the veil, do with that blood as he did with the blood of the bull, and sprinkle it on the mercy seat and before the mercy seat.*

It was the sprinkling of the blood that made atonement for the sins of Israel. And that was repeated year after year for the sins of the people. In the Brit Hadashah, the New Covenant, we find a parallel to this.

I John 1:7 *But if we are walking in the light, as he is in the light, then we have fellowship with each other, and the blood of his Son Yeshua purifies us from all sin.*

NKJV *But if we walk in the light as He is in the light, we have fellowship with one another, and the blood of Jesus Christ His Son cleanses us from all sin.*

So, when we trust that Yeshua's sacrifice was the fulfillment of the sacrificed animals in the Temple, then His Blood cleanses us from the sin that we are all weighed down with, because we've all done things that are against God's will. His Blood cleanses us from it and purifies us. So, there's a cleansing power of the blood in both the Tanakh and the New Covenant.

The Healing Power in the Blood

Second, I'd like to talk about the healing power of the blood. In the Exodus from Egypt, we know that there was blood placed on the doorposts of the houses. The blood of the Passover Lamb was placed on the doorposts. And that protected the people from the plague of death. But it did something more. It's not actually recorded in the book of Exodus. It's in the Psalms.

Psalms 105:37 (NKJV) *He also brought them out with silver and gold, And there was none feeble among His tribes.*

Now, I want you to just think about this a little bit. We learn from Exodus that 600,000 men came out of Egypt. I don't know how many women and children that would be, but probably at least four times that many. So, we're talking about maybe three million people coming out of Egypt. Now, if you were to statistically take a sampling of three million people anywhere in the world, do you think you could find a sampling where none would be feeble? No! That would be supernatural. And it says in the Psalms here that when it came time to leave no one was left behind. That's what we hope when people are fleeing disasters like Hurricanes Katrina and Sandy that none will be left behind! In fleeing from Egypt, all of them got out because none were feeble—not because they had to put them on stretchers and carry them out, but because none were feeble. They were all able to walk out of Egypt!

So, what I see in this is that in the blood of the lambs on the doorposts of the house—in that Passover sacrifice—there was a healing and a strengthening power. It was a miracle! It enabled the children of Israel to ALL walk out. Scripture tells us that some Egyptians came with them, too. It was a mixed crowd. They ALL walked. None was feeble.

Let's look again at the covenant meal equivalent to the Passover in the New Covenant, the S'udat Adonai, The Lord's Supper (Communion). For that ceremony, we are given these instructions concerning doing it with the wrong attitude.

I Corinthians 11:29-30 (NKJV) *For he who eats and drinks in an unworthy manner eats and drinks judgment to himself, not discerning the Lord's body. 30 For this reason many are weak and sick among you, and many sleep.*

So, what does this mean? Well, it's obviously a warning not to take this ceremony lightly. But it is also saying that there is healing power in this ceremony, in the S'udat Adonai—the Lord's Supper. There is a healing power in that. I had an experience with this. It might just seem like a small thing, but to me, it was very big. I have suffered over the past several years with some kind of allergy. It affects me in a very strange way. I don't get teary eyes and runny nose and all that, but my nasal passages completely block up and I can't breathe through my nose. For a long time I found a solution to it in a spray I used. It completely cleared it up, but it had one problem. The spray was addicting. I couldn't stop using it. Whenever I started using it, I'd have to stay on it for months and months before I could get off it.

It had been a couple years since I'd used it. After the Lord started speaking to me about the healing power in the Blood of the Lamb, my allergies started coming back again. The worst time, if you can imagine, is when you're trying to go to sleep because, I don't know about you, but I can't sleep when I can't breathe through my nose! It's absolutely impossible. So, there I was trying to go to sleep and it wouldn't clear up, no matter what position I lay in. No matter what I did. I tried taking some pills but they didn't really work. I prayed and prayed for healing.

Then the Spirit of God was upon me and I did something I hadn't done in a long time, I prayed for the Blood of Yeshua to protect me from whatever it was that was causing this. And it was instantaneous! It was amazing. It was just like that, it cleared up and I was able to go to sleep. Like I said, it wasn't a big thing. It wasn't a broken arm or leg, but, to me, it was amazing.

So, my point is there's healing power in the Blood of the Messiah.

The Covenant Sealing Power of the Blood

There's also what I would call a covenant-sealing power. You know when we make covenants, whether they are between God and His people or between two people, it's very important that the covenant be sealed, in the sense that both parties stick with it and don't decide after a little while, "Well, I didn't really mean to make that covenant. I didn't really want to do what we agreed to, so I'm not going to do it."

What we find in the Scriptures is that all of the covenants were sealed with blood. Let me just remind you of those covenants.

God made a covenant with Adam. But when He did, He killed an animal and made skins to cover Adam and Eve. So, blood was shed.

God made a covenant with Noah. Clean animals were sacrificed in that covenant. That's the covenant with the sign of the rainbow.

God made a covenant with Avraham. It was sealed with circumcision and, of course, there was shedding of blood in that.

God made a covenant with Moses. And this covenant involved the Passover Lamb whose blood was shed.

I'd like to read a passage in Hebrews that speaks about the importance of the blood in the covenant God made with Moses. It's called the Mosaic Covenant or the Sinai Covenant. The author here is actually quoting the Tenakh.

Hebrews 9:18-20 This is why the first covenant too was inaugurated with blood. 19 After Moshe had proclaimed every command of the Torah to all the people, he took the blood of the calves with some water and used scarlet wool and hyssop to sprinkle both the scroll itself and all the people; 20 and he said, "This is the blood of the covenant which God has ordained for you.

So, the blood was the sealing, if you will, of that covenant. Yeshua says almost identical words when He gave us the S'udat Adonai. He said it this way.

Luke 22:20 ... "This cup is the New Covenant, ratified by my blood, which is being poured out for you."

We need to understand that the ratification is the thing God used to say He is going to stick to His covenant. And it's what makes us stick to the covenant. When we participate in that ratification of the New Covenant—when we partake of the Blood of the Messiah, it's our way of saying, "We are committing to this New Covenant."

Now, covenants in the Scriptures are often renewable. What that means is that every so often, usually every year, the covenant has to be renewed. I'm not sure how many of you are aware of this, but the Passover Seder is actually the renewal meal of the Mosaic covenant. So, every Jewish person is supposed to participate in a Passover Seder every year, as a way of renewing their covenant with God in the Mosaic Covenant.

Now, in the Passover Seder, there are four cups. They are called the cups of the Covenant. These cups are a memorial of the blood of the Passover Lamb because we don't actually slaughter lambs anymore. It's stated in the Haggadah that these are the memorial of the Passover Lamb. So, the cups are actually the renewal drink of the Mosaic Covenant. And, of course, in a similar way, the cup of the Lord's Supper is the renewal drink of the New Covenant. This is why Yeshua told us to do it periodically. He said as often as you do this, remember Me. This is the renewal of the New Covenant. So, I hope you've gotten the picture here. The cups in the Passover Seder represent the sealing blood of the Passover Lamb. And the cup of the Lord's Supper represents the Blood of Yeshua that seals the New Covenant. So, you can see that The New Covenant is built on what happened in the Tanakh.

I Am the Bread of Life

Now, I'd like to take you to a passage that has always been very difficult for people to understand. It deals with the Blood. The context of this passage is that Yeshua had been having some open-air meetings with people. They had been coming to listen to Him speak. It got to be late and the people were hungry. So, He did a creative miracle. From five loaves of barley and two fish, He fed five thousand men. Again, Scripture only numbers the men. There were probably at least 15,000 women and children there, too. They were all fed, according to Scripture, from the five loaves and two fish. It's actually humorous to me that Yeshua sent His disciples around to pick up the leftovers and they ended up with twelve baskets of leftovers! I think it was just to show how real this was—that it really was miraculously multiplied. So, He did this incredible miracle and the people who were there were just stunned! They were drawn to Him by this and they were ready to make Him king. But Yeshua didn't want to be made king. He knew it was not His time to be made king. That will come later.

So, He left and He crossed over the Galilee to the other side. When the people found out that He was gone, they also crossed over looking for Him. And when they found Him and wanted to be with Him, He gave them a warning. He said to them, "You shouldn't be following after Me because I gave you bread, but you should be following after Me for eternal life which

I alone can give you." Yet these people, even after experiencing that awesome miracle, said to Him, "Well, give us a sign." Do you catch the irony in that? They had just seen twenty thousand people fed from five loaves and two fish, and they say to Him, "Show us a sign!" So, Yeshua wasn't too pleased with that.

What we find here is that it's one of the best examples in the biographies of Yeshua, (the Gospels) where He speaks in riddles and parables. I read them sometimes and I ask, "Why is He doing this? Why doesn't He just explain clearly what's going on?" But He had a purpose in that He wanted to separate those who were really interested from those who were just there to get a free meal. So, He started speaking about some things that are very difficult to understand.

John 6:35 *Yeshua answered, "I am the bread which is life! Whoever comes to me will never go hungry, and whoever trusts in me will never be thirsty.*

Of course, this is one of the great "I am" passages where He related back to when God spoke to Moses and said, "I am that I am." This is one of those Messianic promises where Yeshua revealed His deity. He revealed that He is God Himself come as a man because what He was saying was far beyond what any man can do. I'm going to give you enough food and drink for the rest of your life if you come to me. But the people began grumbling about Him that He would call Himself the Bread of Life. "Who does He think He is? Isn't He the carpenter, Joseph's son? Didn't He grow up amongst us?" Here's His answer to them.

John 6:47 *Yes, indeed! I tell you, whoever trusts has eternal life.*

Now the promise got even more far-fetched than what He promised before because now He's not talking about being hungry and thirsty. He's talking about eternal, perpetual, everlasting, forever life. Now what does this eternal life mean? It means life in God's presence on this earth and in the place that God has prepared for those who love Him, in heaven. And He promised this. Then He repeated His previous statement.

John 6:48 *I am the bread which is life.*

Then He related back to something they were all familiar with.

John 6:49 *Your fathers ate the manna in the desert; they died.*

Now I hope you know what the manna is. It is the supernatural food that our forefathers ate while they were wandering in the desert. It was miraculous, but it doesn't compare with the awesomeness of the Bread of Life.

John 6:50-51 *But the bread that comes down from heaven is such that a person may eat it and not die. 51 I am the living bread that has come down from heaven; if anyone eats this bread, he will live forever. Furthermore, the bread that I will give* **[Are you ready for this?]** *is my own flesh; and I will give it for the life of the world."*

Now, I imagine that when He said it that way, "The Bread is My own flesh," it shook people up a little bit. Wouldn't you agree? That would've shaken them up.

John 6:52 *At this, the Judeans disputed with one another, saying, "How can this man give us his flesh to eat?*

Is He talking about cannibalism here? What is this? Is He saying He's going to cut off his arm and cook it and feed it to us? This is outrageous! This is ridiculous!

John 6:53 *Then Yeshua said to them, "Yes, indeed! I tell you that unless you eat the flesh of the Son of Man ..."*

[And then He gets even worse!]

... and drink his blood, you do not have life in yourselves.

This is even beyond. This is beyond all because now He's talking about drinking blood. If you are at all familiar with the Torah, you know that the drinking of blood is forbidden, not just for Jewish people, but in Genesis, in the covenant with Noah, it's forbidden for everyone.

Genesis 9:4 NKJV *But you shall not eat flesh with its life, that is, its blood.*

So, it is absolutely forbidden, yet here Yeshua was saying you have to drink My Blood. Then He went on.

John 6:54-55 *Whoever eats my flesh and drinks my blood has eternal life -- that is, I will raise him up on the Last Day. 55 For my flesh is true food, and my blood is true drink.*

What in the world did He mean by true food and true drink? Think about that because we're going to come back to that expression a little bit later.

John 6:56-58 *Whoever eats my flesh and drinks my blood lives in me, and I live in him. 57 Just as the living Father sent me, and I live through the Father, so also who ever eats me will live through me. So this is the bread that has come down from heaven—it is not like the bread the fathers ate;* [Here He's talking about the manna again.] *they're dead, but whoever eats this bread will live forever!" 59 He said these things as he was teaching in a synagogue in K'far-Nachum. 60 On hearing it, many of his talmidim* (disciples) *said, "This is a hard word -- who can bear to listen to it?"*

I can just see them holding their ears. "Who can bear to listen to this!" Now, these were His disciples who were grumbling, not just casual followers. These were the people who had been with Him for a couple years at this point.

John 6:66 *From this time on, many of his talmidim turned back and no longer traveled around with him.*

And even the twelve were now thinking of leaving Him.

John 6:67-68 *So Yeshua said to the Twelve, "Don't you want to leave too?" 68 Shim`on Kefa* (Simon Peter) *answered him, "Lord, to whom would we go? You have the word of eternal life.*

Sometimes Peter seemed a little dense, but here Peter was connecting these words about Yeshua's Blood and His flesh with what He had talked about—eternal life.

John 6:69 *We have trusted, and we know that you are the Holy One of God.*

Do you agree this is challenging? You know some people refer to Yeshua as a great man. They say, "Well, he wasn't the Messiah, but he was a great prophet and a very wise man." But, this is ridiculous teaching. If He was just a man, this teaching is the raving of a lunatic! Really! I mean, we've got to eat his flesh and drink his blood? This is crazy! Unless! Unless He really is the Messiah telling us something of the Spirit that we need to understand!

So, I had the great joy of digging into this part of the Word. This is actually my greatest joy when I come across passages like this and the Lord directs me that I'm supposed to teach on them. I always have to go before Him and just get on my face and say, "What is this all about, Lord?! What does it mean?!" And God is faithful. He always gives me some understanding that I didn't have before. Since I didn't understand this one before, I figure you didn't either. So I get to share my new understanding with you now.

Three Important Meanings

So, here's what I saw. The Lord showed me that there were three meanings to what was going on here.

First Meaning

First of all, from our perspective looking back at what Yeshua did at His last Passover Seder, where He inaugurated the ceremony of eating the Matzah representing His body and drinking the cup representing His Blood, we can see that He was referring to that! He was pointing forward to the covenant meal, of the New Covenant. That's pretty straight-forward. But what we need to understand is that this hadn't happened yet when He was talking to His disciples and to these people. That wasn't going to happen until some time later! So, how were they to understand that?

So, I began praying, what was He trying to communicate to the people there at this time? Because what I see in His riddles is that they're difficult but they're not impossible to figure out. Always when a person wants to know the answer, He shows them the answer. What I also see in His riddles and parables is that He always makes a connection to the Jewish culture that He's living in. So, if you're familiar with the Jewish culture, you can grasp what He's talking about. So, I believe this speaking of eating of His flesh was a riddle pointing to His hidden identity.

What was His hidden identity? Well, it's part of what we were just talking about, the Passover. In Exodus, the instructions for the Passover, is to sacrifice a lamb. After the lamb is sacrificed, it is to be cooked.

Exodus 12:8 *That night, they are to eat the meat, roasted in the fire; they are to eat it with matzah and maror.*

NKJV *Then they shall eat the flesh on that night; roasted in fire, with unleavened bread and with bitter herbs they shall eat it.*

I'm sure you know that verse. It's one we read at the Passover Seder. So, in the times when the Temple still stood and the people sacrificed their lamb for Passover, they ate the flesh of the sacrificed lamb. So, what Yeshua was talking about here by eating His flesh, was His role as the atoning sacrifice. He was saying, "Just like you were instructed to eat the flesh of the sacrificed Passover Lamb, you will eat My flesh because I'm going to be your Passover Lamb."

This is true for more than just the Passover Lamb. For many of the offerings that were made in the Temple, according to the law of Moses, they were instructed to eat the meat. Here's one example in what's called the sin offering.

Leviticus 6:26 *The cohen who offers it for sin is to eat it—it is to be eaten in a holy place, in the courtyard of the tent of meeting.*

So, we understand that in the time that Yeshua was alive, the normal way of making an offering was that they actually ate the flesh of what was offered. So, what He's saying here is that you are going to eat my flesh because I'm going to be a sacrifice for you. Do you follow that?

Second Meaning

What about drinking His Blood, though? Where in the world does that come from? Is there any place in what was being done in their culture that spoke of drinking the blood? Well, there's a connection, but it's a little bit more difficult to find.

Exodus 12:7 *They are to take some of the blood and smear it on the two sides and top of the door-frame at the entrance of the house in which they eat it.*

NKJV *And they shall take some of the blood and put it on the two doorposts and on the lintel of the houses where they eat it.*

It was this Passover lamb's blood placed on the doorposts of the house that protected the people from the tenth plague, the death of all first born sons. But we know something from Jewish tradition about how they celebrated Passover in Yeshua's time. I trust that you have been to a Passover Seder. It's not in Scripture, but it's in the tradition that there are four cups in the order of the Seder. Those four cups of wine are called the cups of the Covenant. And they are memorials of the blood—the blood of lamb. And we know that this tradition was in effect at the time of Yeshua because in Luke, it speaks about Him taking multiple cups.

Luke 22:20 *He did the same with the cup after the meal, saying, "This cup is the New Covenant, ratified by my blood, which is being poured out for you.*

So, Yeshua was participating in the same ceremony that we do now at the Passover Seder with the four cups. So, I believe that what He was saying by "you shall drink My Blood" is that He was pointing to His fulfilling the role of the Passover Lamb, not only eating the flesh of the lamb, but drinking the blood as a memorial of the blood splashed on the doorposts. Here's the awesome part of it. The blood of the lamb protected the people inside the houses from death from the tenth plague. And

Yeshua was saying it's My Blood that will protect you from Death because it's in My Blood that there is Eternal Life.

Now, another place that it's a parallel with this blood is when Moses ratified the Covenant of Sinai with the people and with God. We mentioned this before.

Exodus 28:8 *Moshe took the blood, sprinkled it on the people and said, "This is the blood of the covenant which ADONAI has made with you in accordance with all these words."*

So, he sprinkled the blood *on* the people! It sounds a little gory, but that's what he did. He sprinkled the blood of the sacrifice *on* the people. So, this is a bit of a stretch here, but I believe it's the parallel that He's referring to. When a person drinks the cup that is the memorial of Yeshua's blood, he puts it in his body, which in a sense is "sprinkling" it inside himself. So, I believe He wasn't trying to confuse the people, He was pointing them to something they knew very well: that the Passover offering and sin offerings were eaten and that at the Seder meal they drank the "blood" of the lamb and, in a sense, also the blood of the covenant at Sinai.

The Third Meaning

The third meaning I saw in this was very amazing to me. It's a meaning that can only be seen looking back from the perspective of people who understand the things of the Spirit of God, and that there is a Spirit of God that God wants to put in people.

Again this verse:

Lev 17:14 NKJV *for it is the life of all flesh. Its blood sustains its life. Therefore I said to the children of Israel, "You shall not eat the blood of any flesh, for the life of all flesh is its blood. Whoever eats it shall be cut off."*

So, what God was saying through Moses at this time was that life on this earth is sustained by the blood of the creature, whether it's a man or an animal. The life is in the blood. Now, here's the jump that we have to make in the Spirit. We tend to think of this life that we live here as the real thing. Right? This is the real life. This is the true life. But, according to the Bible, our life here is just a shadow. According to the Bible, our life in the flesh is temporary. Of course, we all know that it's temporary. If we die before Yeshua returns, what's going to happen to this flesh? It's going to decay away! But we also understand that if our spirits have been made alive by God's Spirit dwelling in us, we will live forever. And someday, the Scriptures say, our spirits will inhabit an immortal body. So, I would propose to you that, according to the Bible, Eternal Life from God is the real life and the true life. The true life is the life of the human spirit when it has been filled with the Spirit of God.

So, I want to take you back to the mysterious verse I mentioned earlier where I said, "What in the world does it mean?"

John 6:55 *For my flesh is true food, and my blood is true drink.*

Here's what I think He's saying. Eternal Life—True Life—is not found in the blood of animals that are sacrificed. The blood of the animals sacrificed in the Temple as atonement for sin did not bring eternal life. True Life—Eternal Life—*is* found in blood, but it's in only one kind of blood—in Yeshua's Blood. In Yeshua's Blood there is Eternal Life! Therefore Yeshua's Blood is true drink. That's what I believe He was saying. Similarly, the manna which He mentions in verse 49 was food directly from heaven. It miraculously sustained our forefathers for forty years in the desert. An amazing miracle! But that manna from heaven didn't feed their spirits. It fed their flesh. They died in the desert without receiving the Spirit of God. Yeshua was saying the food of the human spirit is His flesh.

John 6:56 *Whoever eats my flesh and drinks my blood lives in me, and I live in him.*

This is just another way of saying what we just said because Him living "in us" is His Spirit living in us and us being "in Him" is us living in the Spirit. So, when we eat His flesh and drink His blood, His Spirit dwells in us and we live in His Spirit.

Here's another way of thinking about this for those of you who are completely confused by now. When He lives in us, it's like His Blood is in us! He's in us, so His Blood is in us in the Spirit. It's like He gives us a transfusion. We have this natural blood, but when He comes and lives in us, we become adopted children of God, the Father. Normally, when you adopt children, they aren't in the bloodline of the family, but in this case, they are. They get into that spiritual bloodline through a spiritual blood transfusion. Our blood has become blood that sustains the spirit, not just blood that sustains the flesh.

Now let's go back to the verse we started with.

Revelation 12:11 *They defeated him because of the Lamb's blood and because of the message of their witness. Even when facing death they did not cling to life.*

So, how does this all tie together? We as Yeshua's followers are able to have victory over ha-satan, over our adversary, over the enemy, because we have drunk the blood of the Lamb. We have received that holy transfusion. Here's what the holy transfusion does to you. You know you have Eternal Life! Now, there are some reading this book that don't know that. I know there are. But let me tell you that once you know you have Eternal Life, this knowledge changes you! It brings you to the place where you don't cling to this life. The things of this life are not that important anymore—even when facing death. This is why our history tells of people that were willing to die for the Kingdom of God! We call them martyrs. They were willing to die because they knew that this life is not all that there is.

And you know, we have a perversion of this in our world today—a significant perversion! Do you have any idea how many people have died as suicide bombers? I have no idea, but it's huge now! It keeps on happening all over! Why do they do that? Because they believe in the Koran. They believe that if they die as a martyr, they will go to the Muslim heaven—a good place. Now, it's a lie. We know that. I hope you know that. It's an absolute lie! To think that you would go to heaven because you kill innocent people is beyond comprehension. It's certainly not at all what the Bible teaches. But that's ha-satan's perversion of what we have in the New Covenant which says, "I promise you Eternal Life if you will serve Me and follow Me."

I don't know if it has affected you this way, but it has affected me to the point of saying, "I'm not afraid of death." I'm not afraid of it because I know there's something better. That's a very dramatic way of talking about it because not many of us, I hope, are going to face that decision today, that we would have to give up our lives and die for God's Kingdom. But every day we do face many decisions. What are they? They are decisions that we are going to lay down our life and not do the things that **we** want to do, but do the things that God wants us to do. Every day we're faced with this kind of decision. And again, I would propose to you that it's hard to do that unless you really believe that God has a better life coming for you, that if you give up some of the pleasures of this world, you're going to get a lot more because of the promises that Yeshua has made. This is how it has affected me. This is the power of the Blood. It is true drink.

This is how I want to say it to end this point. The Scriptures tell us the life of the flesh is in human or animal blood, right? But the life of the Spirit is in, say it with me, YESHUA'S BLOOD!!

One more thing here, just like we can't eat natural food just once and expect to live the rest of our lives sustained by that food, I don't think we can eat or drink the body and blood of our Lord just once and expect to be sustained. We must continue to keep coming back to Him for His spiritual food and drink. It's more than just the S'udat Adonai—the Lord's Supper. It's more than that. I believe we receive from His body and His Blood every time we read His Word—every time we study His Word—and when we worship Him and when we pray and when we fellowship with His people. Those are ways in which we eat spiritual food for the Life of the Spirit to be strengthened within us.

So, let's pray.

Adonai, we thank You today for Your Blood. We recognize that it is a mysterious, mysterious entity. It's beyond our comprehension. So, we want to thank You today that it cleanses us from sin as we look to it for the sacrifice. We want to thank You today that it has healing power. We want to thank You that it reminds us of the Covenant that we are under and of the riches of that Covenant. We also want to thank You that it is a spiritual weapon, that it strengthens us in our battle against evil and against the forces of darkness. We want to thank You, Lord, that Your Blood is true drink. It is the life of our spirits. And so, Lord, I pray give us this drink. We want Your Spirit in us. We receive Your Blood that gives Life—the Blood that gives Eternal Life. We declare that we are people of the Spirit, not of the flesh. We ask You, O Lord, to help us walk in the power of Your Spirit.

And Father, I also want to pray for those who don't have that confidence—who aren't sure that they have received that gift of Eternal Life—who aren't sure that if they were to somehow, God forbid, die today that they would go to be with You in heaven. Father, I pray that they will receive that gift today. That they will know that they have had a transfusion, that You are in them, knowing that the power of the Spirit is working in them. In Yeshua's Name, Amen.

If you have any doubt—even a tiny, little bit of doubt, please talk to a Messianic rabbi or pastor or a strong believer because they can explain some things to you in only about 5-10 minutes that will make you absolutely sure that you have received Eternal Life. You will walk away a transformed person in the most significant way anyone can be transformed! You will have the Eternal Life of God within you.

Chapter 10

KOL NIDRE

On the Biblical Hebrew calendar, the day begins in the evening, so Yom Kippur begins in the evening. We call it Erev (eve of) Yom Kippur. It is tradition to have an Erev Yom Kippur service, which is also called the Kol Nidre service. The Kol Nidre is a traditional prayer that is recited at the beginning of the traditional Erev Yom Kippur meeting. It was set to beautiful music hundreds of years ago. It is one of the most touching songs you will ever hear. (You can search the web and find some amazing Kol Nidre solos.) The title means *all vows* in Hebrew; Kol means *all,* and Nidre means *vows.* It is a prayer asking God for forgiveness for vows made to God under duress, meaning someone forced you to make the vow. To understand how this prayer became Jewish tradition, you need to understand something about Jewish history. I will show you two things. I will show you what the history of persecution of the Jewish people has to do with the barrier to Jewish people accepting Yeshua, what it has to do with the Kol Nidre prayer, and what it has to do with praying for the peace of Jerusalem.

What has been the biggest barrier to Jewish people receiving Yeshua as Messiah?

To understand the Kol Nidre prayer, you need to know about the persecution of the Jewish people and what they were forced to do at the threat of death *by the church* and/or under the authority *of the church!* This is one of the main things that keep Jewish people from accepting Yeshua as their Messiah. I don't want to offend you in any way, if you are a Christian, but from a Jewish perspective, seventeen centuries of almost non-stop persecution of our people *by the church* is a huge deterrent to embracing what the *church* believes. In fact, it has been the biggest barrier to being open to the Gospel.

Let me give you an example of how impenetrable this barrier is. When the movie "The Passion of the Christ" came out, I was very shaken by what Yeshua suffered. I almost had to leave in the middle of the movie to take a bathroom break or something because it was so emotionally gripping to me. I thought to myself there has never been a more powerful presentation ever made about what Yeshua was all about—the music, the intensity, everything—was so riveting, surely it would convince anyone to believe. Then I met a Jewish gentleman who was visiting a place where I was speaking about the movie. Later I was talking to him, and I asked him what he thought about it. He said, "I spent the whole movie watching for signs of anti-Semitism in it." Incredulous, I asked him, "It didn't touch you at all?" He said, "No, No, I was just watching to make sure there wasn't any anti-Semitism."

So I thought about that for awhile, and I realized what was happening to this man was this. The residue of the seventeen centuries of persecution was so great that he could not even see or appreciate or be impacted by the story! All he could think about was "these people persecuted my people." You know, when we present the Gospel, the veil is so thick. There needs to be something to break through the veil before they will even listen.

Why would the church persecute Jewish people? What is the root of such a terrible thing? Well, it is well documented that there has been this thing called "Christian Anti-Semitism" that has been around for about 1700 years. It's based on a theology which we call "Replacement Theology." What this theology says is that the Jewish people are responsible for the death of the Messiah and therefore God has cast them off. Or it says because the Jewish people have rejected Yeshua, God has rejected them. So, it says that now the church has replaced Israel as the people of God. Therefore it teaches that all the promises in Scripture for Israel are now for the church instead. So, the promises for the Land of Israel are not to be taken literally, instead they are for a spiritual Promised Land. These Replacement Theology beliefs have taken many forms over the years, and have caused much suffering.

In history, the suffering took the form of pogroms and ghettos and expulsions. In fact, in a very real way Replacement Theology contributed to the Holocaust. I'm not saying that the Holocaust was perpetrated by true Christians, but Germany was a strongly Christian nation and yet it happened there. So, this has caused much of the wall in Jewish lives. However, from what we understand from our history, aside from the Holocaust, none of the things that have been done over the years have been more significant than the forced conversions.

The most famous time in Jewish History when there were forced conversions was in the Spanish expulsions and inquisitions. Conversions were forced at other times too, but what happened in Spain, around the time when Columbus set sail to discover America, was infamously horrible.

Here's what happened. There had been hundreds of years of Muslim domination of Spain. It was King Ferdinand and Queen Isabella (who, it is said, hocked her jewels to help finance Christopher Columbus' voyage to the New World) who finally defeated the Muslims and drove them out of Spain, but they were afraid that the Muslims would come back in and try to take over again.

These fears were not unfounded. It is much like the Taliban trying to come back in to dominate Afghanistan. The king and queen's method of preventing this was to declare that everyone in Spain must swear their allegiance to the nation and to the church. Everyone had to do this by a certain day on the Jewish calendar called "Tisha B'Av" which is a day that many catastrophes have happened to the Jewish people. The alternative to swearing allegiance to the church, which meant converting to Catholicism, was expulsion from Spain.

At this time, more than a million Jewish people had been living in Spain. They had prospered under Islam, which is interesting, and they had risen to prominent positions in society. Now they had to choose between converting or being expelled; about half chose each, from what I understand. Those who left went to other parts of Europe, to Turkey, and to South America. They were called "Morranos." Those who stayed and converted to Catholicism were called the "conversos." The conversos were baptized and often changed their names to hide the fact that they were Jewish.

After the successful expulsion, something very interesting happened. The leaders of Spain and the Catholic Church began to doubt whether these conversions were genuine. Isn't it amazing that they would doubt that? After they had forced the conversions, they wondered if the conversions were for real. Imagine that! Since they doubted them, they began something called the "Spanish Inquisition." The Spanish Inquisition had people spied on to see if they had really converted. What they were looking for was people who still practiced their Judaism. If they did things like fast on Yom Kippur or light the Shabbat candles or have a Shabbat meal, they were suspect. If they were caught doing these things, they were brought before the inquisition for trial. If convicted (and most were), their property was confiscated and they were tortured or executed—just for doing things like keeping the holidays or circumcising their sons, or even refusing to eat pork. All this was done in the name of the Church.

So now you can see why history has been one of the biggest obstacles to the Jewish people listening with an open mind to the Good News of the Messiah. Jewish children are taught about this history. I remember growing up wondering "Why would I want to learn about the claims of a religion that persecuted my ancestors? It's the last thing I want to do." As a young child, I already relegated it to something I didn't want to hear anything about.

By the way, as I said, that wasn't the only time of forced conversions. The record is that there were about 80 separate times of expulsions from different cities and nations throughout

Europe over the years. Some of you might be thinking "Well, that was the Catholic Church and even the Catholic Church has changed." But you know, to Jewish people, on the outside looking in, it's all together in their minds. They don't know the difference between Protestants and Catholics. It's just all one big church to them. I'm not necessarily saying it's true, but this is how a Jewish person sees it, that the whole church persecuted us.

The amazing thing is that even after the Protestant reformation happened, this persecution was never addressed, until recently. This particular part of what the church has done was not talked about, and so there was nothing to change Jewish people's minds about Protestants or Catholics. So this persecution is still a primary barrier to Jewish people trusting in Yeshua.

What does this have to do with praying for the peace of Jerusalem?

We pray for the peace of Jerusalem in obedience to Psalms 122:6 *Shalu Shalom Yerushalayim,* Pray for the peace (wholeness) of Jerusalem. But how will peace or shalom come? Can there be shalom any other way unless Yeshua Himself, the Sar Shalom, the Prince of Peace brings it?

Remember that their welcoming Him, saying "Barukh Haba B'Shem, Adonai" "Blessed is He who comes in the name of the Lord" is what Yeshua said must happen before He would return to Jerusalem (Matthew 23:39). But to a Jewish person even listening to anything about Yeshua is repulsive, let alone welcoming Him to Jerusalem. They must believe He is the Messiah before they will welcome Him to their Holy City.

So in obeying the command in Psalms, by default we are praying for the Jewish people to receive Yeshua so He can return to Jerusalem and bring peace. This in turn means we're praying that this barrier built by these persecutions will come down. We are praying for the thick veil to be removed and for the Jewish people to be healed of the pain of this offense.

Part of helping to bring this wall down and promoting this healing would be, I believe, and many others believe, for Christian organizations to do something or say something to renounce what happened in the past and to repent for the sake of their forebears. It's called repentance by identification. There are many Christians and church organizations that have done this already, but there is a need for more.

You might be interested in knowing that there is one group very much involved in doing this. They are called "Toward Jerusalem Council II" (tjcii.org) and they are actually going to heads of different denominations and saying, "In the documents of your denomination, there are anti-Semitic statements—statements condemning the Jewish people. Would you go back and address these things and revise them and make a public statement that you have done this?" And there are groups that have done what the Toward Jerusalem Council II has asked. Many Christian organizations are beginning to understand that, if publicized, something like this would certainly have great healing power for the Jewish people. Also in the Spirit there is something very important about this being done. I believe it greatly increases our prayer power to pray for the peace of Jerusalem.

So, we see what this history of persecution has to do with praying for Israel, but what does it have to do with the Kol Nidre prayer? Let's answer that question next.

Where did the Kol Nidre service and prayer come from?

As I mentioned at the beginning of this chapter, the Kol Nidre is a prayer asking for forgiveness if you were forced to make a vow under duress. Why would you need a prayer like that? Well, the Kol Nidre prayer was developed in the 1400s during the Spanish Inquisition. It followed the time of the expulsions and, of course, the forced conversions. It was first recited in Spain in underground synagogues at the beginning of Yom Kippur. It was a prayer for those who had been forced to convert to Catholicism, renounce being Jewish, and vow allegiance to the church and to Spain.

In the Kol Nidre prayer, they were asking God to forgive them because to them it was a terrible, blasphemous thing that they had been forced to do. It was decided that just as the Cohane HaGadol made atonement for himself and his household, so this Kol Nidre prayer was a way for each person to make atonement for himself and his household if he had made these vows.

The Inquisitions eventually came to an end, but the Kol Nidre prayer stayed. It had become a beautiful and meaningful part of the Yom Kippur tradition. The rabbis just kept it in there. Today it is still part of the regular Yom Kippur liturgy in the synagogue to make sure we don't forget what went on in those days.

Let me clarify something here. This Kol Nidre prayer only applies to vows that were made to God. Because of misunderstanding of the meaning of the Kol Nidre prayer, Jewish people have been accused of breaking vows made between people, but all the Jewish rabbis teach that this only applies to vows made to God. In other words it is not for breaking contracts that people make between each other. The origin is for saying, "Please forgive us for the vows we made under duress during these forced times." The text is actually in Aramaic, not Hebrew, perhaps to keep suspicions down if they were overheard saying or singing it.

KOL NIDRE
Traditional Text

All vows and renunciations,
Promises and obligations,
Bonds and devotions, and oaths
That we have vowed or sworn,
Or that we have promised,
Or to which we have bound ourselves,
From this Yom Kippur until next Yom Kippur
Let them bring goodness upon us.
All these we repent in them.
All these shall be absolved,
Released, annulled,
Made void and of no effect.
They shall not bind us or have power over us.
Our vows shall not be vows.
Our renunciations
Shall not be renunciations.
And our oaths shall not be oaths

Now here's a question for you. Should we Messianic Jews include this prayer in our Erev Yom Kippur services? Not many of us make false vows to God today. None of us in our country today are forced to renounce Judaism. We might be asked to, but we aren't forced to under duress. So, that would not be the reason for including it. One reason we want to keep it because it is such a beautiful tradition. However, there is another good reason. The main reason we have kept it in our Messianic Jewish liturgy is because it reminds us of the veil that was created by the ones who forced those conversions in the past, and inspires us to pray that it would be removed. We have changed the text of the prayer, though. Our Messianic text incorporates what Yeshua said about vows and includes a verse from Romans.

KOL NIDRE
Messianic Text

All vows, bonds, promises,
Obligations, and oaths
Between ourselves and God
Which we have sworn
And taken upon ourselves
From last Yom HaKippurim
To this Day of Atonement,
May God work them together
For good as we repent
Of having made them.
Yeshua said to us,
"Do not swear at all,
Neither by heaven
For it is God's throne,
Nor by earth for it is His footstool,
Nor by Jerusalem as it is the
City of the Great King,
But let your yes be yes
And your no be no.
For whatsoever is more than these
Is from the evil one. Amen.

(Written by Jeremiah Greenberg, author of
Messianic Shabbat Siddur, Messianic Liturgical
Resources; *12th edition*)

In 2002 Robert Stearns of Eagle's Wings and Jack Hayford of Church on the Way decided to make a call to all churches to pray for Israel. They purposely chose Yom Kippur to be the day for everyone to join together to pray. But the date of Yom Kippur changes every year due to it being on the Jewish lunar calendar. Therefore they chose the first Sunday of October as the date which is near Yom Kippur. This Day of Prayer for the Peace of Jerusalem has really taken off. Churches all around the world come together and pray for Israel every year. At the last count, the publicity material said 100,000 churches in 100 nations were praying for Israel on this day!

In 2006, the Day of Prayer for the Peace of Jerusalem actually occurred on Erev Yom Kippur. It was on a Sunday. However, in the non-Jewish way of thinking, the day ends at midnight. In God's design, the day begins at sundown and ends the next sundown. So we had the two days over lapping for only six hours or so from sundown to midnight. So, when I began to see the convergence of these two days, I thought, "It would be interesting to have a gathering in the evening when people from some of the churches around the Rochester region who are supportive of Israel could come together and join us to pray for the peace of Jerusalem as a regional body, seeing as how everybody was praying in their own church that Sunday morning." So we publicized it and lots of people came. Many of them were pastors and leaders in their churches. Several others were people connected to Israel somehow. Some were from Israel. Others were groups of people about to leave for Israel—some for the very first time. One group was going with Eagle's Wings for the sole purpose of praying "on the walls."

Remember, this was an Erev Yom Kippur service—the traditional Kol Nidre service. I thanked them all for coming and I gave them a sermon similar to this chapter. I concluded by asking them this question. "I know I've taken the long way around to explain it, but can you now see a connection between praying for the peace of Jerusalem and the Kol Nidre?" I explained it again quickly to them in summary, as I will also do for you here because it can be hard to grasp. We're praying for the peace of Jerusalem, but Messiah Yeshua must come to Jerusalem to bring that peace, and He said He won't come until the Jewish people welcome Him. They won't welcome Him until they accept Him as Messiah, but the veil is preventing that. And why is the veil there? It's there because of what the Kol Nidre prayer speaks about—because of the forced conversions.

After the sermon, we began praying earnestly together with our visitors for Israel. We had the church leaders and the people going to Israel come up and gave them the freedom to use the microphone to pray. The Holy Spirit led us into some awesome praying. Our praying went on for more than an hour. You can read some of those prayers and join us in the Spirit to also pray for the Jewish people. Add the power of your prayers to ours and watch the answers keep coming!

Prayers for the Peace of Jerusalem

A man who with his wife are leaders of a ministry and state coordinators of a national strategic prayer network, shared and prayed:

"My wife and I were in Jerusalem for the Toward Jerusalem Council II and had the blessing and honor to help plant a church from Ethiopians there in the Land. And we were excited about that.

"Father, I just thank You that in Zechariah 2:8 it reminds us that the Land of Jerusalem is the apple of Your eye. Lord, we lift up the Name of Yeshua, over Jerusalem. Even from the West to the East, we bless Jerusalem. We thank You that You have watchmen set upon Your walls all over the earth. And we are reminded, Lord, that the earth is Yours and the fullness thereof and all those that dwell in it. But You have set a place as the apple of Your eye. And, Lord, we pray the nations that would seek to do Your apple harm, would be halted. We pray that their plans will be thwarted.

"And Lord, we pray for that city where there are Jewish people, Muslim people, Christians, and atheists living together. We pray that the wall of division that has been keeping those separate will come down. And we pray, Father, that the veil that is keeping them from seeing that their promised inheritance of Yeshua, of salvation has already come. Lord, we bless

Jerusalem. We speak peace from the state of New York where there are more Jewish people than any other place besides Israel. We speak peace, in Jesus' Name."

A pastor:

"Father, in Jesus' Name, I count it an honor and a privilege to intercede, to stand in the gap. Lord, I want to identify with and repent of the sins that have been committed against the apple of Your eye, against the Jewish people. We owe our salvation to Yeshua our Jewish Messiah. Lord, I thank You for grafting us in. Lord, we ask for forgiveness from the sins that were committed against Your chosen people that have put a veil over their hearts. Oh God, we pray that the veil be taken away. I speak healing, healing in the Name of Jesus, in the Name of Yeshua."

Another pastor:

"Lord, Jerusalem is surrounded on all sides by their enemies. It's been prophesied, God. It's here right now. We just pray, Lord, for Your ministering angels to minister to those that will inherit salvation, Your chosen people. Bring them into relationship with You, Lord God. I also just speak, Lord, that there would be warring angels to hold back the forces of darkness. Put a hedge of protection around Jerusalem, around Israel, oh, Lord God. We stand in the gap, Lord. Thank You that You allow us to stand in the gap. Jesus, may they experience You, the Prince of Peace. May they come to know You, Yeshua. Hallelujah! Lord, we give thanks to You. We give You praise, Lord God. We pray for freedom in You. Freedom in Jesus' Name."

A senior pastor:

"I've actually had the honor of walking in that part of the world and personally asking people's forgiveness for things that were done in the Name of Jesus, but not in His Spirit. And it's really important that we make that differentiation because so much has been done in His Name, but not in His Spirit.

"So, Father, what we're praying here even as we ask forgiveness for what has been done in His Name, but not in His Spirit, Lord, we're asking for a supernatural revelation as I have seen happen in that part of the world in one on one conversations—a supernatural revelation that separates the act from the reality of who You are— that separates out that historic act that has burned into their psyche. Lord, there is only so far we can go in asking for forgiveness. We rely upon the Holy Spirit to bring revelation.

"Lord, we have heard accounts, many accounts in the Muslim world who similarly were sinned against through the Crusades. But we've heard accounts, Lord, of You appearing to them in dreams and visions, and in healings. Lord will You not do it in Jerusalem? Will You not also do it among the Jewish people throughout the earth? We ask You, Lord, that You will—that You will appear also to Jewish people in their dreams and in visions. Reveal Yourself to them in a real, tangible way that will melt their hearts toward You.

"Father, Your Word says to give You no peace. So we remind You, Lord, of what You have said You will do in the lives of individuals throughout the scattered nation of Israel wherever they may be throughout the earth. You said that in the lands where You scatter them, they will remember You. You said that You will give them a new heart and a new spirit within them. You have said that You will write Your Law upon their hearts. You have said that they will look upon the One whom they have pierced and will mourn as for an only Son. And You have said that all Israel will be saved. We pray, Lord, for these things to come to pass.

"And Lord we pray for Your believers, we pray for Your body in Israel to rise up, to rise up! Let Jesus in them so shine forth that starting in Jerusalem the non-believing Jewish people's eyes will be opened so that Your peace can come in the Prince of Peace. In Jesus' Name. Amen"

A lady prays:
"Lord, we are so grateful for Your salvation. We are so grateful for Your Word that has come down to us through the Jewish people. Lord, You are the veil lifter. It's the Father who gives the bride away. It's the groom that lifts the veil to behold His bride so that she sees Him face to face. So we call upon You, Lord, as the veil lifter of the bride of Jerusalem, of Your people, oh, God. Beautiful Lord, great Father who is not ashamed to call Yourself

the God of Abraham, Isaac, and Jacob, lift the veil, we pray. You are the veil lifter. Lord, we trust in You and in Your purposes, for there is no wisdom, no council, no understanding, but Yours. We thank You that no plans will prosper, but the plans in Your heart towards Your people. In the Name of Yeshua, our Messiah, and our coming King and Bridegroom. Amen."

Young lady from Tel Aviv:
"Lord, I just thank You so much for this time that we are able to come together to lift up Your people, Lord. I know that right now all of Israel, all the religious, and all those that aren't religious are really crying out to You, Lord. There's silence in the Land, Lord, during Yom Kippur. The stores are closed and the TVs are off. There is no traffic in the streets. There's nothing that would be able to distract them. I just pray for Your Spirit to be there. And for people to cry out to You, Lord, that they would ask You why, Lord. Why are You not here with me, Lord, that they would come and knock at Your door. I know that You will answer them, Lord.

I ask that there would be people to speak to them, that You would bring friends and relatives—people that know You, Lord. We pray that people would come to know you, today, Lord, in Israel. We pray that they would come to know You as they read the Scriptures.

Speak to them in the silence, Lord. I pray that You would break through to them. I pray Your spirit would go out in the streets as people go walking, Lord, as they don't have anything to do and nothing is open. I pray that they would be open to You. I pray they would call out to You. I pray that there would be nothing that would keep them back, that there would be nothing blocking their way to You. Take away every obstruction, Lord. I pray that they would see you, Lord. I pray they would see You in people, that they would see You in nature, and that they would see You as they look around at all the things You have done for them, Lord. I pray that they will cry out to You, Yeshua. And that they would know that You are the Messiah and that they would put their hope and their trust in You, Yeshua! Thank You, Lord. Amen."

A new Jewish believer:

"As a new believer and as a person who recently moved to Israel to find the Lord, and who found the Lord in Israel from people who love Yeshua, who love the Jewish people and reached out, I pray, Lord, for all the members of the church that they may be people like Paul, like the people in Acts who reach out to the Jewish people, that they may be people who read, not just the Gospel, Lord, but the Old Testament, too.

Yeshua says that He came not to abolish the Law, but to fulfill it, Lord. He came here for the Jewish people as well as for the rest of the world, Lord. I pray for every church, every believer, every person who knows Yeshua in their heart and in their spirit, Lord, that they would be able to reach out in love, Lord, in the Love of the Spirit, that the Spirit will grow in the Land of Israel, that the deserts will bloom as You promised, Lord, that the people will one day say "Barukh haba b'Shem, Adonai." That we may become one as it says in the Shema Yisrael, the Lord is one. Help us to reach out in love, Lord. B'Shem Yeshua HaMashiakh. Amen."

New York state coordinator for the Day of Prayer for the Peace of Jerusalem with Eagle's Wings:

"I am blessed to be going to Israel for the first time. I thank You, Lord for that opportunity. Lord, we humbly come before You. Father, the God of Abraham, Isaac, and Jacob, in obedience to Your Word, we pray for the peace of Jerusalem. We pray, Lord, that Your Holy Spirit would fall upon Jerusalem. Lord, we call the Jewish people forth into Your Spirit. Remove the veil from their eyes. Open their ears to hear Your Word, oh, Lord God. Soften their hearts. Heal their hearts. We thank You that You are the Lord that heals.

We thank You, Lord, that You are calling them forth from the north, south, east, and west. We pray for a harvest of Your people, oh, God. We call them forth into the saving knowledge of Yeshua. We pray for the armies of Israel, Lord. I pray for a wall of fire of the protection of Your Spirit around them, oh God. I thank You that even though all the nations around them are rising up against them, I thank You that You will protect them and keep them. Thank You that You will surround them with Your holy angels that no harm shall come to them. We thank You that no weapon formed against them shall prosper.

I thank You that Your Word says that You have inscribed them in the palm of Your hand, oh Lord. I thank You that You are a covenant keeping God. I thank You that Your Word goes forth and that it shall accomplish the purpose for which You sent it. Send Your Spirit, Lord, that they would come to know You. Send Your rain upon them. I pray that Your mantle of peace would rest upon them for Your glory and Your honor alone, Lord. We bless them, Lord. ... To the glory and honor of Your Name. Amen."

A lady in our congregation, the coordinator of the Day of Prayer for the Peace of Jerusalem in our city, was leaving with the Eagle's Wings group to Israel:

"The Lord has shown us to study the Word to show our-selves approved unto God and able to answer. Lord, I pray that you would make us articulate ambassadors. Grant us revelation as we study the Word, not only that we would understand Your eternal covenants with Your people Israel, but that we would come into a greater and greater understanding to what it is that You are doing in this time; that Father, a Rhema word would come into our hearts that we would understand how to meet the anti-Semetic spirit that is around us, that we would begin to understand the media distortions, Father, the fallacies, the untruths, that we would become more articulate about the issues that are historically happening, what the enemies are really about.

I pray that You would put a word in our mouth in due season. Call us forth to speak to those around us in one to one conver-sations as we walk in the way. It's going to be in our workplace. It's going to be where we are that we have to address believer and unbeliever who are listening to the news and reading the newspapers and hearing things that are false.

Oh Lord, give us a word of truth. Help us to study to know what is true about the Land, and what is true about history, and what is true about current events.

"And Lord, we pray for reconciliation in the Land between the Arab and Jew that goes back to Abraham's day, to Ishmael and Isaac. We pray for the brothers. We pray for the enmity to come down that You paid a price for. It's down in You, Lord. We pray there would come a light and a revelation that there would come a peace even in that enmity, even to those in the Land of Arab descent, Lord, that You have declared peace. That the middle wall of partition comes down in You. We do declare peace. We pray against that war-like spirit, that violent spirit that comes against the Land and against the believers in the Land and the Jewish people. Your peace is higher and greater over all the acts of violence and terrorism in the Land. Your peace, Your shalom will prevail. We thank You in the Name of Yeshua, the Prince of Peace."

A lady, an intercessor going to Israel soon:
"Lord, we do see those dark clouds of anti-Semitism, and we see and hear the rhetoric in the nations. Lord, we know that the hour is short, and we know, Father, that the call is serious. So, Father, we come before You thankful that You are the King of Kings, that nothing is too hard for You, that You sit enthroned above the circle of the earth, and that You are executing judgment at this time against Your enemies. Lord, we pray that You would pour out those ancient anointings to break ancient strongholds. We are asking, Father, that You would call Your people, Jew and Gentile alike, to attention, and that we would not be side-tracked by things that are fleeting, by vain things that will pass away. But, Lord, may our focus be on You. May we be about Your eternal business, I pray.

Father, we pray for the nations of the earth that there would be an opening of eyes, that there would be a conviction of sin. Lord, even as the evil one would try to change the times and the seasons, we say no. Not till the full harvest is gathered in, not till the Jewish people have had the opportunity to open their hearts and to see You.

So, Father, we pray that we would allow You to move us accurately, that we would be strategic and that more than anything we would be found faithful in praying whenever it is that You call us to pray, that we would pray in the Spirit, in agreement with Your heart. We ask You, Father, to shine Your bright light to expose lies, in the nations, in the media, in Your church, in Israel, and in all of the peoples of the earth, Lord, those who love righteousness, those who love justice, those who are seeking God, that we would see the truth, that we would be people of the truth and we would hate lies. Spirit of Truth visit us. Show us where we are thinking incorrectly, where we are speaking incorrectly, where we are helping the enemy and not helping Your purposes, Lord. Convict us of our sin. Help us to align with Your heart. We ask this in Jesus' Name. "

Lady, coordinator of the northeast of the United States
for the Day of Prayer for the Peace of Jerusalem

"I want to share something that really struck me. I was reading Daniel 10 where Daniel fasted and prayed because he was realizing that there was an appointed time in his day, that there was a prophesy that in his day was to be fulfilled. So he set himself to fast and seek the Lord. And there was a contention in the heavenly realm, and his prayers released something in the spirit realm.

As I was praying what really caught my attention was in verse 20 that the heavenly messenger said (I'm paraphrasing), "I'm going to go back and contend with the Prince of Persia and after he's gone, the Prince of Greece will come." When I read that, I said, "You know, this is the day that we are living in. In our generation, there is a kingdom that has set itself up against Israel and the redemptive plans of God and just as Daniel prayed against the spirit of his age, we are being called to pray against the spirit that is affecting the Kingdom and the redemptive plan going forth in the earth in our day, but targeted toward Israel." And so as we recognize this, we realize that our prayers are really doing battle in the heavenly realm.

"And so, Lord, we contend in the Spirit against the kingdoms that have set themselves up against Your Kingdom, Lord. We ask right now, Lord, that Your heavenly hosts would be released to fight against these kingdoms of darkness, these demonic structures that have set themselves up to hinder Your going forth, that have come forth even to wipe out the Nation of Israel . We are sending our prayers to intercede, Lord, to say, "Let Your Kingdom come, let Your will be done in the Nation of Israel and throughout the earth!" We pray, Lord, raise up the one new man, the work of Your grace, of Jew and Gentile, the army of the Lord for Your plans and purpose. I pray for a shaking up of the Greco-Roman mindset that has come into the church, and the slumbering spirit that has come over the church, I pray that they would be broken. May all that hinders Your Kingdom purposes be shaken off, we pray in Jesus' Name."

A man making his first trip to Jerusalem:
"I pray, Father, as Paul prayed in the book of Romans. It was his prayer and it is our prayer that all Israel will be saved. We pray that all Israel everywhere in the world will be saved. We ask whatever it takes, Lord, in order for that to happen. We know that we have to walk in love for those walls to come down. We pray that they would see the love, the true love of Yeshua that would just draw them in. Lord, use even signs, wonders, and miracles to draw them in. Give them hungry hearts to hunger after You. We pray that they may experience that true, full salvation that You desire for them. We ask this in Yeshua's Name. Amen."

Rabbi Jim praying for the group going to Israel and for current events in Israel, ended his prayer with this:
"... We pray Lord, that You would comfort all the people that mourn for those who have lost their lives in fighting for Israel's safety—for soldiers and for those innocent civilians murdered by terrorist bombs and terrorist violence. We pray for peace, Lord. We pray for peace along the border of Israel, especially the northern border and the border with Gaza, that all the blood that has been shed in the recent battles will not be in vain, that there would be peace all around the border. We pray for wisdom for the Prime Minister and for the Knesset for the dealings with the Palestinians, with the Hezbollah, with Iran, with Syria, and with Egypt. Give them great wisdom, oh, Lord. Thank You, Father. Thank You, Lord."

A Man:
"It's burning in me that we understand something, that there's a spirit behind anti-Semitism and it's an anti-Christ spirit. There's a spirit behind all that's been happening in the Middle

East. It's an anti-Christ spirit. When we're praying for Israel, and when we're praying about all that is happening there, and about the affects of what has happened in history and are praying for revelation there, we need to understand that all that has been done in His Name, but not in His Spirit, is an anti-Christ Spirit. So, it's really not the church. I mean, the church has been the instrument, don't misunderstand me, but we're praying against an anti-Christ spirit because that's the barrier. That's the real barrier. It's the anti-Christ spirit that's keeping the veil in place because it says in Corinthians that in Christ the veil is removed. So that's what we're praying.

"So, Lord, I pray against this anti-Christ spirit that has come right out of the pit of hell that is set against the people that You have dedicated, that You have put Your hand upon, that You have consecrated, and that You have said are the apple of Your eye. Lord we rebuke this spirit and we do not align ourselves with this. Lord we pray for the angel over the Jewish people to push this veil back, that the eyes of their understanding will be enlightened, in Jesus' Name. Amen."

A lady:
"Lord, as we are asking for salvation for the people of Israel, they have a part in the End Time harvest. You have not just called them to be saved for a good time for themselves. You have imparted so much to them, Lord. They have a destiny on this earth. They have nations to touch that we cannot touch. They have kingdoms to come against that we don't even begin to understand. So, Lord, we pray that as Your salvation comes *to* Israel, Your salvation would go out *from* Israel to the nations. That Israel would take her rightful place as fellow workers in this great End Time harvest, that from her hands would also come people from every tongue and tribe and nation to Your praise and glory. Amen."

Israeli student:
"People in Israel don't like to say Yeshua's name, because it means salvation and they don't want to give that title to Yeshua. They don't want to call Him that because they don't believe that He is salvation. Instead they speak a name that is a curse over Him.

"So, Lord, we just lift up the Israeli people and we pray that they would begin to say Your Name and would begin to see that salvation does come from You. We pray that they would embrace Your Name, Yeshua, and that they would come to know You as their salvation. We pray they would not curse Your Name anymore, but they would come to know that You came for them, that You came specifically so that they would know You and have You in their hearts. We break off this thing, whatever it is, Lord, from generations in the past, we break it off in the power and authority of Your Name. We pray for believers You are sending to Israel that they would be able to help people in overcoming that, Lord, and being able to come to know You and not seeing You as a curse, but seeing You as their salvation, Lord. In Yeshua's Name."

Another lady:

"I'm just encouraged. We're the younger brother coming alongside our older brother.

Lord, I want to pray for many associations, many opportunities to befriend and come alongside Jewish people and Jewish organizations. We pray that every organization that is aligning itself to help and support Israel, Father, that You would bless them. Lord, we pray that You are opening the eyes of people in the Israeli government. We thank You, Father, that You are establishing ties and relationships, and that there is starting to be an understanding that Christians are friends of Israel, that we truly do want to pray and support and come along side the people of Israel. Father, I just pray that You bless every friendship that is being established. We pray that You will remove all obstacles to these relationships for the sake of bringing Jewish people to You. In Your Holy Name we pray. Amen.

CHAPTER 11

OUR TONGUES: VOWS AND CURSES

How do we afflict ourselves? Well, I was reading an interesting book, and there was a little testimony in there by an eight-year-old Jewish girl, who was raised in a somewhat observant home. One year at her family was at home observing Yom Kippur, and her friend came and knocked on the door, wanting her to come outside and play. It was a beautiful day. She told her friend, "I can't, because it's Yom Kippur." And her friend asked, "What is Yom Kippur? Why can't you come out?" And she said, "Well, it's a day you're supposed to mope around and think about all the things you've done wrong."

That may have some truth in it, but I think there is more to afflicting our souls than that. I think there's much more. One of the things that has recently led me to understand how to afflict our souls, is the Kol Nidre prayer. We talked about how it developed in traditional Judaism and we saw that it seems a bit strange to us today. Therefore, I wasn't sure if God had called us as a Messianic congregation to do a Kol Nidre service. For a long time, again, as a Messianic Jew, I struggled with the meaning of it, because of what I explained before.

> Let me give you again the actual Kol Nidre prayer.
> All vows and renunciations, promises and obligations, bonds and devotions, and oaths [to God] that we have vowed or sworn, or that we have promised, or to which we have bound ourselves, from this Yom Kippur until next Yom Kippur let them bring goodness upon us. All these we repent in them. All these shall be absolved, released, annulled, made void and of no effect. They shall not bind us or have power over us. Our vows shall not be vows. Our renunciations shall not be renunciations. And our oaths [to God] shall not be oaths.

I think you can understand why we chose to modify that. It makes sense for the people in history that we just learned about in the last chapter who under duress were forced to speak a vow that they didn't want to speak. But thankfully today that doesn't happen to us. So renouncing our vows is not something that we feel we want to do.

And so, again, I said I have struggled with this because I have always thought that we were supposed to keep our vows to God. In fact, in Psalms 15:1,4, it says: "Who may dwell in Your sanctuary? Who may live on Your holy hill? ... Who keeps his oath even when it hurts." So, we are supposed to keep our vows. So, how can we recite the Kol Nidre?

That is why we thought we needed to modify the Kol Nidre prayer in the Messianic way, and we took the liberty to do that. Actually, Jeremiah Greenberg, author of Messianic Shabbat Siddur made that modification when he was our congregation's cantor before he moved away.

Here is the new version again:

> All vows, bonds, promises, obligations, and oaths between ourselves and God which we have sworn and taken upon ourselves from last Yom Kippur to this Yom Kippur may God work them together for good, as we repent of having made them. Yeshua said to us, "Do not swear at all. Neither by heaven for it is God's throne, nor by the earth for it is His footstool, nor by Jerusalem, as it is the city of the great King. But let your yes be yes, and your no be no. For whatsoever is more than these is from the evil one" (Matt. 5:34-37).

Now, I began to think about this, and I wondered is there any application of the Kol Nidre today, besides inspiring us to pray for the Jewish people? If so how can it be applied? Is there any connection between the Kol Nidre prayer and this afflicting of our souls? After all, the keystone of the traditional Erev (eve) Yom Kippur service is the Kol Nidre prayer. It's such an important part of Jewish liturgy. I'd say, it's maybe the second or third most familiar prayer, almost as familiar as the Shema or the Kaddish. So I really wanted to know from the Lord if it is something He wants us Messianics to include somehow—if there was any message we could glean from it—any connection between it and His command to "afflict our souls." Then something happened that brought to my mind what this connection was. All of a sudden I began to see that it could be really important for dealing with our unruly tongues.

Vows We Make Today

I was counseling with someone who was having a hard time in her marriage. She was struggling with nurturing her relationship with her husband. She knew that she should be attempting to be a loving wife, attempting to love her husband, but she just seemed to be unable to do it. It was one of those things where you know what you're supposed to do, but you can't seem to do it. So we prayed for God's help for her to do this. After we had prayed and just been quiet before the Lord for a minute, she remembered that several years before, in a time of anger, in a time when they were having a marital disagreement, she had told herself that at such and such a date she would end this relationship. Can you imagine that? Telling yourself that on such and such a date, I believe this marriage is going to be over. She told that to herself.

And as we prayed about that, the Spirit said to us that that was the reason why she was unable to love her husband. It was like a vow within her, and it was preventing her from doing what she knew that she should do.

She had, in a sense, made a vow, that she was going to end this relationship. So, anything that she tried to do to prevent that from happening, it seemed like it wouldn't work. She was under the power of what she had said with her mouth. Now, she didn't swear to God. She didn't write it down or anything. She didn't hold up a Bible and put her hand on it and raise her right hand and say, "I solemnly swear that I am going to destroy my marital relationship." But somehow this thing that she said to herself gave the enemy the right to bind her in this way, and to cause her not to be able to love. Somehow, by what had come out of her mouth, the adversary was able to come in and begin to manipulate her and control her situation and to destroy her relationship with her husband. She needed to be released from her vow.

Our Oppressor

After that incident, I was praying about this Kol Nidre prayer, and suddenly I saw the application of the Kol Nidre prayer very clearly. This person had made an ungodly vow. It was a rash vow, made in a moment of frustration, of anger, and she needed to be released from it. So to my mind, now, that's what this Kol Nidre prayer is all about. It is a prayer to release us from ungodly rash vows.

Now, when I got that revelation I thought, well, you know, we do make some vows like that, every once in a while, but thank God we are not under duress. Thank God that we don't have an oppressor who makes us make vows like that. And then I immediately had another realization. "Oh, wait a minute, maybe we do have an oppressor like that." His name is ha-satan, the adversary. And I have had some acquaintance with his work. I think some of you have, too. And you'll agree with me that he tries through temptation and deception and through inciting others against us to make us speak ungodly vows. He works hard to get us to say ungodly things with our mouths.

Our Oppressor's Strategy

One of our oppressor ha-satan's primary strategies is that through temptation and deception and inciting others against us, he attempts to cause us to make ungodly vows in times of duress. Or, he incites others to speak words against us, maybe in our presence, that we receive and they affect our lives—sometimes in very, very negative ways. So, what are the effects of some of these ungodly vows or curses? Well, I think they are many of the things that we struggle with. I think they can be the cause of depression, rejection, self-hatred, lack of self-esteem, anxieties, fears, bitterness, unforgiveness, resentment, anger, addictions and the inability to love. Sometimes, even physical symptoms that people experience can be the result of these things.

And you know, here's one that I thought about. I think all of us have some things that we don't like about ourselves. We just sort of accept that we cannot change. But, you know, that could be the result of some curse that has been placed upon you, or some vow that you have made, and God can reveal that and can break that. Maybe that thing that has been your nemesis all your life can be gone.

Our Oppressor's Ally: Our Carnal Nature

Now, ha-satan also has another ally in this way in which he deals with us, and that is our carnal nature. Our old self. Now let me explain what I mean by my carnal nature, for those of you who aren't familiar with this. The Bible teaches that we are triune beings: body, soul, and spirit, and that the real you is eternal. The real you is a spirit. The carnal nature is the soul and the body. Okay? You are a spirit. The real you is a spirit. But you live in a body and you have a soul. The part of you that connects with God, with His Holy Spirit, the Ruakh HaKodesh, is your spirit. That is what connects with God. In Romans, chapter 8, Rabbi Sha'ul tells us that *all who are led by God's Spirit are God's children*. So, we are to be led by the Spirit, but the Spirit leads us through our spirit, not through our soul or our body. Our old, carnal nature, our body and soul, battle for control of us. They battle to oppress us by keeping us from being led by the Spirit of God. Is that your experience? Okay, so you know what I'm talking about.

Now, here's what I came to understand. Ungodly rash vows are weapons which our carnal nature uses in that battle to control us. Let me say that again. Ungodly vows are weapons that our carnal nature uses in its battle to control us. Now let me explain a little further. We know what our body is. Okay? And we know how its demands attempt to control us. We may be hungry, but it may turn to gluttony. We may be lusting, we may be lazy; those are all ways in which the body tries to control us.

How Does Our Soul Control Us?

But what about the soul? How does the soul control us? Well, my definition of the soul is that it consists of our minds, our emotions, and our wills. Remember what we are supposed to be dealing with on this Yom Kippur? We are to be afflicting what? Our souls. *Not* our bodies. That is why I sometimes wonder why the traditional understanding of this in Judaism is that we are to fast on this day when that is really afflicting your body. It's good to fast; I'm not saying you shouldn't fast, but really the Scripture says we are to afflict our souls. Deal harshly with our souls, humble our souls. What does that mean? That means we are supposed to wrestle control away from our souls and give it to our spirits, so that we can walk in the spirit. So that we can be led by the Spirit.

Well, how do we do that? Well, the first step in doing that is to understand how each component of our souls—our mind, our emotions, and our will—control us. It is very important to understand this. So let me talk about that.

Our Minds

First let's talk about our minds. Our minds attempt to control us with reasoning and logic, with what-ifs. Are you a what-if person? You've got to think up all the possibilities and bad things that could possibly happen for anything you are trying to do. You can't help yourself. For all of us, being controlled by our minds is having to think through every problem and being argumentative. It's intellectualism. It's skepticism.   It's not being able to just move in faith, but having to have everything explained to us—everything has to be clearly understood. We can't just trust in God.

Now, our minds are not bad. Minds are wonderful things. Minds are gifts of God. They are incredible. They are very, very valuable. They are the thing that enables us to live in this world. But, we are not to be led by our minds. We are not to be led by our logic or by reasoning. Yes, we are to use logic and reason. We are to figure things out as best we can, but on the bottom line, what are we supposed to be led by? We are supposed to be led by the Spirit of God. God says: *My thoughts are not your thoughts, neither are your ways my ways* (Isaiah 55:8). If you try to do things in your thinking, in your reasoning, you will not be able to follow the leading of God, because He says His reasoning is not like ours. So, our minds—our reasoning—is one of the things that control us.

Our Emotions

Now, what about our emotions? Our emotions attempt to control us with our feelings—like fear, or rejection or anger. Again, it's not that feelings are bad. God gave us our feelings, and He can move through our feelings. Feelings are wonderful. We would be very, very dull people if we had no feelings. In fact, since I've known the Lord my feelings have been freed up. So, I'm not saying anything's wrong about feelings. I'm saying we are not to be led by our feelings. We are to be led by the Spirit of God.

It amazes me, I interact with many people who are Bible-believers, who study the New Covenant, study the Bible. I don't know about you, but I've had many such people say to me, "Well I did that just because I felt so strongly about it." Did you ever have anybody say that to you? Well, what does that mean? How did they direct themselves? Because they felt strongly! It was an emotion! Is that what we are taught to do? No. But so often you hear that. I hear it all the time from people. And yet it's not what we are supposed to do. We are supposed to be led by the Spirit.

Our Wills

Okay, so that's how the mind and the emotions try to control us. What about the will? Now, that's a new one. I had to really seek the Lord about this. I never really understood exactly what our will is before. But I want to look at five questions about the will and answer them, and I think it will help us see how our soul attempts to control us through our will. The first question is: What is the will? The second one is: Why did God create us with one? The third: When is my will a problem in my walk with the Lord? Fourth: How am I to deal with my will? And the last question is: what have ungodly vows got to do with my will?

What, exactly, is the will? Well, we are not talking about our final will and testament where we write to declare to whom we are going to leave our inheritance. Okay? Our wills are that part of our inner make-up, our inner structure, that enables us to stick to a decision we've made. It is the thing that gives us persistence—patience—stick-to-itiveness. Why did God give us a will? Well, it enables us to carry out His will in the face of opposition. We desperately need a will. Some of us are strong-willed. Once we make up our minds *on a course of action nothing can deter us.* Now, Yeshua had the strongest will that was ever created. *It enabled Him to voluntarily go and die this terrible death to make that atonement, to pay the price for sin.* He was able to set His will to do God's will, and even the most incredible opposition did not stop Him from carrying it out—from going to that cross. In the Gospels, in the stories of Yeshua, it talks about Him setting His face to go to Jerusalem. And it just brings a beautiful picture of His determination. *No matter what people are going to do to try to dissuade me, I'm going. There's great danger to go there, but I have set my face to go.* So, a strong will can be a great asset. God can use people with strong wills in powerful ways, because once they know what they're supposed to do, they will carry it through.

Others are weak-willed, easily diverted. I think of Peter, in the Scriptures. He said, "Lord, no matter what, I'll never deny you." But as soon as danger came along he was out of there.

Right?! So he had a weak will. He did get a strong will later through the power of the Ruakh HaKodesh, though.

When we discern the direction of the Ruakh, the Spirit of God, we are supposed to set our wills to follow that direction. And a strong will helps us keep going that way. And that is why I rejoice when I see a strong-willed person come to the Lord. Usually, it takes them a lot longer. It's more of a struggle for them to come to the Lord, but once they get there, they're going to bear a lot of fruit, because they're not going to stop at opposition.

Our Wills Resist Change

When does my will become a problem in my walk with the Lord? Well, when my will is set in ways that are not His ways. I may have a good idea of how I'm supposed to do something and I'm determined to go do it, but that is not necessarily what God has called me to do. My will, in the natural, keeps me on track, but also resists change, and thus makes it hard for the Ruakh, the Spirit of God, to direct me. Walking with the Lord is all about being flexible and changeable. I mean, I have never gone through so much change since I became a believer and started to walk with God. It is just constant change. Because the Scriptures say that we are to be conformed to the image of His Son. Well, obviously I have to change, if that's the case! I've got a long way to go! Walking with the Lord means determining what God's will is and then setting your will accordingly and being strong. But very often we have our will set in a way that is not God's direction for our lives, and the Spirit has a hard time changing us and getting us to go in the way He wants to go. Let me give you some examples of this.

Some of you might have been in a relationship where somebody hurt you. And it caused feelings of rejection and abandonment or betrayal. The result is that you build up walls so no one can hurt you again. You don't let people get close to you. Your will has been set to not let anybody get close enough to harm you. This prevents you from having any good, close relationships. If you have a strong will, these walls are very strong. They isolate you which is not what God wants for you. God has designed us to be in relationships. So strong-willed people can be great and wonderful in the Kingdom of God, but they can also struggle with yielding their wills to the Spirit of God.

So, it is a constant life of change, but our wills resist that. Now, I want to bring you back to a time in the Book of Exodus, to a time when the Israelites had come out of Egypt and they were at Mt. Sinai and they had made the golden calf and all this stuff had happened, and Moses was talking with God and God was saying you're going to go up to the Promised Land, but I'm not going to go with you. And Moses just about flipped out, "How can we go if you don't go with us?" And he wondered, "Why not?" And here's what God answered.

Exodus 33:3 *For I will not go up in your midst, lest I consume you on the way.*

In other words, if God had come down in the midst of the Israelites His holiness was so great and the Israelites were so full of sin that they just would have burned up. He would have consumed them. Remember? We mentioned this earlier in this book. It wasn't because of their sin. It was because they were stiff-necked. Obstinate and stubborn. See, they could always be forgiven of their sin, but you can't be forgiven of sin if your neck is stiff. Because you don't repent.

Put your hand on your neck. Do you feel any stiffness there? Pray with me: Lord, help us make our necks loose. Remove the stiffness from our necks, Lord.

So, you can see this is a big thing. This is the reason God couldn't be among the Israelites. Their unwillingness to change. Now, prior to my coming to know Yeshua as Lord, my will was set by my mind and my emotions, sometimes the desires of my body, but mostly my mind and my emotions. It included my reasoning and my acceptance of worldly philosophies. Here's an example of my set will: I'm never going to let anyone hurt me. The cause of that was that I had been hurt in the past, so I had feelings of rejection and abandonment and betrayal. And the result of it, of my will being set, was I put up walls to prevent other people from getting close enough to me so that they could hurt me. Have you ever experienced something like that? Or have you seen that in somebody else?

So, that's what happens when your will gets set that way. And the stronger our wills are the harder it is to drop those ways of thinking or behaving and yield to the Spirit of God. But, once you begin to yield, the stronger your will is the more God can use you. Because once He tells you what to do you'll get it done.

How Do We Deal With Our Wills?

So how are we to deal with our wills? Well, obviously, it must be yielded to God's will. Once the Spirit reveals that my will is in opposition to His will, my will needs to be reset to His. I want you to read a few verses here about what happened to Yeshua in the Garden of Gethsemane, so you get a grasp of the importance of our wills. Yeshua knew He was about to go to the cross the next day. And He was struggling with that. God puts the will to live within all of us, so it was in Yeshua too. One of the strongest things that we have in us, is our will to live. We also all have the drive to avoid suffering and pain.

Luke 22:42 Yeshua said this to His Father: *"Father, if You are willing take this cup away from me."* [The "cup" was: going to His death.] *"Yet, let not my will, but Yours be done."*

See, His will was opposed to the will of God, and He had to put that aside and say, 'Let Your will be done." And so he struggled with this, and if we read verses 43 and 44 we see what an incredible struggle it was.

Luke 22:43-44 *And there appeared an angel unto him from heaven, strengthening him. 44 And being in agony he prayed more earnestly: and his sweat was as it were great drops of blood falling down to the ground.*

What a struggle. He was struggling against His will. He fought hard to bring His earthly will into alignment with His Heavenly Father's will. And I'm sure that was not the only thing He was fighting. There were most likely evil powers also fighting against Him trying to force Him to give up. Yeshua had to fight so hard because of the opposition He was experiencing that He was sweating profusely. Some translations say He was sweating drops of blood. But in spite of all the hosts of evil against Him and His own flesh against Him, He stayed the course and prevailed.

If He struggled so with His will, how can we hope to deal with our stiff necks? Well, from this story we can see how He dealt with it. He prayed hard, He fought with spiritual weapons, He resisted the devil and His own will. But this was so intense of a struggle for Yeshua that He needed an angel. He needed an intervention from the Father. An angel came down, it says, and strengthened Him. And so it is very clear to me, and I want you to grasp this, that you need help to do this. I need help to do this. We need the help of God to struggle with our stiff necks and our hardened will. We need to pray and ask God for help. Then we fight with God's spiritual weapons. We resist the devil and our own carnal wills with the power of His Spirit, and the devil will flee and our wills will submit.

Giving Our Oppressor a Legal Right

Now for the last question: What have ungodly vows got to do with my will?

Well, when our old nature or ha-satan has deceived us, we may act or speak rashly. Have you ever spoken rashly? Or am I the only one? We often speak out of impure selfish angry motives, prideful motives, vengeful motives, maybe. And we make rash or ungodly vows. And once we have made that vow, our will is set to make that vow happen. So the will and the vows work together. And how do they affect us?

Well, my understanding of the spiritual realm is this: When we make a vow, an ungodly vow, it gives the adversary a legal right, *a legal power to cause us to behave in a way that fulfills that vow.* The enemy somehow acquires the legal right and the legal power in the spirit world to make circumstances occur that cause that vow to come about. *We actually give him legal grounds to bind us by the things that we have said with our own mouths.* Like that woman I was talking about who said that at such and such a time she was going to end this marriage. That gave ha-satan a legal right and power to harm her marriage.

The book of James, or Ya'akov, speaks of the dangers of the tongue all through it. It talks about it as being a deadly fire that lights flames. Here is his prescription for dealing with the tongue.

James 4:8 *Come close to God and He will come close to you. Clean your hands, sinners, and purify your hearts, you double-minded people. Wail, mourn, sob, let your laughter be turned into mourning and your joy into gloom. Humble yourselves before the Lord, and He will lift you up.*

Now, doesn't that sound like what we are told to do on Yom Kippur? Exactly. A time of T'shuvah. A time of repentance and humbling ourselves. And then, if you go back to verse 7 of that passage, though, it says: *Therefore, submit yourselves to God; moreover, take a stand against the adversary, the devil, and he will flee from you.* So we humble ourselves and seek forgiveness of God, and then we take a stand against the adversary, and we're going to learn what that stand is a little later.

The Many Vows We Make

So, what are some of these ungodly statements that we might have made, which legally are vows? Here's a list of a few possible examples which I know is just scratching the surface..

"Nobody will ever correct me again."

Some of you might have said something like that because you did something and somebody ridiculed you or hurt you. A person who experiences humiliation might make a vow like that. That gives ha-satan the legal right to cause you to avoid putting yourself in a situation where you might be subject to correction. And that is a serious thing because every time you step out and take a risk you risk being criticized. Every time you step out and do something that you're not used to doing, you risk being criticized. And if you're afraid of being criticized, you just withdraw and you don't do much of anything anymore. In other words, this vow causes you to avoid taking responsibility, or stepping out in ways in which you might fail.

"I'll never be of any value."

Well, you say that and that gives ha-satan the legal right to make you have no confidence. Then you will be right. You will be of very little value in many situations.

"Nothing can ever save this marriage."

Well, that can come true. Begin saying that and nothing will be able to save that marriage. By your own words, ha-satan now has the right to break up this marriage. He will use the legal right given him to begin to work things that will not allow the marriage to be saved.

"I'll get even with you."

Somebody does something against you, and you say this to them. Now, what does that do? Ha-satan has the legal right to cause harm to that other person, even at your hand, even if in your rational thinking and in your spirit you don't want to cause harm, sometimes you will cause harm to that person anyway. So, that can be a curse that not only affects you, but may affect some other person.

"You'll never hurt me again."

Somebody has hurt you, and you make this vow. And what does that do? Ha-satan has the legal right to cause you to put up walls of withdrawal or rejection or hostility or fear that prevent that person who hurt you from ever being close to you again. You're afraid of that person. You're not going to get close enough so that you would be hurt if they do something. And that can be a curse; especially if it is in a family, where there should be forgiveness, and there should be reconciliation. That can be between husband and wife, and it can cause there to be division there.

"I'll never be embarrassed again."

You do something and somebody brings some correction, and you say: "I'm never going to get myself in a situation where anybody can embarrass me like that again, or correct me like that." Well, what can that do? Well, ha-satan now has the legal right to cause you to avoid putting yourself in a situation where you might require correction.   Well, in a way, that means that you avoid taking on responsibility, because you're always going to be subject to correction if you take on responsibility or step out in faith.   And so you might just have said that "I'm not going to let that happen."

"Nobody's ever going to laugh at me again."

Well, ha-satan has the right, again, to cause you to be afraid to step out and to avoid taking risks.   And faith is really taking risks.   If you're not willing to take risks, you're not going to walk in faith, because that's what it's all about.   You're taking a risk; you're stepping out on the Word of God.   You're stepping out on what you believe God has told you to do; that's risky.

"I'll never love anybody again."

You say this when you've been hurt by somebody you love. Well, ha-satan has the legal right to harden your heart, to cause it to become stony, and not let anybody get close.

"I'll never botch something up like so and so just did."

Well, again, ha-satan may get the legal right to prevent you from ever being stretched.   From ever being in a situation where you're called on to do more than you thought you could do.

"I'll never treat my children the way my parents treated me."

Usually said when your parent has disciplined you.   And how many people have grown up and then had struggles disciplining their kids.   Well, maybe it's because you made a vow that you would never discipline your kids in a way that would upset them. But kids need to be disciplined effectively, which isn't always comfortable.   Sometimes adults, too, need to be disciplined in a way that brings some pain in their lives.

"I'll never get over this sickness."

Uh-oh!   What does that say?   You give ha-satan a legal right to keep that in you.

"This is just part of me, it's my nature." This could block you from becoming more and more like Yeshua.

"I'll never have enough money."
Opens the door for poverty. Right?

"I'm just stupid." Well, ha-satan can fulfill it.

"I'll never be of any value." Boy, that can do a job on your self-confidence, on your self-esteem.

"No one loves me." Brings rejection.

"I'm just a loser." Yeah. That certainly won't help you succeed at things.

"You should have children like you were!"
You say to your son or daughter, and they do.

And lastly, I don't know if you have done this since you've been a believer, probably not, but I know I did it before I was a believer: "God damn this or that." What does that mean? What are you asking God to do? What happens to that thing? It brings a curse on it. You don't really want that to happen. Maybe it's your car that you've said that about! And now your car is cursed.

Weapons Formed Against Us

So, these ungodly vows and curses are weapons formed against us by the enemy of our souls, the oppressor. They are hooks—places where the enemy can get a hook into us and manipulate us and either torment us or deceive us. So, the Kol Nidre prayer is a yearly reminder to deal with these very serious areas of spiritual warfare in our lives.

Our speaker at our congregation one year during the Yomim Nora'im, we'll call him Tim, told the story of having been in a congregation on the West Coast where he was very faithful. He became the pastor's right-hand man. They had a title in that congregation's hierarchy. It was First Warden. He was given that title. It sounds like he was in jail, I know! He was the helper of this pastor.

Tim had school administrative experience. He was the president, actually, of a junior college in California. So he used that experience to start a school for this congregation. He was at a party where they were celebrating the fact that they had this school started, and he overheard two men speaking. Tim happens to be an African American, and he heard these two men saying, "Did you ever think that we would have an African-American as our First Warden?" He just said to himself, "Oh, where did that come from?"

Then something else happened where the pastor evidently took some credit for something that Tim had done and didn't give him any credit. Tim didn't get angry. He didn't speak to anybody. He told us he just subconsciously made a little vow, "I'll never be in leadership in any congregation again." And suddenly while he was worshiping with us, that vow was made known to him. He didn't realize he had done it. It had been twelve years and it had a tremendous effect on him. He had never taken a real leadership role since. He had done lots of things, but he had never since that time ever stepped out and said, "I'll be responsible for that project" or "I'll take on this thing."

So, sometimes these vows bind us, and we don't even know it. They need to be revealed to us, and that is a big part of what we are talking about here.

The Weapons Revealed

So, the first thing we need to do is to have these ungodly vows revealed to us. And how do we do that? Well, I don't think it's possible in the natural. Only the Holy Spirit can reveal these things to us. And I believe that is one of the ways in which we afflict our souls. In other words, we say: "Spirit of God, reveal to me if there are things that I have said that have gotten me into trouble. If there are things that I have said that have allowed the enemy to have a foothold in my life, that have allowed the enemy to begin to manipulate me in some way. Reveal those things to me."

The vows may be things that we are saying all the time. I spoke about this same thing at a meeting in a city near us, and a woman came up to me afterwards. She said, "You know, I'm always using that expression, 'I swear to God' this, and 'I swear to God' that." And that was affecting her. And so she prayed and it was revealed to her at that time to stop saying that.

So, what kinds of things might you expect God to reveal? Well, almost all of us do something called 'self-talk.' Do you recognize that you have self-talk? I don't want to make any rash predictions here, but I would suspect that there is a significant number of people in any crowd who have negative self-talk. Who put themselves down when they talk to themselves. That's not a godly trait. The Lord does not want you doing that. Some of these vows can be reasons behind low self-esteem and protective walls, fears, unfounded fears.

Here is another area: Judgments that we have made about others. I'll have to talk about that a little bit more later, but the Lord tells us that we are not to judge, lest we be judged. And so, when we do make judgments about others something happens in the spirit world, and it's not good. And what is a judgment about others? Well, it's really a prejudice, in a sense, because that word 'prejudice,' comes from pre-judging. In other words, when you draw a conclusion about somebody or some situation without all the facts, that is pre-judging it. And oftentimes it looks the way it does because you don't know all the facts, but you judge the person because of it.

Sometimes when we pray this prayer things are revealed that we have always accepted about ourselves, that God wants us to change. There is one that was revealed in me many years ago that was really interesting. If you know my background, you know that I had a kind of a strange upbringing. My parents were communists, and they brought me up believing in the communist system and hating capitalism. When I got to be an adult I rejected all of that, but I found it very difficult to deal with finances. It seemed like I never could make enough time to actually think about what I should do with my money, or how I should handle it. And then, one day the Spirit of God showed me that was part of my upbringing that had been drummed into me, that it's evil to think about money; especially to think about saving money or investing money. And I prayed against that and it broke and it wasn't like I got rich right away. But what I noticed was that now I could see the importance of sitting down and figuring out what to do with my money—when I had it.

Here's an awful example. A lady came to me once and told me about another aspect of the power of the words of others to bring curses into our lives. This person had been told by her mother that she was unlovable. In fact, she had been told by her mother that she would never be loved, that nobody would ever love her, that there was no hope for her to ever be loved. She had received these as a young teenager, and it had a tremendous effect on her whole life. She was just realizing the spiritual aspect of these words that she had received. It wasn't a vow that she had made, but it was like a curse that had been placed upon her. And she needed to be set free.

Breaking the Weapons' Legal Power

Once the vows are exposed, though, we find out we've got them, like our "First Warden" friend did, then how do we deal with them? How do we break their power? How do we take a stand when the adversary has legal grounds against us, because of the rash things we have said? Well, when we have made a vow like this, I believe it brings a curse on us, or maybe on another person. The definition of a curse is that which brings evil. And so, we need to break these things as if they were curses. Now, the Kol Nidre prayer in the traditional form and, I think, in our form, really does not deal with curses. But I believe that God has given us something in the Bible to deal with them. You should have this marked in your Bible, because this is very important.

Galatians 3:13 (CJB) *The Messiah redeemed us from the curse pronounced in the Torah* [Your translation might say "from the curse of the law."] *by becoming cursed on our behalf, for the Tanakh says,* **"Everyone who hangs from a stake comes under a curse."**

What is the curse pronounced in the Torah? The curse is simply what happens to us when we break God's laws. There is this law of reaping what we sow, and when we sow evil we reap destruction. There is lots of destruction described in the Torah as the consequences or curses for many kinds of sins. But what we are specifically talking about here are the curses due to ungodly vows and the ways our tongues get us into trouble. Now, prior to Yeshua's redeeming sacrifice, I don't believe there was any such power available to deal with curses. But, now God has provided deliverance, for those who will receive what Yeshua did.

Yeshua paid the price to redeem us from curses, and this verse tells us how. He did it by becoming a curse Himself, on our behalf. Now, we know that His atoning death was for the forgiveness of sins, and to purchase a place for us in eternity in heaven, and for our healing; it says *by His stripes we are healed*. But His atoning death was also for redemption from curses. To break the power of us reaping what we have sown when we have gotten ourselves into trouble using our mouths.

What do I mean by that: Well, let's suppose you robbed a bank. Okay, now, you come to your senses and you say, "Oh, what a terrible thing I did, what a stupid thing." You ask God to forgive you in the way you have been taught to do. Then you go back to the bank and return the money, and you ask them to forgive you. Your conscience is clear. But what's going to happen to you? You're going to go to jail. Right? Well, this is how these curses work. We do something that is against the Law of God. In this case it could be we made some kind of a rash vow. We realize it, even, and we repent of it. And maybe we go and apologize to someone, if it affected somebody else, and they forgive us. But, we still reap the effects of what we did—unless the curse is broken. That's what this redeeming us from the curse of the Law is all about. And it is only in this passage in the New Covenant in Galatians.

I don't know if you've thought about this, but Yeshua died in a very specific way. How did He die? On a cross! In this Galatians verse we just read, Rabbi Sha'ul (Paul) is actually quoting from this passage.

Deuteronomy 21:22-23 (NIV) *If a man guilty of a capital offense is put to death and his body is hung on a tree, 23 you must not leave his body on the tree overnight. Be sure to bury him that same day, because anyone who is hung on a tree is under God's curse. You must not desecrate the land the LORD your God is giving you as an inheritance.*

So, now we understand why Yeshua died the way he did. It is one of the reasons He died on a wooden cross, a stake, a tree. (Some translators actually call it a tree in places.) He was dying to break curses over us. The Israelites had a custom that if they executed someone for a crime, they would hang their dead body on a tree. They wouldn't kill them by hanging them on a tree, they would be already dead. Then they would hang them on the tree.

The Romans, of course, in their wonderful kind way, went beyond that, and said we're going to hang the living bodies on the tree. Yet it was for a reason in God's divine plan. That's how Yeshua took our curse upon Himself. That's how He became a curse on our behalf.

So, Yeshua has this power to break these curses! Hallelujah!! And Kol Nidre is a reminder to us of that! We will need Yeshua's power over curses as long as we live because, as we all know, our tongues are unruly organs, and they can get us into trouble over and over again. I really believe that till the day we die, at least for me, but probably for you too, we will struggle with our tongues. We will get better at it, but I don't think any of us are going to be completely perfect and have that complete victory where we will never say anything that gets us into trouble. And I don't just mean with people. I mean in the spirit. In the spirit these things get us into trouble. Oftentimes we don't realize that what we are saying in the spirit world puts chains on us. So, I think praying and breaking curses is a very wise thing to do.

Now, here's the interesting thing, a wonderful thing. This Kol Nidre service is repeated yearly. Even though Yeshua died once, to make an atonement, the Lord said to keep on doing this forever. Why? Because of what I just said. Because we are foolish people. At least I'm a foolish person. if you're like me, your mouth gets you in trouble over and over again. And even though I pray that my mouth would not get me in trouble, it still gets me in trouble. And so, I need to have those curses broken; not just once, but over and over again. I'll probably get myself in trouble again this coming year. I'm likely to make some rash vows. Maybe I shouldn't say that. Maybe that will make me do it! I'm not going to say that! I take that back! There's just a chance. There is just the possibility because I'm human. Ya'akov (James) even says it here.

James 3:2 (NAS) *For we all stumble in many ways. If any-one does not stumble in what he says, he is a perfect man, able to bridle the whole body as well.*

So, next year it will be time for another Kol Nidre service because we need this reminder that we need to have these vows broken. As long as we are living in these mortal bodies we need this kind of help. So let's afflict ourselves. Let's humble ourselves in this way—deal harshly with our souls. Let's chasten ourselves, not by moping around and feeling sad about all the wrong things we've done, but by taking the power away from our souls. That's what real humbling of our souls is. When you humble someone you take the power away from them. So, when you humble your soul it means you take the power away from your soul.

We need to receive the atoning sacrifice of the Messiah in order to experience this power, in order to have it available to us. So, I'd like to lead in prayer for that, for anybody reading this book who would like that power in their lives and that forgive-ness from God. So, you need to pray this prayer with me. It's just a simple prayer of asking for forgiveness and believing that that forgiveness is available because of the atoning sacrifice of the Messiah, but that each individual person has to receive it themselves. So let me give you that opportunity, and pray this prayer together with me:

Lord, I ask You to forgive me for anything I've ever done that has been against Your will. I ask You to cover over my sin with the blood of atonement that You shed as the Messiah, to make me right with You. I thank You for Your forgiveness. I ask You to be my Lord, to guide my life, to be in my heart, guiding and leading me. In the Name of Yeshua. Amen.

Preparing in Prayer for Breaking Curses

Lord, we thank you for the message of Kol Nidre. We know now that there are these things called vows that we have to deal with in our lives. And You tell us that we are to afflict our souls and humble ourselves, and we recognize that this is a way of doing it. It's not the only way, but it is one of the things that we need to do to take control back from our souls and give it to our spirits. And so we do humble ourselves now, Lord God, and we ask that You would reveal to us the ungodly vows that we have made.

Lord, we ask You to forgive us of rash vows, of things that we have said that have allowed the enemy to bind us. And we ask now for the help that we need, even as Yeshua needed help from an angel. We ask that Your Spirit would reveal to us any ungodly vows that we have made, any statements that we have made, any judgmental statements, any ways in which we have allowed the enemy to bind us, any ways in which we have criticized ourselves, called ourselves things that we should not have, and we are going to be quiet right now and ask You to show us, Lord.

And now just take a moment and be quiet and let your mind be opened to the Spirit of God to speak to you about any thing that the Ruakh needs to say.

So, many of you are hearing things. If you're not hearing anything, if something hasn't come to your mind, continue to pray about this every day until the Day of Atonement.

Repenting From Making Ungodly Vows

Father, we ask You to reveal to us things that have been spoken by others about us, possibly in our hearing, or that was reported to us, that we accepted and that have affected us. We ask you to bring those things to our memories right now.

We've been stubborn and stiff-necked and we've stuck with these vows or these curses, believing them, even when we know they are not true, when we know they contradict Your Word, they contradict what You say about us, and so we repent right now of being stubborn, of being strong-willed, being stiff-necked. Lord, we repent of being judgmental. (Can you agree with me on that one?) Forgive me, Lord, for being judgmental. Save me, Father, from the consequences of being judgmental, that I would be judged in the same way. Father, forgive me for other ways in which my tongue has gotten me into trouble. Ways I don't even know of, Lord.

And Lord, I ask You to cleanse me of these things, by the power of Your blood. Cleanse me from these things, oh God. Cleanse me, oh God in the Name of Yeshua.

Breaking the Curses of Ungodly Vows

Now, would you declare with me? Read these declarations out loud. The first is from Galatians 3:13 about the redemption from the curse.

Declaration:
Messiah has redeemed me from the curse pronounced in the Torah by becoming cursed on my behalf, and in the power of that right now I break the power of these curses in my life. I break the power of these vows in my life. I break the power of curses and vows passed down from my parents. I repent of having accepted those things, and I break those powers. I break the power of stubbornness in my life and stiff-necked-ness. I break the power of the curse of ungodly ancestors to the third and fourth generations. I renounce those vows and I declare the opposite of those vows that are ungodly. I declare the Words of God over my life.

Now I would like you to do a little self-talk. Speak blessing to yourself.

Speaking Blessings:
I am a child of God. God loves me. He's created me for a purpose. I am fearfully and wonderfully made. He has a plan for my life. He has made me a person filled with love. Other people love me. I can receive love. I can give love. I am not afraid of being hurt. Thank you, Lord. Thank you, Lord.

Let's pray
Father, I ask that You would show me if I have brought a curse on anyone else through my words, and I would repent of any harsh words, of any ungodly words, of any demeaning

words, critical words, that I have spoken, that have caused someone else to stumble; I ask You to forgive me for that, Lord. And I break the power of any of those curses. I break the power of any curses that ha-satan attempts to put on my children, due to things I have said to them. I break that power right now. I know that I am not perfect, and I break the power of what ha-satan could do. I break that power right now, according to the power of Yeshua, who became a curse for me.

Lord, over the next several days I ask for Your Spirit to be speaking to me, to bring the curses to my recollection. I repent of them, Lord. I repent of rash vows that I made under duress, when I have set my will in ungodly ways. I repent of those things. Lord, I ask You to show me how I've been stubborn, or stiff-necked. I repent of being strong-willed and stubborn. I repent, oh Lord, of being stiff-necked. I want to be yielded to You in the leading of Your Spirit. I humble myself. I humble myself and ask You to cleanse me and make me whiter than snow. I thank you that you went and died on that cross for the specific reason of breaking the curses, because it is written in the Torah, cursed is he who hangs upon a tree. And we are told in the New Covenant that You redeemed us from the curses of the Law because You were hung on a tree. There would have been a lot of easier ways to die than that way which was the most terrible ever devised by man. And yet You chose that way to redeem us from the curses that we bring upon ourselves.

And so now, on the authority of what You did, Lord God, in the authority of Your redeeming curse-breaking power, I break right now the power of every ungodly vow in my life, in the Name of Yeshua, ones that I am aware of, ones that I am not aware of, I break those things. I break the power of those vows and I speak release right now, from the power of those vows, in the mighty Name of Yeshua, I break those curses, in the Name of Yeshua. I break those curses that I have brought upon myself. Thank you, Lord. Thank you, Lord. I break the power of ungodly curses upon my loved ones, that I may have made in a rash moment; on spouses, siblings, children, and parents. In the Name of Yeshua I repent of those things and I break their power in the Name of Yeshua. I break the power of stubbornness in my life.

Especially if I am strong-willed and know it. I break that power. I submit my will to You, Lord, that it might be yielded to Your will, oh God; not my will, but Your will. Let Your will be done. Thank you, Lord.

And Father, I pray for the power to control my tongue. Oh Lord, Your Word says that our tongues are unruly and that they are the things that get us into the most trouble. I pray, Father, for the power to bring forth only sweet water from my tongue, and not bitter water. Do a miracle in me, Lord. Break the power of an unruly tongue in my life. Thank you, Lord. Thank you, Lord, that I can break these things because of Your power. And I pray, father, that as the days go by from here on, the next few days and weeks, that You would bring to my mind the things that I need to be aware of, like You did for that "First Warden", Father. Make me aware of those things that I need to do, Lord.

And finally, Lord, as we conclude this chapter, I ask that You would give me power over this thing in my mouth, here, this tongue. Lord, Your Word says that it is an unruly member, and no one can control it. Well, I can't control it, but You can control it. And help me, Lord, from this Yom Kippur to the next Yom Kippur, to be speaking words of life, words of encouragement and not criticism, words of blessing and not cursing, words of faith and not doubt, words of hope and not despair. Help me to be a light, oh God, to those all around me. In the Name of Yeshua. Amen.

CHAPTER 12

BREAKING CURSES

Generational Curses

Curses can come upon us from more than just our own tongue. Another kind of curses are those from prior generations. In the Book of Exodus, God says this to Moses about Himself:

Exodus 20:5 (NKJV) *You shall not bow down to them nor serve them. For I, the LORD your God, am a jealous God, visiting the iniquity of the fathers upon the children to the third and fourth generations of those who hate Me,*

So, God shows His grace to a thousand generations, but punishes to the fourth generation. Now, that goes to show that there's 250 times more grace of God than there is justice of God. Right? And that is good for us! But the punishment part is like a curse that goes on to three or four generations. So, if your grandfather or your great-grandfather had iniquity, you may still be suffering or reaping the results of that. We call these things generational curses. Have you ever heard of that term? Now this is not an isolated passage about generational curses. When God is speaking to Moses just after the Golden Calf incident, we see Him repeat almost the same thing. Speaking about Himself, He says this.

Exodus 34:7 (NKJV) I am the God who keeps mercy for thousands, forgiving iniquity and transgression and sin, by no means clearing the guilty, visiting the iniquity of the fathers upon the children and the childrens' children to the third and the fourth generations.

So, we see here that this idea of generational judgment, in this case, is caused by iniquity. Do you remember what it was caused by in the second commandment or "word" in Exodus 20 quoted above? Hatred of God! But here in chapter 34 it is just plain iniquity.

What is God saying here? He is saying that if your father was a hater of God, or was somebody who practiced iniquity, or your grandfather, or your great-grandfather, some of that comes down generationally to you. And it's a curse.

Now, there are other curses that we bring on ourselves. In Deuteronomy 28, there are a bunch of beautiful verses about blessings for obedience and then there's a whole long section where it speaks of curses for disobedience.

So, we see this generational pattern. Actually, you can see this with your natural eyes. You don't need spiritual eyes to see this. We know even today that the curse holds. You know, maybe even in your own life, that when a parent does something terrible the kids suffer, and oftentimes they are scarred and dysfunctional because of it. They grow up with all kinds of wounds. A friend of mine was ministering to children who were orphaned and they had lots of problems because of what the parents had done. Think of some examples of how children are affected by their parents' sin. The obvious one that comes to mind is if the parents are abusive. What if the parents are alcoholics? That affects the children. What if they are adulterous? That affects the children. What if the parents are controlling? That affects the children. What if they are negligent? If they're materialistic? If they are always complaining? Or if they're gossiping? All these things, we can see how they get passed down, not genetically, necessarily, but because of the way the children are raised.

Some of these things we have had in our lives, but according to this passage, there doesn't seem to be any way to be free of these curses, because God is saying, "I'm going to put these curses on up to the third or fourth generation." So, in the Mosaic Covenant, there really wasn't any way to break these curses. But, the good news is that there IS a way to break them. There IS the power to break these curses that ha-satan has legally against us because of our forefathers' iniquity, but it is only available through the New Covenant. It was not available before the New Covenant. And here is why I believe this.

The Answer is in the New Covenant

I came across this many years ago. It precedes the very famous and well-known part of Jeremiah 31 where God gives the New Covenant. God proclaimed in the Tanakh, in the Old Testament, to the prophet Jeremiah that there would be a New Covenant. You might be very familiar with that passage. But did you know that when God said this, He actually also said that He will deal with generational curses? This is amazing to me. Starting at verse 31, there is this wonderful passage where the New Covenant is explained. But if you back up two verses from there to verse 29, listen to what it says.

Jeremiah 31:29-30 (NKJV) *In those days,* [in other words, in the days of the New Covenant,] *they shall say no more: "the fathers have eaten sour grapes and the children's teeth are set on edge." But every one shall die for his own iniquity; every man who eats the sour grapes, his teeth shall be set on edge.*

Wow, what does that mean? Well, it's a proverb. He explains it right in the next verse.

Jeremiah 31:30 *Rather, each will die for His own sin; every-one who eats sour grapes, his own teeth will be set on edge.*

What is God saying? He is saying that in those days, in the days of the New Covenant, no longer will people suffer for the iniquity of their ancestors. Why? Because there will be a way to break those curses. And only in the Messiah is there that way to break them

So, I hope you get this. You know when you eat a sour grape, your teeth feel that sourness. He's saying that "it used to be" or actually in the time of Jeremiah when it was written, He was saying—"the way it is *now* is that when the parents sin, the children will suffer the effect, but the day is coming when this will not happen." Now, He doesn't say it in a very positive way. He says everyone will die for his own iniquity. But it is a little bit positive because you won't die for your parents' sins. (smile) So, when those days come, the sins won't be passed on.

Then the question is, "Well, okay, but when are those days?" Well, the answer is easy. Just look at the next verse.

Jeremiah 31:31-34 (NKJV) *"Behold, the days are coming, says the LORD, when I will make a new covenant with the house of Israel and with the house of Judah— 32 not according to the covenant that I made with their fathers in the day that I took them by the hand to lead them out of the land of Egypt, My covenant which they broke, though I was a husband to them, says the LORD. 33 But this is the covenant that I will make with the house of Israel after those days, says the Lord: I will put My law in their minds, and write it on their hearts; and I will be their God, and they shall be My people. 34 No more shall every man teach his neighbor, and every man his brother, saying, 'Know the Lord,' for they all shall know Me, from the least of them to the greatest of them, says the LORD. For I will forgive their iniquity, and their sin I will remember no more."*

This is a passage that you should have memorized because this is an Old Covenant prophet, Jeremiah, giving the New Covenant, and it is just perfect. I mean, it's so descriptive of what the New Covenant would be; the forgiveness of sin, the ability to know God, the pouring out of the Spirit on all people, not just a few; all of those things are wrapped up in this passage.

And just before that he is saying that the generational curses that are passed down will no longer be unbreakable. The children will not have their teeth set on edge because the father ate sour grapes. And I believe he is saying that the power to break the curse of generations is part of the New Covenant. Do you see that?

God promised this around 600 years before the time of Yeshua, that a New Covenant would come. And Yeshua came and fulfilled this promise by dying a sacrificial death. He was wounded for our transgressions, which are intentional sins, and He was bruised for our iniquity. We know that was the fulfillment of that promise. And now we know that he was hung on a tree to redeem us from curses—from generational curses and from other curses that we are going to talk about in a minute.

The Curse is Broken through Messiah

Let's look at that verse once more just to be blessed again.

Galatians 3:13 (CJB) *The Messiah redeemed us from the curse pronounced in the Torah by becoming cursed on our behalf, for the Tanakh says,* (NIV) *"Cursed is everyone who is hung on a tree."*

The New Covenant brings the breaking of the generational curses. This is so important that it bears repeating. Yeshua's method of execution, His hanging on the cross, was specifically designed and ordained by God because He had to take curses upon Himself. Do you see that? The curses that He is taking on Himself are the just punishments or curses that the Torah had determined for sin. And they were to be upon even the children of the sinners, for the sins of their ancestors. But His sacrifice is enough to deliver us from them all!

This helps us understand the amazing power of Yeshua's atonement. He was wounded for our transgression, bruised for our iniquities, rejected for our acceptance, punished with stripes for our healing, and He was cursed—He took the curse—for our deliverance from curses. How incredibly marvelous!!

This is such an awesome revelation from God to Rabbi Sha'ul (Paul). Yeshua became a curse so that He could break the curses that are upon us, so that He would have the power to redeem us from them and deliver us from those hooks that ha-satan has been able to hook into us through those curses.

Now, let's read on. There's something really interesting in the next verse.

Galatians 3:14 *Yeshua the Messiah did this so that in union with him the Gentiles might receive the blessing announced to Avraham, so that through trusting and being faithful, we might receive what was promised, namely, the Spirit.*

So, here Rabbi Sha'ul is talking about breaking the curses, then suddenly, he begins to say "specifically the Gentiles." I began to think about this. "Why do the Gentiles particularly need curses broken more than the Jews?" Well, if you think about generational curses coming down from your ancestors, if you were Jewish and you had Torah (law) abiding ancestors, you didn't get curses from the generations because they were obeying God. Let me ask first. Were there such people? Because I know it's been taught in churches that there wasn't anybody who actually could obey the law. But let's take a look at the verse about Zechariah, father of Johanan the Immerser (John the Baptist) and Elesheva, Yochanan's mother. This is what it says about them.

Luke 1:6 *Both of them were righteous before God, observing all the mitzvot and ordinances of ADONAI blamelessly.*

So, they *were* living righteously before the Lord! And how could they do that? Well, God had put in place a system of animal sacrifice so that when you did fall short or disobey, you sacrificed an animal and repented and you got back into God's good graces. The animal paid the price. So, we did have people living under that law and living righteous lives like them.

But there was no hope for the Gentiles. Right? Thousands of people and generations who never had the Law! Also, depending on the culture, they very well might have been haters of the God of Israel. They might have been enemies of Him. So, this is why Yeshua's taking of the curses is specifically for the Gentiles.

There's no way the Gentiles could have this taken off

because there are so many. It goes back four generations. Each generation would have been just full of curses. So, these curses are why Yeshua had to be executed like He was. And when we understand this, we see why.

The cross was actually not a Jewish means of execution. It was a Gentile means, the Roman way. Of course, we know, the Jews didn't execute Him. They plotted against Him, but who actually executed Him on the cross? It was the Romans. It was the Roman soldiers that actually nailed Him to that cross. So, that fits in, too, that He was executed in a Gentile way to break even Gentile curses—take even Gentile curses upon Himself. So, this is why it speaks in Galatians of Yeshua's crucifixion being for the Gentiles.

Now, today, if you are familiar with Jewish society today, we need it very much too, because there is a huge proportion of Jewish people here in America that are the farthest thing from obeying the laws of God. And in Israel, it is something like 80% that is secular. And because there are no reformed or conservative synagogues in Israel, they don't even make a token attempt to live as practicing Jews because you have to either be secular or you have to be Orthodox. So for people in Israel, there's a lot of passing down of generational curses right now.

How and When are the Curses Broken?

So, how does this work? Yeshua became a curse on our behalf, but does the breaking of the curse happen automatically when a person receives the Lord? Do all those curses from our former generations get broken? Do you think yes? Or no? I think the answer is no because when I came to the Lord, I had to deal with reaping much destruction that I had personally sown in my life, but also I had to deal with a whole lot of things that were there because of the way my parents were.

In my particular family, I had Orthodox grandparents on my mother's side, but my grandparents on my father's side were socialists and atheists. They hated God. They were Marxist. They were anti-God. So, there was that hatred of God. They thought religion was the "opiate of the masses". That was their slogan. So, I had that a lot on that side. And, I don't know about you, but I have no idea what my great grandparents were like.

Do you have any idea of yours? I guess you could if you know your family history. But I have absolutely no idea about what they were doing. And that's the fourth generation, so that could be coming down to me.

So, I went through a lot of deliverance in my walk with the Lord. Later we're going to pray for these things—for generational curses—that we can claim the power of Yeshua becoming a curse for us to break these curses.

Another Kind of Curse

But I want to address another kind of curse. This other kind of curse, I believe, has really been very much ignored in the body of Messiah. I'm going to go back to a passage in the Torah.

Numbers 22:1-6 *Then the people of Isra'el traveled on and camped in the plains of Mo'av* (Moab) *beyond the Yarden* (Jordan) *River, opposite Yericho* (Jericho). *2 Now Balak the son of Tzippor saw all that Isra'el had done to the Emori. 3 Mo'av was very afraid of the people, because there were so many of them; Mo'av was overcome with dread because of the people of Isra'el. 4 So Mo'av said to the leaders of Midyan, "This horde will lick up everything around us, the way an ox licks up grass in the field." Balak the son of Tzippor was king of Mo'av at that time. 5 He sent messengers to Bil'am* (Balaam) *the son of B'or, at P'tor by the [Euphrates] River in his native land, to tell him, "Listen, a people has come out of Egypt, spread over all the land and settled down next to me."*

The people of Moab were in great fear of the Israelites as Israel was coming through their land. Their solution was to have the Israelites cursed. So Balak the King of Mo'av sent a message to a Bil'am.

Numbers 22:6 Therefore, please come, and curse this people for me, because they are stronger than I am. Maybe I will be able to strike them down and drive them out of the land, for I know that whomever you bless is in fact blessed, and whomever you curse is in fact cursed."

This is a long story. We won't go into all the details here. But it is fascinating if you read the whole thing. There are very interesting things in there like a talking donkey and an angel with a sword. In this story, it is quite hard to figure out what Bil'am was. Apparently he was a prophet of some kind, because somehow he had some kind of spiritual power. Somehow he could curse and he could bless. But, if you read on, you will see that he was forbidden by the Lord to curse Israel.

Numbers 22:12 God answered Bil'am, "You are not to go with them; you are not to curse the people, because they are blessed."

In the end, much to Bil'am's chagrin, and to the frustration of King Balak who hired him, he ended up blessing the Israelites instead of cursing them.

Based on this story and on verse 12 above, some believe that a curse against a believer by another person is not possible. They back this up with the following verse.

Proverbs 26:2 Like a fluttering sparrow or a darting swallow, an undeserved curse does not come to rest.

But, notice it says an "undeserved curse," a curse without a cause. But, there may be things in our lives that allow curses to come home to rest. These could be generational curses. They could also be our own sin that opens a door for the curses to gain access.

A Curse through Deceitful, Conniving Advice

If we read further in the story of Bil'am we will see that he did eventually manage to bring a curse on Israel by causing them to sin.

Numbers 31:16 Why, these [women] are the ones who— because of Bil'am's advice—caused the people of Isra'el to rebel, breaking faith with ADONAI in the P'or incident, so that the plague broke out among ADONAI's community!

What happened in that rebellion? It occurred just after Bil'am gave up trying to speak a curse over the nation of Israel.

> *Numbers 25:1 Isra'el stayed at Sheetim, and there the people began whoring with the women of Mo'av. 2 These women invited the people to the sacrifices of their gods, where the people ate and bowed down to their gods. 3 With Isra'el thus joined to Ba'al-P'or, the anger of ADONAI blazed up against Isra'el. 4 ADONAI said to Moshe, "Take all the chiefs of the people, and hang them facing the sun before ADONAI, so that the raging fury of ADONAI will turn away from Isra'el."*

So, these women were enticing the people on the advice of Bil'am, according to Numbers 31:16 above. As an aside note, this happens to be the first time that this god, Baal is mentioned in the Bible. Notice that the leaders were the ones to be hanged, and that it must have been on trees that they were hung before Adonai, facing the sun. I think it was to show that their leadership, or lack of leadership, had brought on a curse on the people. Remember this is the same punishment for those who were cursed.

> *Deuteronomy 21:23 Anyone who is hung on a tree is under God's curse.*

Now, keep in mind that in the Hebrew culture, people were hanged *after* they died. It was their dead bodies that God was telling them here in Numbers to hang in the trees. The leaders had to bear the curse, help bear away the curse. This curse of the plague was punishment for a great sin that the people committed. It was so wicked that it brought a horrible disaster upon the people. Twenty-four thousand people died! Pinchas (Phinehas) saved the people from more destruction by executing a man who took a woman of Mo'av into his tent right in front of all the people (Numbers 25:6-9).

So Balaam cursed the Israeli people through his deceitful, conniving advice, rather than by casting some kind of spell. How was he able to do that? He gave his wicked advice to the Moabite women. He instructed them to tempt the Israelite men to sin. It was the sin that opened the door for the curse. Do you see that? The women talked the people into sacrificing to another god and they tempted the men to commit sexual sin. It was sin that brought the horrible, deadly curse.

Modern Examples of Breaking Curses

I mentioned at the start that I am teaching on this subject because of some significant experiences in my own life. The first example concerns my wife Diane. She suffered from vertigo or dizziness for many years. In 2008 a new physical therapist moved to Rochester who specializes in vertigo. We tried to contact her but we were always unable to make a connection. In the late spring of 2008, we received a word through a friend that non Messianic Jews were speaking curses against leaders of the Messianic Movement. This idea had never occurred to me before. I had never heard anything about that spoken of in the Messianic Rabbi's gatherings.

There had been lots of stuff in the news recently about people involved in Kabballah. But I had never made the connection. Kabalah is a book of the Talmud. It teaches mystical, new age type practices. They take part in mysticism and the occult. They use curses against what they believe is evil. They are Jewish people, so one of the main things they consider evil is Christianity. And what is worse to them than Christianity? The Messianic Movement, of course!

So, I began to realize those engaged in such practices who oppose Messianic Judaism could be speaking curses against Messianic leaders. So, I decided to pray against any curse possibly spoken against us. I figured we had nothing to lose. We confessed our sins and I claimed Yeshua's substitutionary sacrifice, "becoming cursed on our behalf."

Immediately after we did this, the door opened for my wife to visit this new special physical therapist. She was able to show Diane a maneuver that cured vertigo. The therapy took a long time because vertigo can come back and it has. Also her balance system had to be strengthened to function correctly after the vertigo was removed. But she experienced significant improvement within a few months and there was great rejoicing in our house and family. Praise the Lord!!

A few weeks later I was praying for a young woman in our congregation who had annoying, chronic foot and ankle problems that had plagued her for a long time. She was raised in an Orthodox neighborhood and has much knowledge of Judaism. I prayed over her and by the power of Yeshua's atonement, broke curses that might have been spoken against her. She visited the doctor two days later. This time she was examined by a different doctor who knew exactly how to treat her problem and she was healed soon afterward.

Not long after that I prayed for another lady to be delivered from fear. She had started to see some things about one of the leaders of her congregation that were very wrong and deceitful. She saw that the situation was urgent. She feared innocent people would be led astray and get hurt. So she exposed this false leader. Of course, the leader did not like this and she was suffering from fear of what he might do to her. I prayed for her and spoke in the authority of Yeshua's Name against any curses being spoken over her by that leader. She was delivered from that fear.

Next I prayed for one of the main pillar couples in our congregation who have a significant leadership role in the Messianic Movement. They have a café business and their business was struggling. Since we prayed and broke curses over them, their business has turned around.

At the Messianic Rabbi's conference, I shared with a rabbi about what was happening. He told me he knew a rabbi in Georgia who came out of Chabad and who also used to be actively involved in an anti-missionary organization. Chabad is an Orthodox Jewish group. I got the rabbi's phone number and called him. We had a long discussion about what they did in Chabad.

He told me that when he was in the Chabad, they certainly did speak curses over and cast spells against the Messianic Movement and Messianic Jews. He said they often specifically targeted Messianic leaders and their congregations because they believe that the Messianic Jewish people are evil and that God is against us. So, this was real revelation. They are firmly convinced that we are evil and that we are drawing people away from true Judaism. He said they spoke evil against whole congregations and against the whole movement.

So, the next thing I did was to begin praying for our congregation and to break any curses against us. And you know what? Things have turned around considerably since then concerning our growth and our finances.

So we need to always be alert for ongoing battles and come to the Lord in prayer and spiritual warfare.

So, my conclusion is that we are all subject to the curses from our parents and our grandparents and great-grandparents. We are also subject to curses spoken over us, especially if we have any sin in our lives, especially sins of our tongues as we noted in the last chapter that open the door to them. But, now we understand that we are also given the power to break those curses in our lives, and that is exciting. That is absolutely amazing. So, we are going to take a few minutes now and do that. Okay? Are you ready to do that? I'm going to lead you in prayer. We're going to start by repenting from some more of the times that our mouths have gotten out of control, and I trust you will be able to repent with me.

Let's pray

Father, we just come before You and we thank You for being a God of justice—that we reap what we sow both good and evil. Show us the evil we have sown. We repent of it, and we ask you to cover it with the blood of Messiah that we might stop reaping ruin. And Father, now again in obedience to what Your Word says in the book of Ya'akov, or James, we repent of rash vows. We repent of things that have come out of our mouths that have been ungodly, that have been harmful, that we know were not pleasing to You. We repent of things that we have said, even under times of duress, when the circumstances of life and our adversary, ha-Satan, has caused us to be so stressed and under such duress that we say things that we shouldn't say, and even do things that we shouldn't do. We repent of those things, Lord, and we ask Your forgiveness through the blood of Yeshua.

We repent, God, and we acknowledge that these things get us in trouble in the spirit, that they give the enemy footholds in our lives, and allow him to bring curses upon us. We humble ourselves and acknowledge that we cannot extricate ourselves in our own strength from these traps, from these weapons that the enemy has formed against us.

Declaring

So we humble ourselves before You, oh God. We humble ourselves and ask forgiveness in the name of Yeshua, and by His blood. Adversary, ha-Satan, and all of the principalities and powers that are arrayed against us, we declare right now that Messiah has redeemed us from the curse pronounced in the Torah, by becoming accursed on our behalf.

We declare it in the name of Yeshua. We are redeemed. We are redeemed from the curse. The curse can no longer hold in our lives, and in the name of Yeshua, the name that is above every name, we break the curse in our lives that we have brought upon ourselves by our own rash statements or that have been pronounced over us, especially any curses cast over us intentionally by those of false religions, using powers from the enemy. We ask you to redeem us from those curses. Break them off of us according to Your promise of becoming a curse for us.

Breaking Curses Others have Spoken

Thank you for revealing that some of those who oppose us have spoken curses against us, especially those opposed to the Messianic Movement. We break those curses by the same redeeming power of Messiah who became a curse for us. In the name of Messiah Yeshua we break the power of those curses. We break the power of curses that have been brought upon us by anyone else. We break that power. We declare it broken right now, in the name of Yeshua, and by the power given to us. In the Name of Yeshua. Thank You, Lord. Thank You, Lord.

Breaking Generational Curses

We break the power of curses that have been brought upon us by our ancestors, our forebears, in the Name of Yeshua. In Jeremiah 31, it says in those days, in the days of the New Covenant, everyone shall die for his own iniquity, not for the iniquity of his parents, and so we break the power of generational curses that have come down upon us from our parents, in the Name of Yeshua. We declare that according to the Word of God, in these days, now in the time of the New Covenant that everyone shall die for his own iniquity by the power of the redeeming sacrifice of Yeshua. And we break the power of any curses on our children that the enemy would do through things that we have said or done, in the Name of Yeshua. Thank you, Lord.

Thank You for redeeming us from that curse pronounced in the Torah by becoming a curse on our behalf. Thank You for Your redeeming power to break generational curses. Reveal those curses to us. Thank You, Lord.

Sit or kneel quietly before the Lord a few moments and allow Him to reveal any specific generational curses He wants you to deal with.

Father, now, in Yeshua's Name, we break all the curses that have come down on us from our ancestors, to the third and fourth generations, including the specific ones You have just revealed to us; we break those curses right now. We declare them broken, in the name of Yeshua. We put them under our feet. No weapon formed against us shall prosper. No weapon formed against us shall prosper. There is power in Your Word. No weapon formed against us shall prosper. We break those curses. In the name of Yeshua. In the name of Yeshua. We thank you for setting us free right now. In the name of Yeshua. Thank you, Lord. Yes, we break those curses over our children for things that we have done, in the name of Yeshua. We break those curses. We break the curses over any person that we have unwittingly brought a curse upon, by our rash statements and our actions, in the name of Yeshua. We break the power of those curses. In the name of Yeshua. We set them free; we set our children free, in the name of Yeshua. Thank you, Lord.

Prayer for Control Over Our Tongues

Finally, Father, we pray that you would give us greater and greater control over our tongues. Lord, we are realistic and we know that we are going to struggle with this; we don't expect to have complete victory, but we pray that we would see ourselves conformed to Your image and we know that You said nothing that the Father did not give You to say. And so we ask that You would put a guard on our tongues, Lord God, that You would give us that control over our tongues, Father. Help us, Lord God, check us, cause our tongues to be submitted and yielded to You. In Yeshua's name. In Yeshua's name.

Thank You again Yeshua for redeeming us from all curses pronounced in the Torah by becoming a curse on our behalf. Thank You for Your redeeming power. In Yeshua's name. Amen. Thank you, Lord. Thank you, Lord. Amen. Amen.

Now, I feel I need to pronounce a blessing over you. Here's the Aaronic Blessing:

The Lord bless you and keep you. The Lord make His face shine upon you, and be gracious to you. The Lord lift up His countenance to you, and give you peace. A peace of having the weapons formed against you broken. In Yeshua's mighty, everlasting, powerful, overcoming, all-defeating Name. Shalom.

Chapter 13

AFFLICTING OUR SOULS: T'SHUVAH

Leviticus 23:27 *Also, the tenth day of this seventh month (that is the seventh month of the Jewish calendar) shall be the Day of Atonement. It shall be a holy convocation for you. You shall afflict your souls and offer an offering made by fire to the Lord. And you shall do no work on that same day, for it is the Day of Atonement, to make atonement for you before the Lord, your God.*

But we know that Yeshua, the Messiah, fulfilled this appointed time by making a final atonement for us. And it says in the book of Romans, that we who trust in Him are justified freely by His grace, through the redemption that came by Messiah, Yeshua. God presented Him as a sacrifice of atonement, through faith in His blood.

So we know that atonement has already been made, and it has been made once and for all, and we are all very thankful for that. But let's read on here a little bit and see what else the Lord wants to say to us through this.

Leviticus 23:29 *For any person who is not afflicted in soul on that same day shall be cut off from his people, and any person who does any work on that same day, that person I will destroy from among his people. You shall do no manner of work. It shall be a statute forever, throughout your generations, in all your dwellings.*

Now, let's understand that this was written by Moshe (Moses) something like a couple thousand years before the time of Yeshua. Do you think God knew that Yeshua was going to come when He told Moses to write this? Yes! Of course! I mean, God knows the future, so He knew that. So when He told Moshe to write this, why would He have said it shall be a statute forever, throughout your generations, if what He was meaning was when Messiah comes we don't have to do this anymore? It doesn't make any sense, does it? He said to do this forever. Even though He knew that Messiah was going to come and be the final atonement. Now, we can't do some of the things forever. We can't do the sacrifices in the Temple, but many of the things that it says in these verses to do forever, we certainly can do.

Forever in All Your Dwellings

There's another interesting thing in God's command. If you look at it again, you will notice it says in verse 31, "in all your dwellings." So, that says to me that even though Yom Kippur is very connected to the Temple, even though the Temple was destroyed, there must still be things God wants us to do because it says we're supposed to do them forever in all our dwellings. So, it is clear to me, that as Jewish believers in Yeshua, we are to continue to keep this Moad. Not for our salvation, but for our spiritual health, and because God tells us to do it. We're going to talk a little later about why this is needed for our spiritual health.

Now, according to the book of Acts, and you probably have already studied this a lot, in chapter 15 the Holy Spirit spoke to the early believers in Yeshua, and said that Gentiles, non-Jews, who come to believe in Yeshua, are not required to keep all of the laws of Moses. But, they are certainly welcome to do that. Those of you who are grafted into the olive tree, which is Israel, who choose to participate with us Messianic Jews, are welcome to do that. And I am not sure if you realize this, but you are privileged to be able to do that. I, as a Jew who believes in the Messiah, Yeshua, am privileged to be able to keep the Moadim. I have this privilege simply because I am alive at this time. There were many, many hundreds of years when that was forbidden.

We mentioned earlier about the time of the Inquisition when it was forbidden by the Catholic Church to do anything Jewish. Those who were believers in Yeshua who were of Jewish descent were actually investigated to make sure they didn't go back and keep Jewish traditions once they professed faith in the Messiah. Yes, that is what the Inquisition was all about. The Inquisition was actually a board of inquiry (inquisition) by the Catholic Church and, as we said in chapter 10, the people they were inquiring about were Jewish people who had made a profession of faith in the Messiah. They were inquiring whether the "converts" were going back to keeping Passover or refusing to eat pork, etc. If they were doing anything Jewish, they were subject to torture and death.

So that is the sad history of what has gone on, and that is why we are privileged to be alive at this time. It's only been the last few decades that we as Jews can keep these things and not be in fear of our lives. And also, it's only been a couple decades that you who are not Jewish, who are Gentiles, are invited to participate, because that would have gotten you in big trouble, too, back then. So, we need to be thankful for that.

So, now that we understand that God said to do this forever, and we also understand that we can't go into the Temple and sacrifice animals and we can't have a scapegoat, what are we to do? We understand and are very grateful that the Messiah has already come and made that final atonement. So what is left for us to participate in?

Well, we can certainly have a holy convocation. And, we are happy to avoid work. You are probably in favor of that! Those two were pretty easy. But what about afflicting our souls? That is the other thing God is telling us to do at this time. There are times we are told to rejoice, and there are times we are told to party, but here we are told to afflict our souls.

Afflicting Our Souls—Humbling Ourselves

Now, when I first became involved in Messianic Judaism, I had a hard time afflicting my soul on Yom Kippur. Maybe some of you are struggling with that, even as you are reading this. Why should I afflict my soul, since Yeshua has come to be the final atonement and fulfill Yom Kippur, making His once and for all offering of His blood? I should just be rejoicing in having received that wonderful atonement, rather than being afflicted in my soul. But, you know, afflicting our souls can mean to humble ourselves in an attitude of repentance. Yeshua, Himself, says some interesting things about humbling ourselves. He says *everyone who exalts himself will be humbled, but everyone who humbles himself will be exalted.* So, if we don't humble ourselves, we are in danger of having God humble us. That's a lot worse than our humbling ourselves.

And so now I can understand why God would appoint a time once a year for us to humble ourselves in a repentant attitude. He knows we are careless people. We can get to a place where we don't humble ourselves for a long time, unless we are told to do it. And I think that's what happened to me one year on Rosh Hashanah. I wasn't feeling well. I was just starting my message, when I was overcome with so much nausea that I had to leave quickly and someone else had to take over the service and give the message. I got a little lesson in humility in that. Maybe I hadn't humbled myself enough. So, if you want to avoid those kinds of humbling experiences, humble yourself.

But how do we do this? How do we afflict ourselves? Well, I don't think we have to be gloomy and mopey like the little Jewish girl thought we were supposed to do. Remember her? She wouldn't go out to play because it was Yom Kippur but instead just moped around all day and thought about the things she had done wrong. There is a much better way.

Afflicting Our Souls—Repentance

How much did it cost Yeshua to atone for our sin? Once we begin to comprehend this, we will be humbly repentant and begin to love Him much as the woman with perfume.

Luke 7: 47 (NLT) *I tell you, her sins—and they are many—have been forgiven, so she has shown me much love. But a person who is forgiven little shows only little love.*

True humility before God always involves love and an attitude of repentance, being conscious of how much our sin cost Him. "Repent" is "shuvah" in Hebrew, which is *"to turn back (hence, away), return, reverse, withdraw."* In Greek, it is "metanoia" which means: *compunction (for guilt, including reformation), repentance.*

Repenting is more than apologizing. I've had a lot of experience with repenting over the years. I remember, as a child, my mother refusing to accept apologies from me. She would say, "You're always saying you're sorry, but then you do the same thing again." It doesn't do any good to say you're sorry, if you don't change your behavior, it's just hypocrisy.

I never confessed or repented to God until I put my trust in Yeshua. Repentance is how we must come to Him initially. We must repent of sin and ask for His sacrifice to pay our penalty. We all sin in different ways from which we need to repent, but there is one sin that we have all committed. Everyone who comes to Him must repent of the sin of not humbly submitting to His Lordship. That's the sin of violating the first commandment—not loving Him and making Him our only God.

I have realized recently that many people don't fully understand repentance (T'shuvah). The essence of T'shuvah is having a humble, contrite heart or spirit

Isaiah 66:2 *For all those things My hand has made, and all those things exist," says the LORD. "But on this one will I look: on him who is poor and of a contrite spirit, And who trembles at My word.*

A contrite spirit is something greatly prized by God. What is a contrite spirit? It is a *humble* heart open to change. A heart that is teachable, seeking, open to correction, willing to admit when wrong. (For a much more in depth look at a contrite heart, see my book, *Yom Teruah, The Day of Sounding the Shofar.*)

Is your heart open to hear the truth about yourself? Is it open to see yourself how God sees you? If it isn't always open, the Days of Awe and Yom Kippur are a special time to seek that openness.

T'shuvah starts by asking God to show us what we've done, said, or thought that's been displeasing to Him; how we've broken His Law even if it's been accidentally or in ignorance. Once we realize there are things about our behavior and attitudes that don't please God, the next step in T'shuvah is to confess with a contrite heart, to tell God we're sorry, to apologize and be truly remorseful over our actions. Why? Because we love Him!

Many find it difficult to sincerely say they're sorry to God or other people. Instead of apologizing, they make excuses, or they blame others, or they blame circumstances.

An Example of T'Shuvah From Today

In sports, there was a public example of an insincere repentance that turned to sincere repentance a couple weeks later. During a semi-final tennis match at the US Open in the fall of 2009, Serena Williams, the best woman tennis player in the world lost her temper over a call that went against her. The call cost her a very important point in a close match. She was so angry she threatened the umpire who made the call. When she did that she was penalized another point and lost the match.

The next morning Serena issued a statement to the public saying her behavior had been inappropriate, but she excused her behavior by saying it happened because she is so passionate about tennis. When I read her statement, to me it was clear she was not at all sorry. She didn't apologize to the umpire, or show any sorrow. Reporters also immediately saw she wasn't really sorry for what she did. They said she had no remorse, and they were highly critical of her behavior.

Her lack of an apology or true remorse caused the reporters to call for her suspension from the game. I was amazed because she had her sister, her mother, and her father with her at the Open. They should have looked at her statement and told her it wasn't going to work.

I prayed for her

A couple weeks later, Serena realized, or the Ruakh HaKodesh (the Holy Spirit) convinced her that she needed to issue another statement to the public. This time, she really apologized to the umpire, her opponent, the tournament officials, the spectators, and to the fans. Immediately all the commentators' and reporters' attitudes changed toward her. They all were relieved that she had truly repented.

My thought was if sports reporters can tell when a person is really sorry, how much more can God, who sees directly into our hearts, tell?

BIBLICAL EXAMPLES OF
TRUE AND FALSE T'SHUVAH

First Example of True T'shuvah

There are many examples of true and false T'shuvah in Scripture to help us understand what true T'shuvah is. First let's glean from a Scriptural example of true repentance.

King David committed adultery with Bat Sheva (Bathsheba) and later had her husband murdered. God sent David's friend Natan (Nathan) to confront him.

Speaking for God, Natan said in II Samuel 12:9 *"So why have you shown such contempt for the word of ADONAI and done what I see as evil? You murdered Uriyah the Hitti with the sword and took his wife as your own wife; you put him to death with the sword of the people of 'Amon."*

David showed contempt for the Word of the Lord by violating His commandments that forbid adultery and murder. He murdered Uriyah by sending him to the most dangerous part of the battlefield.

II Samuel 12:10 *Now therefore, the sword will never leave your house— because you have shown contempt for me and taken the wife of Uriyah the Hitti as your own wife.*

God pronounced judgment on David's sin that showed contempt for Him.

II Samuel 12:11-12 *"Here is what ADONAI says: 'I will generate evil against you out of your own household. I will take your wives before your very eyes and give them to your neighbor; he will go to bed with your wives, and everyone will know about it. 12 For you did it secretly, but I will do this before all Isra'el in broad daylight.'"*

Natan prophesied David's son Absalom's rebellion as judgment.

II Samuel 12:13-14 *David said to Natan, "I have sinned against ADONAI." Natan said to David, "ADONAI also has taken away your sin. You will not die. 14 However, because by this act you have so greatly blasphemed ADONAI, the child born to you must die."*

David had covered up his sin and had not repented. Natan's confrontation brought David to true repentance. Often we need confrontation to force us to repent. We call this accountability – a goal of our Khavurah Groups (our "Friend" groups—our small groups).

God was able to immediately forgive David because He saw his repentance was sincere. David expressed his repentance in one of his most beautiful psalms.

Psalm 51:1... *God, in your grace, have mercy on me; in your great compassion, blot out my crimes.*

He calls on God's grace, mercy, and compassion.

Psalm 51:2 *Wash me completely from my iniquity, and cleanse me from my sin.*

He cries out for cleansing from his sin and his iniquity.

Psalm 51:3 *For I know my crimes, my sin confronts me all the time.*

His conscience was constantly accusing him and tormenting him.

Psalm 51:4 *Against you, you only, have I sinned and done what is evil from your perspective; so that you are right in accusing me and justified in passing sentence.*

He had sinned against Bat Sheva & Uriah but saw it as sin against God Himself.

Psalm 51:5 *True, I was born with iniquity, was a sinner from the moment my mother conceived me.*

He recognizes his iniquity, his inclination to evil—that sin is in his nature.

Psalm 51:6 *Still, you want truth in the inner person; so make me know wisdom in my inmost heart.*

He recognizes his need for greater wisdom to keep from sinning again.

Psalm 51:7 *Sprinkle me with hyssop, and I will be clean; wash me, and I will be whiter than snow.*

Hyssop was used to sprinkle the blood of the sacrifice on the altar and the Mercy Seat.

Psalm 51:8 *Let me hear the sound of joy and gladness, so that the bones you crushed can rejoice.*

David was experiencing physical symptoms from his sin. Bones are where our immune systems are generated.

Psalm 51:9-10 *Turn away your face from my sins, and blot out all my crimes. 10 Create in me a clean heart, God; renew in me a resolute spirit.*

He is crying out to be born again, to have a new heart or spirit that can follow Torah, God's instruction. He is resolute. He wants a steadfast spirit—one that doesn't give in to temptation.

Psalm 51:11 *Don't thrust me away from your presence, don't take your Ruach Kodesh away from me.*

He recognizes the Ruakh HaKodesh cannot dwell in the presence of sin. He also recognizes that the Ruakh is needed to resist temptation.

Psalm 51:12 *Restore my joy in your salvation, and let a willing spirit uphold me.*

Uphold me with Your spirit.

Psalm 51:13 *Then I will teach the wicked your ways, and sinners will return to you.*

When You forgive me, I will witness to others of Your great love.

Psalm 51:14 *Rescue me from the guilt of shedding blood, God, God of my salvation! Then my tongue will sing about your righteousness.*

He specifically cries out for removal of the guilt of murder. This is so hard because restitution can never be made.

Psalm 51:15-17 *Adonai, open my lips; then my mouth will praise you. 16 For you don't want sacrifices, or I would give them; you don't take pleasure in burnt offerings. 17 My sacrifice to God is a broken spirit; God, you won't spurn a broken, chastened heart.*

A broken spirit and a chastened heart equal a contrite heart which is precious to God.

Second Example of True T'shuvah

Here is a second example of true repentance in Scripture. This is a Biblical account of what happened during the Days of Awe following the return from the Babylonian captivity.

Nehemiah 8:1 *When the seventh month arrived, after the people of Isra'el had resettled in their towns, all the people gathered with one accord in the open space in front of the Water Gate and <u>asked</u> 'Ezra the Torah-teacher to bring the scroll of the Torah of Moshe, which ADONAI had commanded Isra'el.*

Note the people asked for the Torah to be read to them.

Nehemiah 8:2 *Ezra the cohen brought the Torah before the assembly, which consisted of men, women and all children old enough to understand. It was the first day of the seventh month. 3 Facing the open space in front of the Water Gate, he read from it to the men, the women and the children who could understand from <u>early morning until noon</u>; and all the people listened attentively to the scroll of the Torah.*
This was a six hour reading.

Nehemiah 8:8 *... They read clearly from the scroll, in the Torah of God, translated it, and <u>enabled them to understand the sense</u> of what was being read.*

That is exactly what we do when we read and explain a passage of Scripture.

Nehemiah 8:9 (NKJV) *And Nehemiah, who was the governor, Ezra the priest and scribe, and the Levites who taught the people said to all the people, "This day is holy to the Lord your God; do not mourn nor weep." For all the people wept, when they heard the words of the Law.*

Nehemiah 8:9 *Nechemyah the Tirshata (Governor), 'Ezra the cohen and Torah-teacher and the L'vi'im [Levites] who taught the people said to all the people, "Today is consecrated to ADONAI your God; don't be mournful, don't weep." For all the people had been weeping when they heard the words of the Torah.*

Why did they weep? They were convicted of their sin because they had not been obeying the Laws of Moshe—they were ignorant of what was in the Torah scroll. They needed to study and remember and they were doing that on Rosh Hashanah—the day of remembrance.

II Corinthians 7:10 (NKJV) *For godly sorrow produces repentance leading to salvation, not to be regretted; but the sorrow of the world produces death.*

Their behavior of weeping and mourning indicated their T'shuvah was truly sincere. Rabbi Sha'ul gives some other indicators of true repentance in the next verse.

II Corinthians 7:11 *For observe this very thing, that you sorrowed in a godly manner: What diligence it produced in you, what clearing of yourselves, what indignation, what fear, what vehement desire, what zeal, what vindication! In all things you proved yourselves to be clear in this matter.*

What are the other fruits of repentance? They are: diligence to make restitution, indignation at yourself, fear of God, and a strong desire for reconciliation with God.

Now let's go back to Ezra and the people in Yerushalayim.

Nehemiah 8:10 *Then he (Ezra) said to them, "Go, eat rich food, drink sweet drinks, and send portions to those who can't provide for themselves; for today is consecrated to our Lord. Don't be sad, because the joy of ADONAI is your strength."*

This is a greatly misunderstood verse. Most of us have sung this verse as a song—"The joy of the Lord is my strength. If you want joy, you must praise, sing, shout, dance for it." I knew the song was a verse in the Bible, but I had understood the song and verse to mean God gives us joy. That joy is the joy of the Lord, and His joy gives us strength, which it does! It is true that

His joy gives us strength, but that's not the meaning at all of this verse when we look at the context.

"Strength" in Hebrew is "maw-oze." It means *a fortified place; figuratively a defense:—force, fort (-ress), rock, strength (-en), (X most) strong (hold).* So it's a fortified place—a fortress. It's not talking about our own strength at all. So now let's look at the verse again. Looking at the contextual meaning, we now see that what it is saying is, "because you made the Lord joyful by your repentance, His joy is your protection. His joy is your defense from the judgment you deserve for you disobedience.

Nehemiah 8:11 *In this way the L'vi'im [Levites] quieted the people, as they said, "Be quiet, for today is holy; don't be sad."*

Clearly it was the Ruakh HaKodesh or Holy Spirit's direction for the L'vi'im (Levites) to declare the day consecrated. A day when all the people repent is indeed holy! It is a true revival.

Nehemiah 8:12 *Then the people went off to eat, drink, send portions and <u>celebrate</u>; because they had understood the words that had been proclaimed to them.*

Amazing! They went from weeping to rejoicing. True repentance will bring joy to the Lord and that joy will be the repentant person's fortress of protection from God's judgment, and that knowledge of being protected brings great joy to the person repenting!

The Third Example Of True Repentance

Yonah was sent by God to preach repentance to Nineveh. After trying to hide from God to avoid going, he walked through the city for one day preaching.

Yonah (Jonah) 3:5 *When the people of Ninveh believed God. They proclaimed a fast and put on sackcloth, from the greatest of them to the least.*

To have everyone fasting and wearing sackcloth is quite amazing! It was a sign that all the people were humbling themselves.

Yonah 3:6 *When the news reached the king of Ninveh, he got up from his throne, took off his robe, put on sackcloth and sat in ashes.*

Including the king!!

Yonah 3:7-8 *He then had this proclamation made through-out Ninveh: "By decree of the king and his nobles, no person or animal, herd or flock, is to put anything in his mouth; they are neither to eat nor drink water. 8 They must be covered with sackcloth, both people and animals; and they are to cry out to God with all their might - let each of them turn from his evil way and from the violence they practice.*

Not just sorrow and humbling themselves but turning from their evil ways

Yonah 3:9-10 *Who knows? Maybe God will change his mind, relent and turn from his fierce anger; and then we won't perish." 10 When God saw by their deeds that they had turned from their evil way, he relented and did not bring on them the punishment he had threatened.*

God responded to their repentance and spared the city from judgment

The Fourth: A Strange Account From Ephesus

In Ephesus, there were some Jewish men doing some exorcism. Yes, Jewish rabbis used to do exorcisms. They were not followers of Yeshua, but they had heard that there was power in His Name. So they used His name to try to confront a demon in a man.

Acts 19:15 *and the evil spirit answered them. It said, "Yeshua I know. And Sha'ul I recognize. But you? Who are you?"*

The demon then caused the man to attack them. He beat them and took their clothes.

Acts 19:17-18 *When all this became known to the residents of Ephesus, fear fell on all of them, Jews and Greeks alike; and the name of the Lord Yeshua came to be held in high regard. 18 Many of those who had earlier made professions of faith now came and admitted publicly their evil deeds;*

These were people who had turned to Yeshua before but were now brought to a deeper level of repentance by the fear of the Lord. True repentance can lead to public confession of sin.

Acts 19:19 *and a considerable number of those who had engaged in occult practices threw their scrolls in a pile and burned them in public. When they calculated the value of the scrolls, it came to fifty thousand drachmas.*

True repentance causes a person to want to get rid of all ungodly things in their lives, including books teaching occult religions and other things used in ungodly practices.

The Fifth Example of True T'shuvah: Job's Repentance

The reference for this story is the whole book of Iyov (Job, pronounced *ee-yohv*). No I'm not going to give you the whole book here. I'll just paraphrase the incidents and give you key verses. Iyov was a righteous man whom God allowed to be greatly tested through sickness, loss of family, fortune, and home.

After all that tragedy, and after the unhelpful, not comforting attempts at comfort from his so-called "friends," while he was still suffering miserably, finally in Iyov chapters 38-41, God revealed Himself in a storm to Iyov. Here's how Iyov responded.

Job 42:1 *Then [at last,] Iyov gave ADONAI this answer: 2 "I know that you can do everything, that no purpose of yours can be thwarted. 3 [You asked,] 'Who is this, hiding counsel, without having knowledge?' Yes, I spoke, without understanding, of wonders far beyond me, which I didn't know. 4 'Please listen, and I will speak. [You said,] 'I will ask questions; and you, give me answers' - 5 I had heard about you with my ears, but now my eye sees you; 6 therefore I detest [myself] and repent in dust and ashes."*

Iyov is repenting of his previous attitude toward God. In his great distress, Iyov had questioned God's judgment, fairness, and love. When God revealed Himself to Iyov in these 4 chapters, Iyov was overwhelmed by God's power and saw his previous ignorant attitudes as sin

So, Iyov repented of his ignorance "*I spoke, without understanding, of wonders far beyond me, which I didn't know.*"

In verse 6, *therefore I detest [myself] and repent in dust and ashes,* the Hebrew word, "n'kham-ti" is used for "repent" which means: *repent, to be sorry.* Repenting in dust and ashes was the cultural way at that time to show that you were genuinely and deeply sorry. Iyov was completely humbling himself. The Hebrew word used for "detest" is "em-ahs" which means: *detests, abhors, despises, disdains, loathes, rejects himself.* Iyov was very ashamed of his previous ignorant arrogance toward God. The Lord was very pleased with Iyov's attitude of repentance. In fact, He was so pleased that He sent Iyov's three uncomforting friends to Iyov.

Job 42:8 So now, get yourselves seven young bulls and seven rams, go to my servant Iyov, and offer up for yourselves a burnt offering. My servant Iyov will pray for you—because him I will accept—so that I won't punish you as your boorishness deserves; because you have not spoken rightly about me, as my servant Iyov has."

There is something very important to notice here. Do you know what I'm referring to? What significant thing do we see about Iyov after he repented? We can see here in verse 8 that after his repentance, his prayers had power. Don't we all long for power in our prayers? Well, it looks here like one of the prerequisites to having powerful prayers is to fully, completely, and genuinely repent.

Now for Some Examples of False T'shuvah:

Adam and Eve

Adam and Eve disobeyed God's command not to eat from the tree of the knowledge of good and evil. When God confronted them, they began to blame everyone but themselves.

Genesis 3:12 *The man replied, "The woman you gave to be with me—she gave me fruit from the tree, and I ate."*

Adam blamed God for his sin. That does not go over well with God. It most certainly is not true repentance.

Genesis 3:13 *ADONAI, God, said to the woman, "What is this you have done?" The woman answered, "The serpent tricked me, so I ate."*

The woman blamed the serpent. This also is not true repentance. Blaming the devil also does not go over big with God. It is good to see that, after the fact, Eve began to have great discernment to know ha-satan works through deception. It's too bad she didn't realize this before she partook of the tree.

Cain and Abel

In Genesis 4, Kayin (Cain) murdered his brother Hevel (Abel) and God confronted him.

Genesis 4:9 *ADONAI said to Kayin, "Where is Hevel your brother?" And he replied, "I don't know; am I my brother's guardian?"*

Kayin didn't repent at all. He didn't seem to have even a drop of remorse for what he did. Instead he thought he could outwit God. He thought he could make God believe he wasn't the one who killed Cain. He tried to cover his crime by claiming not to know where his brother was. He defied God by rejecting his responsibility to protect his brother.

Comparing False and True Repentance

Our final example shows the contrast between repentance that's pleasing to God and false repentance and prayer that is displeasing to Him.

Luke 18:10 *"Two men went up to the Temple to pray, one a Parush* (Pharisee) *and the other a tax-collector.*

The Pharisee was a pious, religious man. The tax collector was a despised secular man who was considered a collaborator with the occupying Romans.

Luke 18:11 *The Parush stood and prayed to himself, "O God! I thank you that I am not like the rest of humanity—greedy, dishonest, immoral, or like this tax-collector! 12 I fast twice a week, I pay tithes on my entire income, . . ."*

There was no repentance here! There was just self justification based on pride and religious activity. And there was a very judgmental attitude toward the tax-collector. This is definitely an example of false repentance.

Luke 18:13 *But the tax-collector, standing far off, would not even raise his eyes toward heaven, but beat his breast and said, "God! Have mercy on me, sinner that I am!"*

This was true humility! He didn't even consider himself worthy of raising his eyes to heaven! He also beat his chest which in that culture was another sign of humility. Do you think this is true repentance or false repentance? Let's see what Yeshua said about it.

Luke 18:14 *I tell you, this man went down to his home right with God rather than the other. For everyone who exalts himself will be humbled, but everyone who humbles himself will be exalted."*

True repentance keeps us right before God.

Gleanings From All These Passages.

The meaning of repentance is turning from sin and turning to God out of guilt. That is what true repentance is.

When do we need to repent before God?
When we disobey even if it is out of ignorance
When we have a bad attitude toward Him like blaming Him for our sins
When we are not trusting Him
When we are considering Him unfair
When we've sinned against other people
When we've sinned against God
When we realize we have iniquity—inclination to evil—even if we haven't given in to it
When we have judgmental attitudes toward others who seem clearly more sinful than we are
When we have pride

What produces repentance?
Godly sorrow, revelation of God's holiness and power, and confrontation by other people. This is one of the reasons we encourage everyone to participate in small groups, which we call Khavurah groups (friendship groups). Small groups provide accountability. When we are in fellowship regularly with a group of people, it's hard to hide our sin.

How should we feel when we need to repent?
We should detest, abhor, despise, disdain, and loathe ourselves.

What behavior does true repentance produce?
Weeping
Mourning
Sitting in sackcloth
Turning from evil and sin
Fasting
Destroying things used in ungodly practices
Making restitution when possible

What attitudes does true repentance produce?
> A broken spirit
> A chastened heart—a contrite heart, precious to God
> Indignation at yourself
> Diligence to make restitution
> Fear of God
> A strong desire for reconciliation with God
> Humility

What is God's reaction to true repentance?
> He gives us Joy that's like a fortress protecting us from our deserved judgment from Him.
> He cleanses our sin and guilt.
> He clears our conscience.
> He will answer our prayers.
> He will do a cleansing of our hearts.
> He will give us His Ruakh HaKodesh to help us resist temptation.
> He will give us a steadfast spirit that can resist temptation.
> He will uphold us.
> He will make us right before Him.

What is the effect of not repenting?
> A guilty conscience that torments us
> Physical ailments and diseases
> The absence of the Ruakh HaKodesh

How should we feel after true repentance?
> Joy
> Relief
> Joy of salvation
> A desire to share His love with others

Why should God accept our repentance?

He made the way in the B'rit Hadashah by giving His only Son, Yeshua, whose blood was shed as a sacrifice, just as the blood of innocent animals was shed in the Mosaic Covenant.

Is repentance for believers or unbelievers?
It is for both. The Ephesians were believers, but they had to repent of occult practices even though they had already made professions of faith.

What do we learn from the examples of false repentance?
We can't hide our sin from God.
We can't blame God or others as an excuse for our sin.
We can't claim we're not responsible as an excuse for sin when God has made us responsible.
We can't justify ourselves by our religious activity.
We can't be in pride.

When we ask God's forgiveness with genuine sorrow in Yeshua's name, He promises to forgive us.

1 John 1:9 *If we acknowledge our sins, then, since he is trustworthy and just, he will forgive them and purify us from all wrongdoing.*

When we ask in Yeshua's name, we are acknowledging that we need His sacrificial death to pay the price for our sin. Isaiah 53:5 says of Yeshua *But He was wounded for our transgressions* (pesha, our intentional sins), *He was bruised for our iniquities (avone); the chastisement for our peace was upon Him, and by His stripes we are healed.*

He paid the penalty for our sins and iniquities by His sacrificial death. The Ten Days of Awe only come once a year. Celebrating those Ten Days involves lot's of repenting and reconciling. Over the years the Ruakh HaKodesh has done much work in me during this Moadim season. One year I realized that I need the Days of Awe to happen more frequently. God, who knows us so well, also saw that a time for introspection was needed more frequently.

New Covenant Days of Awe

When God promised us there would be a B'rit Hadashah—a New Covenant. He said it would be a better covenant. In a powerful connection between the two covenants, He made the B'rit Hadashah better in its provision to have Days of Awe more often. You are probably thinking, "What? Where do you find the Days of Awe in the B'rit Hadashah? Well, it's there and it is very prominent. In 2009, I saw this for the first time.

First let me give you a brief summary to refresh your memory of what is supposed to happen during Days of Awe. We're to remember God's holiness and our unworthiness. We are to remember our sin and the ways we have not followed God, and to repent. We are to remember those we've offended or who've offended us and make reconciliation. We are supposed to do all this, so that when Yom Kippur comes and we focus on His atoning sacrifice, we will appreciate how much sin we've been forgiven and how much it cost Him to atone for our sin.

God gave us something in the B'rit Hadashah with the same purpose. Do you know what it is? It's the S'udat Adonai, the Lord's Supper!

If practiced scripturally, whenever we participate in the Lord's Supper, that day <u>becomes</u> a Day of Awe for us. It becomes a day of remembering what Yeshua did for us and of reflecting and doing inner soul searching to make sure we partake in holiness. Rabbi Sha'ul had a revelation of the need to prepare our hearts before the Lord's Supper. He tells us we need heart preparation before we partake of the bread and the wine.

1 Corinthians 11:26 *For as often as you eat this bread and drink the cup, you proclaim the death of the Lord, until he comes.*

Next read the following *very important* instructions for preparing our hearts for meal.

1 Corinthians 11:27 *Therefore, whoever eats the Lord's bread or drinks the Lord's cup in an unworthy manner will be guilty of desecrating the body and blood of the Lord! 28 So let a person examine himself first, and then he may eat of the bread and drink from the cup; 29 for a person who eats and drinks without recognizing the body eats and drinks judgment upon himself.*

This recognizing of "the body" is what makes the Lord's Supper like the Days of Awe. It is appreciating the awe inspiring cost of His sacrificed body and the awe inspiring power of His sacrifice.

1 Corinthians 11:30 *This is why many among you are weak and sick, and some have died! 31 If we would examine ourselves, we would not come under judgment. 32 But when we are judged by the Lord, we are being disciplined, so that we will not be condemned along with the world.*

Examining ourselves to determine if we're worthy to partake requires the same contrition, humbling, and repentance as the Days of Awe. It requires confessing our sin, turning from it, and reconciling our conflicts.

Yeshua said He came to fulfill the Torah and the Prophets. He also fulfilled many of the traditions that developed around keeping Torah. For example, He fulfilled the tradition of keeping two Passover Seders. He kept the first Seder with His disciples and gave the B'rit Hadashah covenant meal at it. He fulfilled the second Seder by dying His sacrificial death at the same time the lambs were being slaughtered. Now we see that He also fulfilled the tradition of the Ten Days of Awe that developed around keeping Rosh Hashanah and Yom Kippur, by giving us the Lord's Supper and inspiring Sha'ul to instruct us in this passage how to prepare for it.

There's no clear direction on how often we are to keep S'dat Adonai. Opinions range from once a year on Pesakh to every time we come together, as the Catholics do. Our practice at Congregation Shema Yisrael is to come to the Lord's table whenever the Ruakh HaKodesh leads us, which usually results in it happening several times per year. The Shabbat during the Ten Days of Awe, traditionally called the, Shabbat T'shuvah is an awesome day to partake of the Lord's Supper.

CHAPTER 14

THE TORAH OF YESHUA

One year in preparing a sermon for the Shabbat T'shuvah, the Sabbath during the Ten Days of Awe, I was asking the Lord "Is there any Biblical account of what went on during the Ten Days of Awe that will give us an idea how to observe this Moad (Appointed Time)?" And I found one that is so amazingly perfect for that. I wonder if you can guess what it is.

Well, it is in Nehemiah chapter 8. (I will be looking at this story from a different angle here than I did in my book, *Rosh Hashanah, Yom Teruah, The Day of Sounding the Shofar.*) The context is this. Our ancestors were conquered by the Babylonians and were taken off into captivity. After 70 years they came back under the leadership of Ezra and Nehemiah and at this point in time they actually had built the Temple again with a wall around it. Now look what happens in chapter 8.

Nehemiah 8:1 *When the seventh month arrived, after the people of Isra'el had resettled in their towns, all the people gathered with one accord in the open space in front of the Water Gate and asked Ezra the Torah-teacher to bring the scroll of the Torah of Moshe (Moses), which ADONAI had commanded Isra'el.*

The first thing I want to know is, "Why did this happen?" The answer is, the people initiated it! They gathered together and said to the leaders,. "Bring us the Word and read us the Word"

Nehemiah 8:2 *Ezra the cohen brought the Torah before the assembly, which consisted of men, women and all children old enough to understand...*

The kids were with the parents.

Nehemiah 8:2 *...It was the first day of the seventh month.*

It was actually Rosh HaShanah or Yom Teruah—the first day of the seventh month in line with exactly what they were doing

Nehemiah 8:3 *Facing the open space in front of the Water Gate, he read from it to the men, the women and the children who could understand from early morning until noon; and all the people listened attentively to the scroll of the Torah.*

Would you like your rabbi's sermon to take four hours? Would you stay and listen? We should do what it says, right? They listened attentively for hours and hours as the law of Moses was read from the scroll.

Nehemiah 8:8 *They read clearly from the scroll, in the Torah of God, translated it, and enabled them to understand the sense of what was being read.*

Other translations, rather than saying "translated" they say "gave a sense of it" and so I feel this is what we do at our synagogue. Every Shabbat we read from the Word and we give an understanding of what the passage is all about.

Nehemiah 8:9 *Nechemyah (Nehemiah) the Tirshata, Ezra the cohen (priest) and Torah-teacher and the L'vi'im (Levites) who taught the people said to all the people, "Today is consecrated to ADONAI your God; don't be mournful, don't weep." For all the people had been weeping when they heard the words of the Torah.*

Why do you suppose they were weeping? It's because they hadn't been following the Torah for years—for decades—for the whole 70 years of captivity. Now they were all being convicted. God's law says to do this and this, and they hadn't been doing it. They were weeping out of shame and remorse. And why had they not been doing it? It was ignorance. They had not been reading from the scroll. Maybe it wasn't possible, but if it was, they could have been reading from the scroll even in Babylon, but they hadn't been.

Nehemiah 8:11 *In this way the L'vi'im* [Levites] *quieted the people, as they said, "Be quiet, for today is holy; don't be sad."*

When I read this, I just got chills. This is so much being led of the spirit by these readers. Can you see what was happening? Thousands of people were repenting. This is a wonderful day. This is what we've been praying for. Let us rejoice! Then, even though they had just been repenting in tears, they were apparently comforted by what the leaders' said.

Nehemiah 8:12 *Then the people went off to eat, drink, send portions and celebrate; because they had understood the words that had been proclaimed to them.*

So, this is an amazing passage. Let's take it a little further. What did they do first? They read the Word of God—the Torah, and the person who was reading it—actually in this case it was several persons—gave explanation of each law of Moses as it was being read!

So that is what I intended to do in this chapter. But I was thinking. Why should I give an explanation of the Torah, when Yeshua Himself explains it? Did you know that? Did you know that Yeshua explained the Laws of Moses? He made sense of them. The longest passage of His interpreting and explaining them is a very famous passage. Yes, it is the Sermon on the Mount.

The Sermon on the Mount

So, we're going to go through the Sermon on the Mount starting in Matthew chapter 5. If we went through the whole thing this book would be very thick and heavy! But I'm just going to go through several verses and then I'm going to suggest that you read the others. I believe for all of us as we read this, it will be like the Israelites that all of a sudden remembered, "This is the Word of God, and we've been breaking it!" And it will bring us to repentance and then that joy of revival. So, we'll start at Matthew 5:20 where Yeshua tells us how He interprets the law. And I tell you, it is a little scary!

Matthew 5:20 *For I tell you that unless your righteousness is far greater than that of the Torah-teachers and P'rushim (Pharisees), you will certainly not enter the Kingdom of Heaven!*

That is really scary, because the Torah teachers and the scribes were experts in the Word. They had it memorized. Really! They could recite any verse to you. They could recite the whole thing, the whole Law of Moses.. They had it all stored in their heads. Not only that, they spent their entire lives trying to keep every commandment. In fact, they had developed a whole set of traditions that helped them not break the commandments. We call them the "fences around the laws." And they obeyed those traditions.

You have to understand this about the Pharisees. We look down on them sometimes. But the Pharisaic movement was actually a revival movement in Israel. The core of the revival was that the Pharisees came to this revelation that every Israelite should be like a cohane, like a priest.

There were a lot of laws in the Torah that spoke about the purity of the cohanim, of the priests. And the Pharisees said "Everybody should live that way." Then they said, "Our homes are like the Temple and our tables are like the altar." It was a powerful revival. They actually began to live that way.

According to the Torah, a normal Israelite from the different tribes didn't have to keep the same level of purity that the cohanim did, but the Pharisees kept them. They wanted to do this. So, they were incredibly well versed and worked very hard at keeping the laws of God. But Yeshua says, "You've got to be much better than them."

Do you like that challenge? That is really something. How can anyone hope to do better than these people who were spending their whole lives focused on keeping the laws of God?

Yeshua answers this question very simply. "You have to obey the laws of God in the way I interpret them, not the way they interpret them, because many times they have interpreted them according to the letter and not according to the Spirit. I'm going to tell you how to obey this according to the Spirit." But it's not going to be easy! I can tell you that right now.

So, let's look at some of these things that He has told us. Of course, in the verses immediately following, as Yeshua explains in His interpretation, it's meant to bring us to repentance so that we will call out for His mercy. And of course, He explains also that He has made atonement for us so that as we go into this, we don't start thinking, "Now this is condemnation upon me." It's not condemnation. It is to make us appreciate how great our need for His atonement is. So, do you follow where we're going? Okay. SO, let's start out in the next verse

Anger Equals Murder

Matthew 5:21 *"You have heard that our fathers were told, 'Do not murder', and that anyone who commits murder will be subject to judgment."*

This is the sixth of the Ten Commandments. Now when you first read it, obeying it seems pretty easy. I mean, are you a murderer? I hope not. But Yeshua has something more to say about how to interpret this commandment.

Matthew 5:22 *"But I tell you that anyone who nurses anger against his brother will be subject to judgment; that whoever calls his brother, 'You good-for-nothing!' will be brought before the Sanhedrin; that whoever says, 'Fool!' incurs the penalty of burning in the fire of Gey-Hinnom (hell)!"*

WOW. So, what Yeshua is saying here is "I have a much higher standard. Those people are spending their lives trying to live up to the Law of Moses. Hey, that's nothing. I've got a higher standard than that." Now when he uses the term "brother" here, he really means all fellow Israelites. If we look at this, we could say "all fellow Americans." So, it's not exclusive here. I like the term "nurse anger" as David Stern translates it. I've always seen it as allowing anger to fester in your heart, as holding a grudge and maybe seeking revenge.

So, what has happened here is that Yeshua has made this commandment, the sixth commandment, much more difficult to obey.

Then He goes on to talk about using demeaning or derogatory names toward people, not just nursing anger. And He says, "You'll be judged for that!" Which is even harder! Now let's think about this a little bit. Some translations say "being angry *without a cause*" and some translations don't have that phrase "without a cause" in there. So it could be even when you *do* have a cause if you nurse anger against someone. I admit, I've been angry with people. Sometimes I think I have a good cause. Do you ever get angry for a good cause? But, you know sometimes that cause is because they've offended me. They're late for an appointment. They've mistreated me in some way, but later I learn about the circumstances. Their car broke down or some emergency happened. What they did had a cause, so my anger is really without a cause and I'm convicted of that.

He goes on about the demeaning names for which we'll receive judgment. I have to admit that I've used some demeaning names at times. Are you willing to admit that you have too? Sometimes it's about politicians. Other times it's about others.

So do you see how much more stringent Yeshua's interpretation of the law is? If the Israelites at the Water Gate in the time of Nehemiah started to weep because of their interpretation, perhaps we need to do some weeping when we hear Yeshua's interpretation.

I have to tell you. Thirty years ago, when I didn't know the Lord but had started reading the Bible, I read the book of John. I thought, "I want to follow this man. This man is amazing. This is the person I've been looking for to follow all the days of my life. I want to be one of His disciples." I told this to my wife and I asked her, "What shall I do now?" She suggested I read another book. She suggested the book of Matthew. So that's what I did and I got to this verse (Matt. 5:22). And I tell you, this is amazing. Up to that point I had no idea I was a sinner.

I was raised in a Jewish home and in our Jewish culture only the BIG evils were bad. The little things weren't considered so bad because everybody does them. I thought I was living in a way that was generally pleasing to God. I hadn't done anything to intentionally hurt people. I wasn't a thief. I wasn't a liar most of the time. This passage gave me my first realization that I was not coming up to Yeshua's standards. I wasn't even close to living up to Yeshua's standards. I was falling short. I was, perish the thought, — A SINNER! And I had never thought of myself that way before. It was a very important revelation because it showed me I needed Yeshua's sacrifice to make me right with God. There was no way I could achieve it on my own.

There's an interesting thing about the Sermon on the Mount. Christians preachers or speakers sometimes say things like, "Oh the poor Jewish people. They have to keep so many laws. There are 613 laws the Jews have to keep. It's so hard for them to do that." When I hear them talk like that I wonder, "Didn't they ever read the Sermon on the Mount? I mean, the commandments there are so much harder than the laws of Moses!"

I saw a very interesting study that maybe you have also seen. There are 613 laws in the Torah. But did you know that there are over 1100 commandments in the New Covenant? That's almost twice as many! So why do Christians think it is harder to be Jewish?

Why were these more stringent laws given to Yeshua's followers? To those who would enter the Kingdom of God? Well, the Kingdom of God is a holy place. God is a holy God. And no sin will be allowed to enter into that place. The Kingdom of God comes when God's Spirit—The Ruakh—takes up residence in our hearts. Therefore we need His atoning sacrifice, desperately, to cleanse us so that the Spirit of God can dwell within us.

Now the other thing about Yeshua's explanations or interpretations of the law is that they go beyond actions and deal with our hearts and our spirits. For instance, in this matter of anger, the person we are angry at might not know that we are angry, but if we nurse anger in our hearts what does it do to us? It is harmful to us, physically, emotionally, and spiritually. It can be connected with ulcers, high blood pressure, heart attacks, and headaches. Nursing anger or resentment can cause all of those things.

So Yeshua tells us to deal with our anger and not let it fester. Why? He can see inside our hearts. There is a song that we sing, "Open the eyes of my heart, Lord." He can see in that spirit realm. He can see every thought, every word. All our thoughts, words, and deeds have an effect in the spirit realm. This can only be seen with the eyes of the spirit. We need to get rid of anger immediately. We can't have it hanging around.

So how do we get rid of anger? Well, I have learned in my thirty eight years of walking with Him that He doesn't command us to do anything that He doesn't enable us to do. Do you agree with me about that? But that help from Him depends on us committing ourselves to be followers of Him, coming before Him in prayer and repenting.

When I've done that, He helps me deal with that anger. And very often He shows me that I don't have a reason to be angry. It very often is not the person's fault. And He shows me also that when I am angry with a person, when I am holding on to that anger, I am blocking, in the spirit, His judgment from moving on that person which will bring redemption in that person's life. Forgiving the person and letting go of my anger frees God's Spirit to move on that person concerning what they did, if they really did something wrong, and bring redemption out of that.

Another thing He does when I repent and I pray for that person, He shows me how much He loves that person. Have you had that experience? You are angry with a person and He shows you how much He loves them? Oooh, you have to break down. And God is saying, "You need to love them the way I love them."

Make Peace with Your Brother

So, Yeshua continues to deal with this condition of our hearts and He deals with our relationships.

Now, if you think that was tough, we're going to read the next two verses where He makes it even tougher.

Matthew 5:23-24 *So if you are offering your gift at the Temple altar and you remember there that your brother has something against you, 24 leave your gift where it is by the altar, and go, make peace with your brother. Then come back and offer your gift.*

You need to know that "offering your gift at the Temple" means worship. This was the means of worship in those days. So what this means is you are trying to worship God. You're trying to pray to Him. You're hoping He'll hear you. You're trying to receive His blessing. You're expecting your prayers to be answered and suddenly you remember that someone has something against you. Someone is angry at you. Someone has been hurt by you. Someone doesn't trust you. Someone is upset with you. Not that you have something against someone. No, that was dealt with in the previous verse.

You can be very happy with this person. You're saying "I love this person. I don't have a problem with this person." But they have something against you. See what I mean? This is even tougher, and He says, "Don't even try to worship God. Don't even try." Leave your gift at the altar. It wouldn't do you any good to worship God. Go make peace with your brother.

Now, usually that means that you have to go to someone and say, "Have I offended you?" and "If I have, I'm sorry." That's a very difficult thing for most of us to do, and it is more important for you to do that than for you to come worship God. Isn't that what Yeshua is saying here?

Now let me temper this by saying that there are times when our attempts at reconciliation don't work. But we are obligated, according to what Yeshua's saying to go and try. If it doesn't work, that's not on us. It's like the blood is off our hands. But we have to go and make our attempt, and God will put us in right standing. Pretty heavy stuff, isn't it?! Well, there's more! We're going to skip over verses 25 and 26.

Lust Equals Adultery

Matthew 5:27 *"You have heard that our fathers were told, 'Do not commit adultery.'"*

That's the seventh commandment. Adultery by all definitions, in any dictionary, is defined as a married person having sexual relations with someone other than their spouse. Or a single person having sexual relations with a married person. But Yeshua is saying, "I've got a higher standard."

Matthew 5:28 *But I tell you that a man who looks at a woman with the purpose of lusting after her has already committed adultery with her in his heart.*

So, Yeshua redefines adultery making it much harder to avoid than either the dictionary or Moses, and I'm assured that this applies to both men and women. He defines adultery as when a person lusts, whether it's after a real person or after an image of that person which we call today, pornography. This is much more stringent than the seventh commandment the way most people understand it. You see this higher standard? And I must admit that thirty eight years ago, this had one of those heart piercing effects on my life. When I thought back about my youth and my 20's, lusting is what I had spent most of my time doing! But, before I read this I didn't know it was sin! So, again, I was incredibly convicted when I read it.

Why does Yeshua say this? Well, He sees our hearts and He knows what's good for us, and what's destructive. Lusting after another person, even without a relationship with them, is incredibly destructive. If you're married, it's destructive to your marriage. If you're single, it's just plain destructive. And by the way, lusting over other things is equally destructive. There are people who lust after food, after cars, after power, after control, after money.

Lusting is trying to fill that hole that only God can fill with something else. And when you do fill it, you find it is always a lie, it's a deception, it's a failure. But lusting sexually is what we are talking about here. It gives rise to strong sexual feelings and urges, and then indulging those lead down the road to greater sin, adultery, fornication, and homosexuality.

So again, this is a much higher standard and I believe that it is much harder to keep this commandment today than it was in Yeshua's time. You know why? All the pictures that are all around us. All the movies and television, and the newspapers and the magazines. It's so available. Let me say gently, the way people dress today is also a factor in this. They didn't dress like this in Yeshua's time, especially in Israel, and still there was lust. But Yeshua seems to take this seriously. If you want to see how serious, look at the next couple of verses.

Matthew 5:29-30 *If your right eye makes you sin, gouge it out and throw it away! Better that you should lose one part of you than have your whole body thrown into Gey-Hinnom* (Hell). *30 And if your right hand makes you sin, cut it off and throw it away! Better that you should lose one part of you than have your whole body thrown into Gey-Hinnom.*

Now He's not meaning this literally, so don't let anyone say that I teach you to gouge out an eye or cut off a hand, but what He's saying is that we need to realize that sin is serious and sin can keep us out of heaven and land us in hell. We need to do everything we can to stop sinning because it would be worse to spend eternity in hell than to be blind in one eye or be one handed.

How to Overcome Lusting

So, how do we stop lusting? Many have tried, but are unable. The same remedy is there. Repent, receive His forgiveness, make Him Lord. Offer your lives to obeying and serving Him and He'll fill you with His spirit and give you the power to overcome sin. One of my favorite verses is:

Romans 6:14 *For sin will not have authority over you; because you are not under legalism but under grace.*

You will have authority over sin. Let me tell you. This whole area of lusting is like having a hole that we try to fill with things and no matter what things you try to fill it with, it will never satisfy because there is only one thing that can fill that hole and that's God and His Spirit.

The thing is not just to try to stop lusting, the thing to do is replace it by doing and serving the Lord and letting Him fill you up. Let the things about the Kingdom of God be the things you are passionate about, the things that you are involved with because those are the things that will take away this craving.

Now I don't have the space to go through the whole Sermon on the Mount. That was just a quarter of the first chapter. There are two more whole chapters! But let me just call out to you some of the other things Yeshua says as He interprets the Law of Moses.

Pride, Treasure, Worry, Judging, Golden Rule, Obeying

Then He goes on to speak about giving, praying, or doing good deeds so that others will think more highly of you. Ohhhhhh. Check your heart as you're doing those things. Giving, praying, helping someone—what's the motivation? Do I want to look good in front of others? Yeshua says you get no credit from God for that.

Striving to store up wealth on earth rather than in heaven. A whole passage on that. Letting the desire for wealth influence your life and guide your life in these passages.

Now here's a really tough one. Worrying. About 8 or 10 verses are about this one. Worrying about food, clothing—and here's the big one—the future. Worrying about tomorrow. That's a big one..

Judging others. Ooooooohhhh. What does judging others mean? Finding fault with others without knowing all the facts. That's really what it means. Looking at somebody and saying, "Look at how they look." "Look at the dumb thing they're doing" without knowing why they're doing what they are doing or what their background is. That's judging others.

And then the one we've always heard: treating others the way you want to be treated. Remember that commandment! It's called the Golden Rule.

And finally He ends the Sermon on the Mount by speaking about those who call Him "Lord, Lord" and even doing miracles in His Name but not obeying what He says, claiming to be followers of Yeshua, but not listening to Him. He will say to them, "I never knew you."

I suggest you read through the Sermon on the Mount during the Ten Days of Awe. You will be doing what they were doing on Rosh Hashanah in the time of Nehemiah. They were interpreting the laws of Moses. Now if I had to interpret the laws of Moses, I wouldn't interpret them the way Yeshua did. But that's Yeshua's interpretation of them. Let's look at some more of Yeshua's expounding of the Torah.

Being Salt

Matthew 5:13 *"You are salt for the Land...(of the Earth) But if salt becomes tasteless, how can it be made salty again? It is no longer good for anything except being thrown out for people to trample on.*

Yeshua is making an analogy here, referring to some uses of salt. People in the Holy Land probably weren't familiar with one of our greatest uses for salt here in the northern hemisphere, to melt snow and ice. When He says "for the land" (or earth as in other translations), it makes us think He is referring to ice melting. But, in the Hebrew that He would have been speaking, the word "Land" or "earth" can mean "dirt" or it can mean *a nation, region, community, or culture.*

Yeshua's followers are to be like salt. I can think of several uses for salt. How many can you think of? Following are all the uses or properties that come to my mind. Yeshua's followers are to be like salt in all of them.

1. Taste – Salt makes food taste good.

   Yeshua's followers are to be like salt to make the Word of God taste good. Just a sprinkle of salt is used on a large portion of food to make it taste good. So, we are to be scattered among the people around us to make our community taste good, to make it loving, just, truthful, fun, creative, and beautiful.

2. Preservative — Salt preserves things.

   Yeshua's followers are to be like salt, preserving the culture we live in, keeping it from becoming decadent, deteriorated, uncivilized, barbaric, evil, cruel, and deceptive. We can do this by taking stands for righteousness, by helping the poor and handicapped, etc, and by standing for justice.

3. Making thirsty — Salt makes people thirsty.

There is an old saying that you can lead a horse to water, but you can't make him drink. That is not necessarily true. If you put a tablet of salt in his mouth, he will definitely drink! Yeshua's followers are to be like salt by making people around them thirsty to know God. How? By showing people the love of God, by helping them, forgiving them, being kind to them, and by letting them know you are doing it because of God's inspiration.

4. Melting — Salt melts ice and snow.

Yeshua's followers are to be like salt by softening hearts that are cold to the love of God, by melting cold hearts to allow God's love to enter people's hearts. How can we possibly do this? By being a vehicle of God's love and letting people know it is God's love.

Matthew 5:13...*But if salt becomes tasteless, how can it be made salty again? It is no longer good for anything except being thrown out for people to trample on.*

If we as followers of Yeshua don't function as salt, we are worthless. This is a big issue because in many places and at many times Yeshua's followers have failed to be salt. They have withdrawn from the culture they lived in to became monks or hermits. Some have become as decadent as the rest of the people. Others forced people to believe what they did.

Being Light

Matthew 5:14 *"You are light for the world. A town built on a hill cannot be hidden."*

Yeshua's followers are also to be like light. What does light do? It enables us to see clearly. It reveals beauty, but also ugliness. It helps us to see the truth, but also to see what is not the truth. It helps us see what is good, but also to see evil. Light helps us to not be deceived, to find our way, and to not stumble. Light sustains life. Without light plants would die. Without light we would all be blind. In the Bible light represents the Truth of God. His Truth dispels the darkness of evil.

John 8:12 *Yeshua spoke to them again: "I am the light of the world; whoever follows me will never walk in darkness but will have the light which gives life."*

We are to be like mirrors reflecting His light, like the moon reflects the sun's light.

Yeshua's followers are to be like light by speaking the truth to people who have been deceived by the enemy. The devil's main tactic is deception.

John 8:44 *You belong to your father, ha-satan, and you want to carry out your father's desires. From the start he was a murderer, and he has never stood by the truth, because there is no truth in him. When he tells a lie, he is speaking in character; because he is a liar—indeed, the inventor of the lie!*

Yeshua's followers are to be like light revealing God's beauty,
   Bringing insight so we can see the Kingdom of God,
   So people can see things they couldn't see before, such as
      hidden evil.
Yeshua's followers are to be like light,
   Bringing the light of the Good News to people walking in
      darkness.
Yeshua's followers are to be like light,
   Bringing life to people.
Yeshua's followers are to be like light,
   Lighting the path that God has for them,
   So they can fulfill their destiny.

Matthew 5:14 *You are light for the world. A town built on a hill cannot be hidden.*

I never fully understood this expression until I visited Israel. Here in the US, we build our towns in the valleys, near a water source. When you are flying over the US, you will see that often the towns are hidden by trees. But, in Israel, because their greatest concern was always defense, the towns are built on the tops of hills. Standing in the valleys, you can see the white stone walls of the towns on the surrounding hilltops. There are very few trees so they are easily seen.

Yeshua is saying His followers should not hide their light. They should be as visible as an Israeli town. They should not be ashamed to be known as His followers. They should not fear criticism for being a believer.

Matthew 5:15 *Likewise, when people light a lamp, they don't cover it with a bowl, but put it on a lampstand, so that it shines for everyone in the house.*

This passage is further emphasis of His point. Yeshua has given His followers the light of God and the ability to reflect His light. He didn't do that so they could cover up that light to avoid being seen for who they are, out of fear.

Matthew 5:16 *In the same way, let your light shine before people, so that they may*
see the good things you do and praise your Father in heaven.

In the same way a lamp shines or an Israeli town is easily visible, Yeshua commands us as His followers to let our light shine. Then He tells us how to do that when He says, "so that people may see the good things you do." We let our lights shine by doing good things for people. Our light is the good things we do: good works and acts of kindness or compassion. Then He tells us what the effect will be of people seeing His followers doing good things.

Matthew 5:16...*and praise your Father in heaven.*

People will praise God when they see us doing good things! Other translations say they will glorify God. This means they will see Him as wonderful and good. For this to happen, Yeshua's followers must do good things. But they must also let people know they are doing the good things because they have experienced God's love themselves. This is the foundational verse for our outreach program called Sharing Our Bread. I first heard a sermon on it by Joel Chernoff, founder of the Joseph Project, and it had a tremendous impact on my thinking. This is what we do at Sharing Our Bread. We do a good thing and we tell people we are doing it, not because we're such great people, but because the God we serve commands us to do good things for others.

He Came to Fulfill

Matthew 5:17 *"Don't think that I have come to abolish the Torah or the Prophets. I have come not to abolish but to complete.*

When Yeshua refers to the Torah or the Prophets He is referring to the entire Tenakh. Other translations use other words in place of "abolish." They use "destroy." In place of "complete," they used "fulfill." This is the foundational verse of Messianic Judaism. For 1700 years the church has taught the opposite of what Yeshua was clearly saying here. They were interpreting Yeshua's statement that He was completing or fulfilling as meaning He was bringing an end to the Law of God. In other words they thought He was saying that people don't need to obey God's laws anymore. But, if you look at it carefully laying aside what you've been taught about it, you will see that is clearly not what He meant! The next verse makes it even more clear.

Matthew 5:18 *Yes indeed! I tell you that until heaven and earth pass away, not so much as a yud or a stroke will pass from the Torah—not until everything that must happen has happened.*

The yud is the smallest Hebrew letter. Other translations say "jot or tittle." Here He says that the Torah will stand (have influence) until heaven and earth pass away or until all of God's plan is fulfilled.

Matthew 5:19 *So whoever disobeys the least of these mitzvot (commandments) and teaches others to do so will be called the least in the Kingdom of Heaven. But whoever obeys them and so teaches will be called great in the Kingdom of Heaven.*

Yeshua is about to interpret several of the most important commandments. We need to understand that Yeshua was sent to the Jewish people who were given the commandments by God in the Torah. We believe they are still the commandments of God to us today.

Later, when the Good News went to the Gentiles, non-Jewish people were not given all of these commandments, but they were expected to keep many of them. Everyone is, of course, required to keep the moral commandments. But they were not required to keep the commandments that were given specifically to the Jewish people. These are things like the Kosher food laws, circumcision, keeping the Moadim (Appointed Times).

Divorce

Matthew 5:31 *"It was said, 'Whoever divorces his wife must give her a get.'"*

A "get" is Hebrew for a certificate of divorce. This is not one of the Ten Commandments. Deuteronomy 24:1 mentions a get but does not specify its contents or conditions. Yeshua states His position on the conditions very strongly.

Matthew 5:32 *But I tell you that anyone who divorces his wife, except on the ground of fornication, makes her an adulteress; and that anyone who marries a divorcee commits adultery.*

In that culture it was not thinkable for a woman to divorce her husband. Women didn't have legal rights. So today, Yeshua's statement must also be reversed:

Matthew 5:32 *But I tell you that anyone who divorces [her husband,] except on the ground of fornication, makes [him] an adulterer; and that anyone who marries a divorced [man] commits adultery.*

Keep in mind that women in that culture could not live on their own. So the divorced wife would have to re-marry. In doing so she would be committing adultery because in God's eyes, the marriage covenant with her husband was still valid. Yeshua was challenged about this position later in Matthew.

Matthew 19:3-5 *Some P'rushim (Pharisees) came and tried to trap him by asking, "Is it permitted for a man to divorce his wife <u>on any ground</u> whatever?" 4 He replied, "Haven't you read that at the beginning the Creator made them male and female, 5 and that he said, 'For this reason a man should leave his father and mother and be united with his wife, and the two are to become one flesh'?*

He is quoting Genesis 2:24 there.

Matthew 19:6 *Thus they are no longer two, but one. So then, no one should split apart what God has joined together."*

Here Yeshua tells us how He interprets what God said in Genesis. God makes the two into one—man and woman into a married couple. No one, not even the husband or the wife, not lawyers or judges should separate what God has joined together.

Matthew 19:7 *They said to him, "Then why did Moshe give the commandment that a man should hand his wife a get and divorce her?"*

They are referring to Deuteronomy 24:1. Permission is not given for divorce there. It is only saying that if it happens, the wife should get a written notice.

Matthew 19:8 *He answered, "Moshe allowed you to divorce your wives because your hearts are so hardened. But this is not how it was at the beginning.*

Yeshua is saying God allowed divorce in the Mosaic Covenant because their hearts were hard, but divorce is not God's intention.

Matthew 19:9 *Now what I say to you is that whoever divorces his wife, except on the ground of sexual immorality, and marries another woman commits adultery!"*

Here Yeshua again makes it even tougher to enter the Kingdom of God. In Matthew 5:32 He said if you divorce your spouse and your divorced wife remarries, she and her new marriage partner are committing adultery, and He says you caused it. Here He says if you divorce your spouse and you marry another person, you commit adultery. It sounds very strict and it is!! But understanding this verse is also key to understanding God's position

What is the key? The key is that God considers marriage a sacred covenant between husband and wife that He, God, makes between them. God does not grant a husband or a wife the power to break that covenant made by Him. So, if you divorce your spouse and marry another, you are committing adultery. Why? Because your first marriage covenant is still valid in God's eyes.

In Matthew 5 & 19 Yeshua does give one valid reason for divorce. If there is infidelity by one spouse, then the other spouse is allowed to divorce the adulterous spouse. Why? Because infidelity by one partner breaks the covenant. So, the other spouse is permitted to divorce the unfaithful spouse. But, repentance, forgiveness, and reconciliation is much preferred by God than divorce. Yeshua's position is further supported by Malachi.

Malachi 2:14 (KJV) ...*Because the LORD has been witness Between you and the wife of your youth, With whom you have dealt treacherously; Yet she is your companion And your wife by covenant. 15 But did He not make them one, Having a remnant of the Spirit? And why one? He seeks godly offspring. Therefore take heed to your spirit, And let none deal treacherously with the wife of his youth. 16 "For the LORD God of Israel says that He hates divorce, For it covers one's garment with violence," Says the LORD of hosts. "Therefore take heed to your spirit, That you do not deal treacherously."*

Violence – khamas – also means wrongdoing
Garment – l'voosh
It covers one's wife with wrongdoing

We see Yeshua has interpreted the law according to the heart of God. God hates divorce. There had been much debate in ancient Israel over divorce. There were two positions, lenient and strict. Yeshua took the strict position. What should you do if you are considering divorce or separation? You should seek counseling to reconcile.

What should you do if you are already divorced? If it was for infidelity it is valid in God's eyes. If not, every marriage breakup has two sides. Repent for your part in it. God will forgive you. And, if possible, try all you can do to reconcile. It may be impossible to reconcile.

You might already be remarried. Perhaps your divorced spouse has already remarried. God will forgive you when He sees your repentance.

Making Vows and Swearing

Matthew 5:33 *Again, you have heard that our fathers were told, "Do not break your oath," and "Keep your vows to ADONAI." 34 But I tell you not to swear at all -- not "by heaven," because it is God's throne; 35 not "by the earth," because it is his footstool and not "by Yerushalayim," because it is the city of the Great King. 36 And don't swear by your head, because you can't make a single hair white or black. 37 Just let your "Yes" be a simple "Yes," and your "No" a simple "No"; anything more than this has its origin in evil.*

The Bible teaches there are valid kinds of swearing or vows or oaths

1. If I swear to God that I will do something, it is binding on me to fulfill it.

2. If I swear to a person that I will do something, it is a binding oath or vow. I must fulfill it.

Yeshua says the problem is people take these statements lightly. It's not wrong to swear to God or to make vows to people, but it's foolish and not necessary because circumstances can change, and you might not be able to fulfill it. When a vow is made to God or man, the Torah says it must be fulfilled or the person who made the vow will experience judgment.

So, Yeshua says, don't swear at all.

There are two more valid forms of swearing.

1. I swear a statement is true and add I swear to God it is true.

> So help me God – sworn in US courts.
>> We are really saying – if I am swearing falsely may God never help me again.
>> It is valid when used in court but again it should not be done lightly.

2. I promise or swear something as assurance my statement is true.
>> If I don't fulfill my promise, I will give you this thing of great value.
>> We call this a guarantee. It backs up my statement.
>> It is like a money-back guarantee today. If this TV doesn't please you, we'll refund your money.
>> This is a valid way of assuring a promise. God has no problem with it.

Matthew 5:33 *Again, you have heard that our fathers were told, "Do not break your oath," and "Keep your vows to Adonai (the Lord)."*

Vows—oaths are not wrong, but Yeshua once again raises the standards for His followers.

Matthew 12:34 *But I tell you not to swear at all.*

The problem Yeshua is addressing is misuse of swearing, oaths, and vows.

1. Swearing to God or a person that I will do something without being sure I can do it. Changing circumstances could prevent me from fulfilling the vow. But I will be bound to that oath. It is better to not have sworn at all.

2. Swearing or vowing to do something that is trivial, like I swear I'll call you to chat tomorrow.
3. Swearing in our common talk, or swearing lightly, or swearing to curse. Yeshua is warning us that we throw words around without thinking about them.

Matthew 12:36 *Moreover, I tell you this: on the Day of Judgment people will have to give account for every careless word they have spoken;*

Not only will we be judged by our words, but our idle words can give ha-satan an opening to bring destruction into our lives. In addition people often bring God into their misused vows. This is where the third Commandment needs to be understood.

Exodus 20:7 *"You shall not take the name of the LORD your God in vain, for the LORD will not hold him guiltless who takes His name in vain.*

Taking God's Name in vain means not treating it with the respect it deserves. This reflects on God. It insults God. This is huge. People have many, many ways of taking God's Name in vain, including cursing people or things with it. Another example is swearing to God for trivial, doubtful, or deceitful reasons. "I swear to God, I never did anything like that." All this is taking His Name in vain.

Jewish tradition takes the third Commandment very seriously. Not wanting to take God's Name in vain, the Name God gave Himself is never pronounced by Jewish people. In the Hebrew Bible God's Name is spelled yud hey vav hey many times. No vowels are given, so we don't know how to say it. Jewish people substitute "Adonai" which means "Lord" when reading it, or they say, "Hashem" which means "the Name." When a document containing God's Name is worn out, their tradition is that it cannot be thrown into the garbage. To avoid taking His Name in vain, it must be ceremonially buried. This is the reason we have the Dead Sea Scrolls. They were buried this way.

According to the Bible, Yeshua (Jesus) is God come as a man. So using Yeshua's Name in meaningless exclamations is another common way people take God's Name in vain.

Frequently people avoid using His Name by swearing or making exclamations that sound like His Name: Jeez, gee whiz, etc. For "God" they use, by gosh or by golly. Similarly for the Holy Spirit, you hear things like, Holy Smoke or Holy Cow. This is one of the advantages of calling the Lord by His Hebrew Name, Yeshua. I have never heard anyone use the Name, Yeshua, like they use the Name, Jesus.

Matthew 12:*34 But I tell you not to swear at all—not "by heaven," because it is God's throne; 35 not "by the earth," because it is his footstool; and not "by Yerushalayim," because it is the city of the Great King.*

Yeshua is saying these things belong to God and are not yours to swear by.

Matthew 5:*36 And don't swear by your head, because you can't make a single hair white or black.*

People also swore by something they thought they owned– their own head. But Yeshua said even that belongs to God. So, how are we to speak or promise?

Matthew 5:*37 Just let your 'Yes' be a simple 'Yes,' and your 'No' a simple 'No'; anything more than this has its origin in evil.*

Yeshua is simply saying his followers should tell the truth. When they say yes, they should mean yes, and when they say no, they should mean no. Consequently, people can trust and believe each other. Those who add to their words with an oath imply that their words cannot be trusted. The person who constantly swears is constantly perjuring himself. Such a person should never be trusted. Yeshua's followers, however, know that they are accountable to God for every word they speak, so they will speak truthfully and do what they promise.

CHAPTER 15

GOD'S CHOSEN FAST: BREAKING BONDS

In this chapter, we will get some more insight about Yom Kippur by looking at Isaiah 58. I tell you, there have been more than twenty times, since I became a Messianic Rabbi, that I've gone before the Lord, asking for a message to give for each Appointed Time, and He has always given me something new! I keep thinking I'm coming to the end of the new things! But I haven't yet. This revelation we are going to look at in this chapter is really different and really new. I'm looking forward to sharing it with you.

Leviticus 23:27,29 *The tenth day of this seventh month is Yom-Kippur; you are to have a holy convocation, you are to deny yourselves, ... Anyone who does not deny himself on that day is to be cut off from his people;*

Nefesh – *soul or life or self,* nafshotechem – *your (plural) souls,* from the root word "nefesh"

Anah - *humble or deny or afflict*; Anit*em - you (plural)shall* humble, from the root word "anah"

Anitem et nafshotechem (You shall afflict your souls) you know has traditionally been understood to mean fasting food—not eating food on this day. So the traditional reading for this day is Isaiah 58 because it talks about fasting. This chapter in Isaiah describes the fasting that God approves and the fasting that He disapproves. However in verse three we have a very interesting situation.

Isaiah 58:3 *"Why should we fast, if you don't see? Why mortify ourselves, if you don't notice?"*

Another word for fasting is used. Both the word, tzamnu – *we are fasting food,* and the words used in Leviticus, aninu nafshenu – *we are afflicting our souls* are here in this verse. So here's how I understand this. The people evidently were obeying God's command to afflict their souls by fasting on this day of Yom Kippur. Perhaps they were also doing something in addition to fasting since they mention both. However, they were not being blessed by God for afflicting themselves or for their fasting. In fact, it seems to them that not only did God not reward them for it, He didn't even notice it.

Why Fast?

So, let's just take a minute here, before we get into the dynamics of this, and talk about why someone would fast. Obviously on Yom Kippur, it would be done out of obedience because the Lord commands it. By the way, I want to make this clear. If you are not physically able to fast due to some medical condition, that is fine. There is no pressure on you to fast. Also, you can fast something other than food. TV is a good thing to fast.

Usually, in our culture and in Israel, when we call for a fast, we call it a time of prayer and fasting. People fast in hopes that God will respond to their prayers that they pray during this time. So, how does that work? Why is fasting something that enhances our prayers?

Well, I've experienced this and maybe you have, too. It's a

very practical answer. It actually frees up time, because I think it takes about two hours out of our day to prepare, eat, and clean up our food. So, if we take those two hours and spend it praying, that works really well. But also, here's how it affects me. When I pray and fast, it gives me a really strong incentive to make sure I get lots of prayer time. Because I'm making this sacrifice of going without food all day, and if I end up at the end of the day and I didn't spend any time praying, I'm going to be really mad at myself. I gave up food and I'm struggling, and then I didn't even do what I was supposed to do.

Fasting and praying for a particular need is a way of demonstrating to God that we are serious. It shows that we are desperate about that situation. It is so important that I'm going to give up food for it. I believe that fasting enables us to hear from God better because it takes our mind off of the things of this world—the physical—the things of the flesh.

In Mark 9:25-28, we have an interesting incident. Yeshua's disciples had been unable to cast a demon out of a young man. Yeshua was away and He came back and saw what was going on and said to them:

Mark 9:29 (KJV) *And he said unto them, This kind can come forth by nothing, but by prayer and fasting.*

The way I understand that is that fasting was needed for power over the stronger spirits. The disciples had cast demons out of other people, but they couldn't cast this one out. There's something about fasting that gives us spiritual power for spiritual warfare, which is where we are going to go in the end here, but you need to be patient as we look at some other things first.

There's much more about fasting. People have written whole books about fasting. But now that we understand a little bit about it, I want to go back to Isaiah 58.

When Fasting Does No Good

In the rest of verse 3, God answers the people's question about why He didn't notice their fasting—why there was no power.

Isaiah 58:3b *"Here is my answer: when you fast, you go about doing whatever you like, ..."*

So while the people were fasting, supposedly afflicting their souls, they were still finding pleasure some other way. We don't know what that was, but in our time we know what kinds of things we could be doing. It could be watching television, listening to music—all kinds of things—taking a nap, maybe—things that are pleasurable. God was saying that is not the idea.

But then He gets into some other very interesting things.

Isaiah 58:3b *"... while keeping your laborers hard at work."*

Yom Kippur was supposed to be a Shabbat. But evidently those people who owned businesses or farms and had people working for them, weren't giving them the day off. They were saying, "No you've got to work in the field today because we are getting behind." God was saying, "You've got to give them the day off."

Isaiah 58:4 *Your fasts lead to quarreling and fighting, to lashing out with violent blows. NIV: Your fasting ends in quarreling and strife, and in striking each other with wicked fists.*

I looked up "strife." It also means "criticizing, putting others down." "Debating" means "quarreling." "Striking with the fist" basically also means "hurting people." So, the people evidently were being divisive. They were being cruel to each other, even on this day when they were supposed to be holy. They were supposed to be fasting unto the Lord.

Isaiah 58:4b *You will not fast as you do on this day to make your voice heard on high.*

So He's saying, "I won't hear your prayers if this is the way you behave during your fasting." Then He addressed some other very interesting things. What He addresses in the next verse are the religious things the people were doing—not necessarily that they were being mean, but this is very interesting.

Isaiah 58:5 (NKJV) Is it a fast that I have chosen, A day for a man to afflict his soul? Is it to bow down his head like a bulrush, And to spread out sackcloth and ashes? Would you call this a fast, And an acceptable day to the Lord?

It looks like the Lord is being sarcastic here. It's not an acceptable fast. So what's this all about? Well, these were things that people in that culture traditionally did when they were fasting to demonstrate that they were humbling themselves. They were bowing low to demonstrate humility. They were wearing sackcloth which is like burlap—very coarse clothing—uncomfortable to demonstrate that they were afflicting themselves. And they were placing ashes on themselves also to publicly demonstrate humility. So what's God saying in this verse? Even if you humble yourself publicly, it's not necessarily an acceptable fast to Me. Do you see that? That's really amazing.

The Fast the Lord Likes

Loose the Chains

Then the Lord began to describe what makes a fast acceptable and chosen.

Isaiah 58:6 (NIV)   "Is not this the kind of fasting I have chosen: to loose the chains of injustice and untie the cords of the yoke, to set the oppressed free and break every yoke?"

Different, isn't it? Well, what are these bonds of wickedness and heavy burdens and yokes? Who are these oppressed? As I read it, it sounded to me like people in slavery. That's on the first level. There are other levels to it. Slavery was not necessarily evil in the times when the Bible was written. It was legal in those days, and it was the means that people had to pay off debts that they couldn't pay. Bankruptcy like we have it today is a relatively recent invention. In times past, if you couldn't pay your debtors, you went into servitude to them until you worked off what you owed. But the Bible commanded that slave owners treat their slaves well. Bonds of wickedness—these heavy burdens and yokes—I believe these would've been on the people who were either unjustly enslaved or were being treated cruelly while they were slaves. This is very clearly directed at people who were oppressing their slaves.

That's the first thing that makes a fast acceptable to the Lord: Set free those who are unjustly or cruelly treated in bondage.

Isaiah 58:7 (NIV) *Is it not to share your food with the hungry and to provide the poor wanderer with shelter-- when you see the naked, to clothe him,*

So what's the second thing that makes a fast acceptable to the Lord? It's very clear. Care for the needy. This passage has been very important to us who have served in "Sharing Our Bread" over the years. This is one of the motivating passages for our ministry of giving away food. He goes on in verse 7 to say something else very interesting.

Isaiah 58:7b (NIV) *and not to turn away from your own flesh and blood?*

How do you turn away from your flesh? That's kind of weird. Well, He's talking about family here. The third criteria for an acceptable fast is to take care of your family responsibilities. Take care of the elderly in your family. Take care of those who are poor. Take care of the widows. Take care of the children.

Then the tone changes. God begins to tell us the rewards for His kind of fasting. They are incredible.

Isaiah 58:8 (NIV)   *Then your light will break forth like the dawn, and your healing will quickly appear;*

Healing and wholeness! Physical, mental, emotional healing will come quickly when you have an acceptable fast to the Lord.

Isaiah 58:8b (NIV) ... *then your righteousness will go before you, and the glory of the LORD will be your rear guard.*

That verse always gets me. Can you imagine that? The righteousness of the Lord breaking the way for you as you go into battle, and your rear guard the glory of the Lord.

Isaiah 58:8b-9 (NIV) *Then you will call, and the LORD will answer; you will cry for help, and he will say: Here am I—hee-neh-nee—here I am.*

This is an incredible promise regarding our prayers being answered. When you call on the Lord, He will answer, "Here I am." This means so much more because this is what Abraham said when he responded to God. He said, "Here I am." In other words, it's not saying I'm located here. It's saying, "Here I am ready to do your will." Look at what God is saying! "Here I am, ready to answer your prayer." In fact it's the only place in the Bible when God says Henani. It's an awesome promise.

Isaiah 58:9b (NJKV) *If you take away the yoke from your midst, The pointing of the finger, and speaking wickedness,*

So, the taking away the yoke, God already talked about. But here He adds two new things to get rid of. He kind of went back and forth here. He gave a promise and then said, "But wait a minute. Here are a couple more things you have to get rid of." *Pointing the finger.* What's wrong with pointing the finger? I give directions to people that way. No, this is about judging others—accusing others of evil—shifting blame. "Oh, no, it wasn't my fault. They made me do it." *Speaking wickedness—avone*—speaking iniquity. Wow, that's pretty big. That includes all ungodly speech. That could be being critical, grumbling, gossiping, slander, threatening speech, deceiving speech, doubting speech, fearful speech—all kinds of negative speech.

Let me kind of wrap this up. When I saw this, it was really amazing to me because I saw here a new definition of what a real fast is. This is what God is saying through Isaiah. God's chosen fast is to treat each other in a Godly way, without strife, criticism, accusations, or other hurtful words or behavior. To break the yoke of oppression, set slaves free and those who are depressed. (We're going to get into what that means at a deeper level in a few minutes.) To care for those in need, providing food, clothing, and shelter, and provide for your family. All this rather than pursuing your own desires. That's what God calls an acceptable fast to Him. Is that amazing? Is that different? It's incredible.

Five Levels of Breaking Yokes

Now I want to focus on the instructions about breaking bondage—breaking yokes of oppression. They were given in verses 6 and 9. I want to look into how they apply to us today. What I saw as I began to study this is that they apply on several levels. Actually I found about five different levels. In each of these levels, as we fast, we are called to pray for, work towards, speak out, and take a stand to break these yokes.

First Level: Slavery and Oppression

So, let me tell you the first level. Did you know that in our world today, there are up to 27 million people who are actually in slavery? Is that outrageous? There are actually more people in slavery right now than at any time in the history of the world, even though it's outlawed. Some of the countries that still have slavery in them, even though it's outlawed are: Sudan, India and Nigeria. Secondly, there are billions of people who are oppressed and heavily burdened and kept in wicked bondage by their governments. It's true. Communist governments, dictatorships all around the world—billions! And thirdly, there are other billions who are oppressed by the lies of false religions. Billions! Hinduism, Islam, Christian cults. And of course you know about ISIS. People are oppressed because of the lies they've been taught and the bondage that they're in because of it.

So a fast that is acceptable to God includes praying and speaking and working toward freedom to people in all of those places. I don't know how we do it other than to pray at this point in time. It's huge how much slavery there is in the world.

As you do pray for this, there's this dangerous principle. If you pray for God to do something somewhere, sometimes He sends you! So be careful when you pray for this! (*smile*)

The fourth area is the United States. Even though slavery is illegal here—we live in a free country—people still oppress each other. They do it with threats of violence, blackmail, and removal of provision. If you've ever read the stories of people who are addicted to drugs or are stuck in prostitution, do you know why they're stuck there? Often times it's because of threats of the people who control them, or threats of removal of the drug they're addicted to. And, sadly, we know that there are parents who oppress their children. There is lots of child abuse that still goes on in this nation. We know there are husbands who oppress their wives. And there are some wives who oppress their husbands. There are older siblings who oppress younger siblings.

A while back it was big in the news about bullies. People are starting to realize this is a problem. There are children all around who bully other children. And there are adult bullies. So we can pray and speak out and work toward freedom to those who are oppressed in these ways in our homes and schools and neighborhoods.

Some of you reading this right now, you may be oppressed by someone—by a spouse or a parent, or an older sibling, or a boss, or a bully. God's word to you today is that it is His will for you to be free. When I think of freedom, I think of this verse in II Corinthians.

II Corinthians 3:17 *Where the Spirit of ADONAI is, there is ... what? Freedom!*

Here's the most significant thing that jumped out to me as I studied this. Yom Kippur is a Moad, meaning an Appointed Time of the Lord. But what is the Appointed Time for today? We know it was a time for atonement back in the days of the Temple, but since Yeshua made atonement for us, what is it for today? Well, I began to see that it is a time for setting people free. It's a time for breaking bondages. That's what God calls His chosen fast! So we're going to pray later to set you free. If you're in some kind of bondage that some other person is putting on you, today is the day for your freedom.

Also, I wouldn't put it past belief that some of my readers, either in person or through the internet, might be oppressing someone else. We're going to pray later for the convicting power of the Ruakh—the Holy Spirit to be upon us. Anyone who is reading this who is holding someone else in bondage, God's message to you today is to let that person go free.

Now let me make a caveat here, this does not refer to the normal authority that parents have over their children! Or that older children have over their younger siblings when it is delegated by their parents. Those are necessary and important areas of authority.

Let's go back and look again at those verses in Isaiah and we will see an even more incredible level.

Isaiah 58:6 (NIV) *"Is not this the kind of fasting I have chosen: to loose the chains of injustice and untie the cords of the yoke, to set the oppressed free and break every yoke?"*

There's another important understanding of the "bonds of wickedness." Many of you reading this are bound in bonds of wickedness. You are heavily burdened and oppressed by the adversary—by ha-satan through his deceptive means. An acceptable fast to the Lord is to break those bonds.

When I was first giving this message, I started getting a lot of phlegm in my throat at this point. It was like opposition as we got to the real crux of this message. I had no problem with my voice till we got to this point. I asked one of the elders to pray for me to combat the enemy. His prayer battle worked. I was able to continue. If there is anything happening to you right now as you are reading this, it is only the enemy trying to keep you from getting this message. Just rebuke the enemy in Yeshua's name to make him flee.

How Do We Break These Bonds?

So, how do we break those bonds? First of all by teaching and proclaiming deliverance. Then by taking authority over the enemy and his henchmen—evil spirits—who would hold us in this bondage. So I'm rejoicing because my day of fasting is acceptable to God because I'm speaking to you now about His delivering power! I'm bringing forth that. Later we are going to pray that those bonds of wickedness—yokes placed on you by ha-satan be broken. We will do prayer warfare that will focus on breaking bondages.

If you are agreeing with me as you read the prayers, you can speak it and pray for it and command it and your fast will be acceptable to the Lord. I need agreement for this. So are you with me? Are you ready for this to be a day of breaking bondages?

Our Soul Needs to Submit to Our Spirit

But there's another side to this from the Lord.

Leviticus 23:27 Hebrew: *Anitem et nafshotechem*

Do you remember what that means? Other translations translate that as "deny yourseves" or "humble yourselves." Remember that the Hebrew "nafshotechem" can also be translated as "souls." The New King James Version translates it as *you shall afflict your souls.* So "afflicting your soul" is the same as "denying your soul" or "humbling your soul." But let's remember how the Bible describes human nature. It starts out with the understanding that God is a Spirit. The Bible also says that You and I, everyone of us, are made in whose image? God's! So, if God is a Spirit and we are made in His image, what are we? We are spirits. We are immortal. Our spirits will not die. Ever since your spirit was born from above, your spirit has been longing to be immersed in or flowing with God's Spirit.

Now your spirit lives in a body. The thing that many people get confused about is that your spirit—you—has a soul. Your soul is your mind, your emotions, and your will. It includes things like your reasoning ability, your gifting, all the memories that you have, the habits that you've developed—both good and bad—the regrets, fears, and doubts you might have, iniquity which are things like envy, bitterness, greed, or lust. The soul is actually called something else in the New Covenant. It's our carnal nature or our old man or old woman or old person. It's our flesh.

So, if you put this together. To deny yourself or humble yourself is the same as afflicting your what? Your soul! What does it mean? It means to humble your soul by reducing—listen to this carefully—the power or control your soul—or your carnal nature or your flesh—has over your life. Let me say that again. To deny yourself means to reduce the power or control your flesh has over your life. It means for the real you—the immortal spirit to take control of your life—to take control away from your soul or your flesh. You've probably heard this described in another way. It's called walking in the Spirit. Be led by God's Spirit rather than be led by your soul or your carnal nature. And what does the Bible say those who are led by the Spirit are? They are the children of God!

So, what I'm getting to here is that this is the deeper meaning of a fast that is acceptable to God. It simply means to walk in the Spirit! Not in your flesh! Not in your carnal nature! After I realized that, I thought, "I should be fasting every day!" If that's what it means! How about you?! That's a fast that is acceptable to the Lord.

First Admit Our Own Soul-Bondages

But as I meditated on this, it came to me that we've got these two things here showing what it means to humble our flesh. One is, in a sense, to have control—to be led by the Spirit, and this other one about breaking bondages. But how are they related?

Well, to set others free from ha-satan's bonds, we need to be free ourselves. But to be free from the bondages of the enemy, we need to humble ourselves. We need to recognize and admit that we ourselves have areas where the enemy is still oppressing us—where ha-satan himself has us in bondage. There are areas in our lives where we are not always led by the Spirit, but where we are led by our emotions or our fears or even our reasoning or our habits or bitterness or lust or envy. We find in those areas that we are being manipulated by ha-satan's messengers whispering deceptive thoughts in our minds.

So humbling ourselves involves dealing with that—taking responsibility for that and realizing that somehow I let that come in and I've got to get rid of that bondage. That's the proper response rather than the reaction of most people which is blaming other people, blaming circumstances, or even blaming God for these things.

So how do we become enslaved by the bonds of wickedness? Well, I think it is pretty simple.

John 8:34   *Yeshua answered them, "Yes, indeed! I tell you that everyone who practices sin is a slave of sin."*

So if we have made it a practice in some area of our life to disobey God, ha-satan gains power or control over us and eventually that control becomes bondage. Let me give you an example. If I were to get drunk frequently, what do you think would happen? I would become addicted to alcohol. Right?

Actually, that's part of my past. That was me more than forty years ago. It was a long time ago. I was addicted! I couldn't do anything without having a beer in my hand. That beer and other alcoholic drinks had power over me. The same holds true for drug addiction. But it also holds true for many other ways of disobeying God. If we use His Name in vain, or lie or steal or lust or covet or hate or are bitter or are in fear all the time or have envy or jealousy or if we hate ourselves or if we have pride—if we give in to those things, the enemy gains power over us. And the big one, the really hard one which is the first commandment—do you know what that is?—worshiping other gods. Of course, you are saying, "But I never do that!"

Well, I believe the definition of worshiping other Gods is to consider anything more important than the Lord. So, that's a tough one. ha-satan gains control over us through those things. We can worship cars or houses or money or clothes, if that's really, really important to us. You know, these things can gain control over us in life. We are deceived by ha-satan in these things and it gives him access to our lives.

There is another big area that I'm just going to touch on. Ha-satan also gains access to us through other deceptive tactics to enslave us and bring curses upon us. He deceives us by speaking wickedness to us. What's the wickedness? Temptations. You think of temptation as, "Oh, eat that cake." Right? Or "Take that nap." But how about these temptations? You might not even think of these as temptations. "I can't forgive that person." "If I only had what he has, then I'd be happy." "If I only looked like her!" "You have *every right* to be bitter about that!" How about this one? "No one loves me." "God doesn't love me." "I'd be better off dead." Those are the words of the enemy—wicked words. They are temptations to believe lies that are against God's Word.

Then, of course, there's that pointing of the finger. He gets us to point our fingers at others and blame them. Many even blame God. Our enemy, ha-satan, points his finger at others and says, "It's their fault. It's not your fault." And the Scripture tells us that one of the things he does is he accuses us before the Father. "Look what she did! You can't forgive her!" Or he accuses us directly, "You can never be forgiven for that." "You'll never be any good." "You're ugly." You're stupid." "You'll never amount to anything." Have you ever heard any of those things?

Freedom From Bondage

These are all bondages. But Yeshua came to bring us freedom from them. How?

John 8:32 *"You will know the truth, and the truth will set you free."*

It's simple. All you need is the Truth and you will be set free. So what's the Truth? Well, you probably know this verse by heart.

John 14:6 *Yeshua said, "I AM the Way—and the Truth and the Life; no one comes to the Father except through me.*

He is the Truth. How is He the Truth? He is the Living Word. He's the Word of God made flesh. And the Word is His Truth. But to be set free you need to hear it more than once. That's been my experience. Maybe you have a photographic memory. All you have to do is flip open the Bible and you've got it. Not me. We need to receive the Truth. We need to memorize it. We need to meditate on it. And we need to put our trust in it and act on it. We need to see it as the most important thing in our lives. And His Words will renew our minds so that we will begin to recognize where those wicked thoughts come from—from the enemy. "God wouldn't say that. That's either ha-satan or it's my habit of thoughts. And I don't need to think like that anymore. I can be rid of that bondage."

When we put our trust in God's Word, ha-satan's bonds of wickedness can be broken off and those heavy burdens can be lifted because he will no longer have a right to inflict us or to keep us in bondage.

Every yoke! I believe that every yoke that the enemy tries to put on us can be broken. Of course though, for those of you who have tried this know, he will resist tooth and nail, every attempt that you make to break those yokes. But with the Truth in our minds and in our hearts, we will be victorious.

So, which of His Words are we to trust in? Well, the entire Bible is the Living Word of God! But especially the Good News that Yeshua sacrificed His life to set you free from ha-satan's bondage—not just to be forgiven by God, which is wonderful, but also to set you free from the chains of the enemy.

Acts 10:38 *Yeshua went about doing good and healing all the people oppressed by the Adversary, because God was with him.*

And you know what? God is still with Him! Because He is still alive and He is still doing this! He is still healing and delivering all the people oppressed by the adversary!

Bondage of Guilt and Shame

So, we are going to have prayer for all kinds of bondage that you might have. But I want to focus on one kind of bondage that affects many people's lives and it really has a lot to do with Yom Kippur. I taught on this before so this is going to be just a short digging into this.

I believe from a lot of counseling that I've done that many people find it hard to forgive themselves—to forgive their past sins—even though they believe that God has forgiven them. They have what's called a guilty conscience. I believe this is an area of bondage in which ha-satan sends spirits to us called spirits of guilt and shame and condemnation to keep us in the place of having a guilty conscience. When we have a guilty conscience, we can't truly experience God's presence. We think, "How can God really dwell in me? I'm so bad. I did those things." Believe me, I used to struggle with this. I didn't think God could dwell in me because of some things I did. But we're going to see what a lie it is.

Also, ha-satan convinces people weighed down by guilt that they really can't serve God. They're not fit to serve God. They're not fit to stand up in front of people. They're not fit to teach. They're not fit to represent God

Now in Temple times, on Yom Kippur, two goats and a heifer were sacrificed. This passage in Hebrews talks about this and you will see how this all ties together.

Hebrews 10:1-2 *For the Torah has in it a shadow of the good things to come, but not the actual manifestation of the originals. Therefore, it can never, by means of the same sacrifices repeated endlessly year after year, bring to the goal those who approach the Holy Place to offer them. 2. Otherwise, wouldn't the offering of those sacrifices have ceased? For if the people performing the service had been cleansed once and for all, they would no longer have sins on their conscience.*

This verse is saying something was missing. But it's a little mysterious. What is the goal in verse one that people could not be brought to?

The goal is a clear conscience. Verse two says that the animal sacrifices did not have the power to clear the conscience. People knew they were forgiven by God. They could worship. They were provided a covering for their sins. They could enter Temple to worship God and God could dwell in the midst of the people, but it did not cleanse their consciences. They still carried the guilt, remorse, condemnation, and shame around.

Here's what I see the difference as. That meant that they weren't cleansed enough for God's presence to dwell in them in the form of His Holy Spirit. He could dwell in their midst in the Temple but not in them, in their hearts. But Hebrews tells us that something does have the power to cleanse the conscience.

Hebrews 9:14 *Then how much more the blood of the Messiah, who, through the eternal Spirit, offered himself to God as a sacrifice without blemish, will purify our conscience from works that lead to death, so that we can serve the living God!*

Will what? "Purify our conscience from works that lead to death." "Works that lead to death" is another way of saying sin. So Yeshua's blood sacrifice is the only thing that also purifies our conscience. It doesn't cover over sins. According to Micah 7:19, it casts them into the depth of the sea, and according to Psalm 103:12, it removes them as far as the east is from the west.

So, the final thing before we pray is that this understanding of God's Moadim, His chosen fast for this Appointed Time is that today is the day for breaking bondage. We are going to specifically pray now for a bunch of things, but we are going to end up praying for those who still suffer from shame and condemnation—for freedom from guilty consciences.

Pray with me

Lord, we ask right now for your Ruakh to reveal to us if we are holding anyone in bondage in some way. If so, we repent, and we promise to set them free. We also repent of quarreling and strife, accusing others, judging others, speaking evil.

We pray, Lord, help us to keep Your fast today and every day, that every day would be an acceptable fast to You. Caring for others rather than pursuing our own desires. Walking in the Spirit and not in the flesh and setting captives free.

We thank You for those promises of those great rewards, oh Lord, of Your glory being our rear guard and of Your righteousness going before us, and of You saying, Hee-neh-nee.

And Lord we want to do what You want us to do.

Prayer Against Slavery

Father, we pray for the 27 million people that are actually in slavery today. Father, we don't know how that could possibly end, but we pray that You would begin to move to set those people free. And we pray for the billions living under oppressive governments who are being spied on, who are being jailed because of their disagreement with their government or the potential disagreement with the government, we pray that You would set these free.

And we pray for the other billions in bondage to religion. We pray even for that pastor in Iran that we've been praying for. It's amazing to me, Lord. First they accuse him of having turned from Islam to Christianity so they were going to execute him for that. Then after the outcry over that, they accused him of adultery and were going to execute him for that. After another outcry over that, they accused him of being a danger to the state—being a spy—all this after his trial—amazing! Father we pray for those oppressed in this way for their beliefs. And Father, we thank You for the freedom that we enjoy in our country.

Reveal the Bondages

Father at this time, we put our trust in the Truth of Your Words and the bondage breaking power of Your sacrifice. And we forgive anyone that we are holding something against. According to Your Word, Lord, You said that we must forgive others before we can be forgiven. And we ask, Lord, that You would reveal any areas of bondage in our lives—things that we struggle with—things that we know are not quite right—things we've tried to get over and we haven't. We take responsibility for them. They are not someone else's fault. We allowed this bondage to somehow get a hold of us. We repent for whatever we did or thought or what attitude we had that allowed ha-satan to bring us into these bondages.

So at this time, I'm going to command bondages to be broken in several things. If you can agree with me in anything that you recognize has had power over you, just claim that for yourself.

Commanding Bondages to Be Broken

In the Name of Yeshua—the Name above all Names—the Name at which every knee must bow, I command all the following bondages to be broken:

The bondage of stress.

The bondage of worry and anxiety.

The bondage of nervousness and fear, we break those bondages.

We bind the spirit of bitterness.

We break the bondages of unforgiveness, resentment, retaliation, and anger.

The bondage of hatred, we break those things.

Even the bondage of violence and murder, we break those off of Your people.

We break the power of bitterness and command all these to leave.

We break that spirit's power that makes us unable to receive love or to give love—unable to believe that God really loves us. In the Name of Yeshua, we break that power. We break that spirit of self-hatred's power over us.

We break the power of addictions over us in the Name of Yeshua.

We break the power of lust in the Name of Yeshua.

We break the power of envy and jealousy and covetousness and pride in our lives in the Name of Yeshua.

We break the power of rejection in our lives. We are accepted in the Beloved. We break every spirit that would say we are rejected and not wanted.

We break the power, that spirit that gives us low self esteem. We are ambassadors of the King—children of the King—royal priests. Thank You, Lord!

Prayer for Cleansing our Conscience

And Father, finally, we believe that You came as the Messiah for the purpose of cleansing our conscience. And so we ask right now, Father, that You would cleanse our conscience, every reader of this book that has guilt, remorse, condemnation, and/or shame over something that they've done, that they've confessed, and that they've asked for forgiveness in the Name of Yeshua. We know that the Word says that You are faithful and just to forgive us and cleanse us of all unrighteousness, if we confess our sins.

Any of us that still has that guilt hanging around—that bondage—in the Name of Yeshua, we break the power of the spirits of shame and guilt and condemnation. In the Name of Yeshua, we repent of letting those things still bother us. In the Name of Yeshua, we renounce shame and guilt and condemnation and command them to leave us in Yeshua's Name.

Prayer for Protection

And finally, Father, we know the tactics of the enemy. We know that he's going to try to get back in. And he's going to try to bring seven spirits more with him. So we pray for protection from the enemy. Lead us not into temptation. Deliver us from the evil one. We pray for Your wall of fire around us, and we plead the Blood of Yeshua over us. And in the power of the Blood and in the authority of the Name of Yeshua, we resist the devil and he must flee from us. We crush him like ashes under our feet in Yeshua's Name.

We thank You, Lord, that today is a day of freedom! Today is a day of bondage breaking! And we are going to go forth from

this place in freedom!! Thank You, Father. Thank You, Yeshua!!
Hallelujah!!

[Lift up your hands and thank Him.]

Thank You for freedom, Oh God! Thank You, Adonai! Thank
You, Lord! Thank You, Father!
Amen. Amen.

Chapter 16

STEPS TO COMPLETE T'SHUVAH AND THE AL CHET

In Leviticus 16:31, it says that Yom Kippur is to be kept forever. Right? Didn't we read that? It said forever. As we have said, the Biblical holidays are Moadim—Appointed Times. These are times that God makes appointments with us and so God sets the agenda.

In the Messianic Movement, we have been coming into the understanding of what God's agenda is for us for these days. We started out by doing most things in our services that came from the church and then some of us began to do very syna-gogue-type things. We are still growing as Messianic believers. And we are still coming into the understanding of what we are *appointed* to do for the Moadim, especially Yom Kippur.

God knew that the Temple was going to be destroyed. Right? I mean, He predicted it. Yeshua predicted it when He was talking with His followers. So, why did He tell us we are to keep this day forever, unless He had something for us to do on this day, without a Temple. Do you see that? Why would He have said forever? Well, we talked about this in previous chapters and have come up with some answers. We've talked about breaking curses and wrong vows we've inadvertently made. We talked about doing T'shuvah and fasting to afflict our souls. And we just talked about breaking bonds as a way to obey this command. Let's see if we can now further answer that question.

Remember what God calls Rosh Hashanah—the Feast of Trumpets? He calls it a "shabbaton zih-kh'ron teruah," a Sabbath of remembrance with the blowing of the Shofar and the shouting for joy. And what do we remember and shout for joy about? God's goodness, His might, His power, and His awesomeness. And what comes after that? The Ten Days of Awe. In Judaism there are two names for these ten days. The first one you already know by now. Do you remember what it is in Hebrew? It is the Yomim Nora'im, the Days of Awe. In my opinion, what that means is that we are to appreciate who God is and be in awe of Him. The Scriptures say that the fear of the Lord—the awe of the Lord—is the beginning of wisdom.

But there is another name for these ten days, and you probably don't know it, so I will just tell you. It is Aseret Yemei T'shuvah (Hebrew: עשרת ימי תשובה), meaning the Ten Days of T'shuvah or Repentance. Appreciating who God is and being in awe of Him on Yom Teruah, transitions into these days of T'shuvah. So let's take a closer look at what T'shuva is.

We've already learned that T'shuvah means to turn, or to return. And we know that it means to turn to God from sin, or to return to God from being away from Him. So now, if we think about this a little bit, and go back to the Temple times, why would there need to be T'shuvah before the Day of Atonement? Do you remember? It seems obvious to me. If you didn't realize that you needed atonement, the Day of Atonement would have been meaningless. It wouldn't have meant anything to you. So, God put into His calendar, that still applies today, ten days for you to think about how much you need Yeshua's atonement—how much you need to have your sins and iniquity atoned for, so that you can come into God's presence. Otherwise Yeshua's atonement would be meaningless to us.

As in the Temple, when atonement was finished, there was great joy. Remembering Yeshua's once and for all atonement is, of course, also accompanied with great joy. We rejoice in our salvation! Remember, His name means salvation.

Cleansing the Temple Today

Now, I want to go back to something we learned earlier. The Cohane HaGadol (High Priest) did something else when he went in and out from the Holy of Holies. He made atonement for all the parts of the Temple, right? He made atonement for the furniture, made atonement for the altar, and made atonement for the sanctuary itself, besides making atonement for the people. So I believe that we are appointed in this day and age by God that this should still be a day for Yeshua, the Cohane HaGadol, the High Priest, to cleanse the Temple. But you say there is no Temple, it's destroyed. Ahh, but you know where I'm going. Yes, there is a Temple. In the B'rit Hadashah, the New Covenant, it says: *Don't you know that your body is a Temple for the Ruach Ha-Kodesh, the Holy Spirit, who lives inside you, whom you have received from God* (I Corinthians 6:19).

Now, here's the question: Does this fleshly temple need periodic cleansing? Yes! It does. Absolutely. Mine does. It definitely needs periodic cleansing. So why would God want us to keep this day as an Appointed Time (a Moad)? Well, I believe it is first of all, as I just said, to remember Yeshua's atoning sacrifice, and then to teach us that we need to periodically allow our Cohane HaGadol to cleanse His Temple. So that is what we are appointed to do. So in the rest of this chapter, I would like to talk about how we do that. How does God cleanse the Temple today?

Just as the people were to spend ten days in T'shuvah to prepare for atonement, we need to prepare ourselves. Yes, we have been doing a lot of T'shuvah already in the previous chapters, but now we are going to look at it from a different angle. We are going to look at what leads to T'shuvah and the steps to true and complete T'shuvah. And then we are going to look at the traditional Yom Kippur prayers of confession.

So, first of all, what leads to T'shuvah? Well, in Romans 2:4, it says, *Perhaps you despise the riches of His kindness, forbearance, and patience, because you don't realize that God's kindness is intended to lead you to turn from your sins.* So it is God's kindness and His goodness that lead us to T'shuvah. Sometimes people wonder why God doesn't just destroy all the evil in the world. Well, it is because He is holding off His judgment so that those who are willing will turn from their sins and be cleansed by Him.

Now, I want to focus a little bit on this phrase "turn from your sins." That is from the Jewish New Testament. If you have a different translation, the word that is used there is repentance. In his commentary on the Jewish New Testament, David Stern talks quite a bit about how he believes we need to really understand that a lot more. So I want to share with you, because in my mind, and maybe for some of you, the word "repent" brings the image of an emotional preacher threatening people with fire and brimstone, and people quaking and saying on their knees, "We repent!" Just an emotional experience—not that it shouldn't be an emotional experience—not that fire and brimstone preaching is bad either, but maybe some of us have seen it misused.

Do you remember what the word "repent" is in the Greek? It is *metanoeite*, and it really means *change your mind.* Change your mind—have a complete change of heart. The underlying Hebrew concept, which is very valuable, is the word we've been using, "T'shuvah," and it, of course, means *turning* or *returning.* Turning from one's sins and turning to God. Not only a "from," but a "to."

Judaism teaches this very much, that turning from sins is impossible unless at the same time one turns to God. Many of us have had that experience where we have tried to stop doing something that we desperately want to stop doing, but we couldn't until God intervened. Many, many people have testified about addictions and bad habits that they were not able to break. But when they gave it to the Lord, when they asked God to help them, they were able to. So, it is a turning away from sin and a turning to God, which each individual must do. It is not something a group can do for you. Each person must do it, and even though we have to do it as individuals of our own free will, it requires God's grace to be able to do it. There is a verse that this is based on in the traditional Judaism teaching. I know you're familiar with this verse, but it never really was clear to me before how it applied. It's Lamentations 5:20, where it says: *Turn us to you, oh Lord, and we will be turned.** That says it right there! Unless you, God, by Your grace, turn us to You, we can't even turn to you. We need Your grace.

*[That's how I remember learning the verse. The exact quote is: *Turn thou us unto thee, O LORD, and we shall be turned* (KJV).]

Continual Contriteness of Heart

So, that's the start. God is the one who wants us to participate in T'shuvah, to turn to Him.

As we noted earlier, we need a contrite heart. Psalms 34:18 says: *The Lord is near to those who have a broken heart and saves such as have a contrite spirit.* This word "contrite" means broken, or humble. What it means is a willingness to be corrected—a desire to change. Now, all of you who have given your hearts to Yeshua have experienced an initial contriteness in coming to the Lord. Just in saying, "I need Your help, Lord, I need Your forgiveness" shows a contrite heart. But I believe that Yeshua and all of his disciples very clearly taught that there is a continuing need for contriteness. And I find often amongst the Lord's body it gets lost. There is a pride that comes in there that says, "I don't need to continue to be open to my own sin." "You know, I've been forgiven, so I don't need to be repentant anymore."

But remember this in Romans 8:29: *Those whom he knew in advance He also determined in advance would be conformed to the image of His Son, so that He might be the firstborn among many brethren.*

So we need to realize that all of us are in the process of being conformed to the image of Yeshua. And that means that whatever image we are conformed to right now needs to change. Right? And we can either cooperate with that work, or we can resist that work. But the changing doesn't ever stop. It starts when you first come to know the Lord. It goes on until the day that you die. It doesn't stop even when you're mature.

Nine Steps to True T'Shuvah

So let me give you the nine steps of T'shuvah that the Ruakh HaKodesh has shown me. Complete T'shuvah is not a simple process. There are nine steps that I have found to true T'shuvah.

The first step is to have that attitude of being willing to be shown your sin, being willing to change.

The second step is to forgive others who have offended us.

In Matthew 6:14-15, Yeshua says: *If you forgive others their offenses, your Heavenly Father will also forgive you. 15 But if you do not forgive others their offenses your Heavenly Father will not forgive yours.*

And God's part in this is giving us the grace to forgive, because sometimes we find it hard when we've been hurt to forgive, but the grace is there.

The third step to true T'shuvah is introspection.

Psalm 139:23 (NIV) *Search me, O God, and know my heart; test me and know my anxious thoughts. 24 See if there is any offensive way in me, and lead me in the way everlasting.*

This is a prayer that we need to pray for God to do this and reveal to us if there are things in us, attitudes, thought patterns, habits, that are offensive to God, and then the hard part is not praying the prayer, the hard part is being willing to listen and see what He says. He will show you those things if your heart really wants to know them. So I call that introspection, the third step.

The fourth step is a new word that I just made up; it's called "extrospection." What is extrospection? Extrospection is finding out if you need to apologize to someone else for something that you are unaware of.

In Matthew 5:23-24, Yeshua says this: *So if you are offering your gift at the Temple altar and you remember there that your brother has something against you, 24 leave your gift where it is by the altar, and go, make peace with your brother. Then come back and offer your gift.*

So here we have the picture of somebody who is trying to worship God. He's at the altar in the Temple, and he remembers somebody has something against him. Now he has to go and make that right. So that is extrospection. What do I mean? How do you do that? Well, how I do it is sometimes I'm with somebody and I notice they just don't seem to be acting toward me the way they should. They seem to be a little cold, a little distant, maybe, or they snap at me or they just act a little funny. I believe those are little hints that we need to go to that person and say, "Have I done anything to offend you?" This is because a lot of times people won't tell you. Often they will just keep it in even though they have been offended. For example, if somebody who used to be real close to you is not calling you any more. Maybe you've done something that has hurt them. You need to go to them and say, "Have I done something? I want to make it right." So that's, by my definition, extrospection.

The fifth step: We need to accept the blame. The classic example of this is in the Garden of Eden when God confronted Adam. Immediately, he shifted the blame. He said: "The woman You put here with me, she gave me some fruit from the tree and I ate it." That's blaming others. Adam blamed Eve—and God for putting Eve with him. We have to accept the blame when the Spirit of God shows us something we've been doing wrong. I can think of how when we were raising our children, that was one of the things that we always looked for. When we caught them doing something wrong I remember we would take them and discipline them, and I know some of you who are parents can relate to this, they would always have a lot of excuses. Oh, my sister made me do it. Oh, my friend made me do it. And he did it to me first. But when we had to discipline our kids we always would make sure we got through that and made them realize that they had to be responsible for their own evil actions.

The sixth step: Once we accept that we are guilty, then comes a very important phase, and that is remorse. Some people think that once you're a believer, remorse is something that you're not supposed to experience. But I don't believe that's true.

I Corinthians 7:10 Rabbi Sha'ul says: *Godly sorrow brings repentance that leads to salvation and leaves no regrets.*

So we need to have remorse, and I believe that the bigger the transgression; the greater the remorse should be, the greater the time of tears and mourning. What do we have remorse for? Well, usually when we've done something wrong, we have hurt somebody. First of all, we have hurt God when we have transgressed His laws and disobeyed him. We've betrayed His trust in us. Secondly, a lot of times we have hurt another individual, sometimes many individuals, by the things that we have done. Then, sometimes we dishonor God. We, who are professing to be followers of God, do something and somebody sees it and knows about it and God is dishonored by that. Or we dishonor other people. So, that's the remorse that has to come upon us, and it has to be real. It has to get down to your heart. I think tears are appropriate, groaning too, depending on the magnitude of this. It's something that you should really feel; this should be an emotional thing.

The seventh step: There needs to be a willingness to suffer the consequences of your sin. We read of the thief who was on the cross with Yeshua. He was a great example of that. It says that he rebuked the first thief who was railing at Yeshua and he said, *"Have you no fear of God? You're getting the same punishment as He is. Ours is only fair, we're getting what we deserve for what we did."* And then that man was welcomed into Paradise by the Lord. He was recognizing that he deserved what he was getting. I've done some terrible things, and I know when I really get to that place of remorse I don't care who knows about it. I don't care if I'm humiliated. Because it's just I've done such a terrible thing that I just want to get rid of it, I just want to be cleansed of it. And if everybody in the world needs to know, that's fine. Now, that doesn't mean everybody always needs to know about it; there are things that don't need to be revealed, but some things need to be revealed. We need to be humiliated because we've done something wrong. And then sometimes there is punishment. Just because we are believers and God forgives us, that doesn't mean that there is no punishment. If you steal something you're going to go to jail, even though you repent, and the Lord forgives you, you're still going to go to jail. So there has to be that punishment. We need to be willing to accept it and not try to get out of it.

The eighth step: Confession. First of all, there needs to be confession to the injured party. That's always necessary, and in the Jewish tradition sins against people are doubly weighty, because they are also against God. All sin is against God, but the ones that we do against people are twice as bad. So we need to confess to the people we hurt. And if the injured party is God, sometimes I think we need to confess that to other people, just to make it real that we're confessing before God. I know there have been times when I have had to do that. It just didn't seem like I had expressed my sorrow to God unless I did it before another person.

James 5:16 *Therefore, openly acknowledge your sins to one another and pray for each other so that you might be healed. The prayer of a righteous person is powerful and effective.*

I believe he is speaking there of either confidential confession, like to somebody that you trust who won't tell other people, but sometimes it can be public confession. If it is something that has injured many people or has brought shame to a community, it might need public confession.

Finally, the ninth step is reconciliation, first of all with God. What do we base that on? How do we know that we can be reconciled with God? Well, in the Tenakh, in the book of Jeremiah, in the explanation about the proclamation of the New Covenant, the Lord says this:

Jeremiah 31:31,34 *The time is coming, declares the Lord, when I will make a new covenant with the House of Israel and with the House of Judah. ... 34 No longer will a man teach his neighbor or a man his brother saying, know the Lord, because they will all know me, from the least of them to the greatest, declares the Lord, for I will forgive their wickedness and will remember their sins no more.*

And how does he do that, with there being no Temple?

Acts 13:38 *Therefore, brothers, let it be known to you that through this man* [referring to Yeshua] *is proclaimed forgiveness of sins. That is, that God clears everyone who puts his trust in this man, even in regard to all the things concerning which you could not be cleared by the Torah of Moses.*

Even those things you could not be cleared of by the Torah of Moses. So that is how we can expect this reconciliation with God. We need to confess it to Him, ask for forgiveness, and receive His forgiveness. But, of course, there is another side to that, and that is we need reconciliation with people, too, when we've wronged them. And with people it requires confession and asking forgiveness and receiving their forgiveness. And I know for me, what I find really interesting is that when I do something that offends someone and I ask for forgiveness, oftentimes I don't get it, until I go to God first. But if I go to God and ask for forgiveness, it seems like then they forgive me. So, I don't know if the rest of you have had that experience, but that's just how it works for me. First I go to God and ask Him to forgive me, and then it seems like He moves upon the person I've offended and the grace is there to forgive me.

And then finally, beyond the nine steps, there is something else about T'shuvah that is very important, and that is that true T'shuvah bears fruit. Okay? It's not just a one-time act. The firstfruit of true, complete T'shuvah is restitution. In the Bible, Luke talks of a man, Zacchaeus, who was convicted of his sin and turned to Yeshua and immediately, because he had cheated a lot of people, he said the following.

Luke 19:8-9 *"Here, Lord, I am giving half of all I own to the poor, and if I have cheated anyone I will pay him back four times as much." 9 Yeshua said to him, "Today salvation has come to this house."*

So we need to make up for what we've done that has been wrong. If we've cheated someone, we need to recompense them for their loss. If we have slandered someone, if we've said something about them that is not right and said it to other people, we need to go back and tell those people that it is not right. If we've hurt them in some way, we need to make up for that. That's restitution. But also, there is changed behavior. Because all this means nothing if you just go right back to the behavior that you are repenting of. Repentance means absolutely nothing if you go back to that same behavior. This makes me think of Yochanan, John, the Immerser (the Baptist). When he came and preached repentance here's what he said.

Luke 3:9 *Already the axe is at the root of the trees, ready to strike; every tree that doesn't produce good fruit will be chopped down and thrown in the fire!*

Now, what is the fruit He's talking about here? He is talking about the fruit of repentance. Every person who does not produce the fruit of repentance will be like a tree chopped down and thrown into the fire. In verse 10 the crowds asked him: *So then what should we do?* And he answered: *Whoever has two coats should share with somebody who has none. And whoever has food should do the same.* What he is talking about is changed behavior. Be generous. Don't be greedy. Help those in need. And then he goes on in the next three verses and talks about other changes in behavior. If you've been extorting things from people, stop doing that. If you've been complaining about your paycheck, or if you've been accusing people falsely, stop it; turn away from these things. So T'shuvah means nothing and it's hollow and empty unless there is a change in behavior.

Now, T'shuvah is also an ongoing attitude. An ongoing attitude for the rest of our lives. The early believers in Yeshua, His first followers kept their Jewish lifestyle. And so, once a year they would have had the Ten Days of T'shuvah, and they would have had the Day of Atonement. They knew that the final atonement had been made, but they would have continued to do these things. I believe it would have helped them to have a proper heart attitude, because every year they would be reminded of their need for T'shuvah..

But, we know that around the year 325 the church lost its Jewish roots; that there was a decree made at the Council of Nicea by the Roman Emperor, Constantine, that said, "Church, you can no longer practice anything Jewish. If you do you're going to be excommunicated." So this Appointed Time, along with all the other Appointed Times, went out the door. And so the church no longer has that annual reminder. Yes, within the church, people are reminded that they need to be repentant, that they need to be contrite, but it isn't at God's Appointed Time. It isn't when God specifically appointed that it be done. I believe there is a certain power, there is a certain timing of the Spirit there. We as Messianic believers can be thankful that we are alive in the times such as this. It has only been since the 1970's that we can experience this special call to T'shuvah yearly at God's Appointed Time because now we are keeping all His Appointed Times.

So I would like to help you get primed for this day. We are going to recite the traditional Jewish Yom Kippur prayers of confession. First there is the Amidah, which is like a prayer. Amidah means "standing" because this prayer is traditionally recited while standing. Then there is the short confession called the Ashamnu, then the long confession, the Al Chet (pronounced ahl khet). Ashamnu means "we are culpable or guilty"— in other words, "we have sinned." Al Chet means "for sin" or "for the sin"— "chet" being a form of "*khatahah.*" The traditional Jewish Al Chet brings to mind some of the things that we might need atonement for. They are listed below. I want you to read them out loud because, you know, it is important that we hear our voices saying these things. Read them loud and clear. It is going to start out with a prayer from the Amidah, just acknowledging God, acknowledging who He is.

The Al Chet Prayer of Confession

Our God, and God of our fathers, and God of our Master, Yeshua, forgive us, pardon us, and grant us atonement through Yeshua's sacrifice. For we are Your people and You are our God. We are Your servants and You are our Master. We are Your congregation and You are our portion. We are Your inheritance and You are our lot.

You know the mysteries of the universe and the hidden secrets of all who live. You search out the heart of man and probe all thoughts and aspirations. Nothing escapes You. Neither is anything concealed from Your sight. May it therefore be according to Your Word that Your mercy would triumph over judgment. Extend Your forgiveness towards us. Do not count our iniquities against us.

For the sin which we have committed against You under compulsion, or of our own free will.

For the sin which we have committed against You by hardening our hearts.

For the sin which we have committed against You unknowingly.

For the sin which we have committed against You with the utterance of lips.

For the sin which we have committed against You by un-chastity.

For the sin which we have committed against You openly or secretly.

For the sin which we have committed against You knowingly or deceitfully.

For the sin which we have committed against You in speech.

For the sin which we have committed against You by wronging our neighbor.

For the sin which we have committed against You by sinful meditation of the heart.

For the sin which we have committed against You
by association with impurity.

For the sin which we have committed against You
by confession of the lips.

For the sin which we have committed against You
by spurning parents and teachers.

For the sin which we have committed against You in
presumption or error, by violence.

For the sin which we have committed against You
by profaning Your name.

For the sin which we have committed against You
by unclean lips.

For the sin which we have committed against You
by impure speech.

For the sin which we have committed against You
by the inclination toward evil.

For the sin which we have committed against You
wittingly or unwittingly.

For the sin which we have committed against You
by denying and lying.

For the sin which we have committed against You
by scoffing.

For the sin which we have committed against You
by slander.

For the sin which we have committed against You
in commerce.

For the sin which we have committed against You
with our taxes.

For the sin which we have committed against You in
eating and drinking.

For the sin which we have committed against You
by idle words.

For the sin which we have committed against You
by gossip.

For the sin which we have committed against You
with sensual looks.

For the sin which we have committed against You
by immodesty.

For the sin which we have committed against You
with haughty eyes.

For the sin which we have committed against You
by casting off the yoke of Your commandments.

For the sin which we have committed against You
by being contentious.

For the sin which we have committed against You
by envy.

For the sin which we have committed against You
by levity.

For the sin which we have committed against You
by being stiff-necked.

For the sin which we have committed against You
by running to do evil.

For the sin which we have committed against You
by tale-bearing.

For the sin which we have committed against You
by vain oaths and promises.

For the sin which we have committed against You
by causeless hatred.

For the sin which we have committed against You
by breach of trust.

For the sin which we have committed against You
with confusion of mind.

For all of these, oh God of forgiveness,
forgive us, pardon us, and grant us atonement according to Your Word. If we confess
our sins You are faithful and just to forgive us
our sins and to cleanse us of all unrighteousness. Amen.

That was a priming of the pump for your Day of Atonement.
Now I would just like to lead you in prayer.

Let's pray

Father, we pray along the lines of what we have just read.
We ask for Your grace, first of all, Lord, to lead us to T'shuvah.

Turn us, oh Lord, and we will be turned. Father, we pray for contrite hearts—hearts willing to be shown what needs to be changed. Give us contrite hearts, oh Lord. Father, give us the grace to forgive those who have offended us; that we might be forgiven by You. Search us, oh God, and know our hearts. Try us, and know our thoughts, and see if there is any wicked way in us, and lead us in the way everlasting.

Reveal to us, oh Lord, that which is unpleasing to You. Lord, we ask that Your Spirit would show us right now if there is someone whom we have offended that we don't know about. Show us, Lord God, just bring it to our minds. Show us the little signs of a broken relationship. Show us the signs of a hurting person, and give us the grace to go to that person and apologize and give them the grace to forgive us, Lord. Father, during this day, as You reveal to us our sin and our iniquity, help us to just accept the blame and not make excuses. Help us to just say, "I'm guilty," and not put the blame on someone else.

And God, whatever level of remorse we need, we pray that You would lead us into that. Whether it be tears, whether it be moanings, whether it be sadness for a season, we yield to Your Spirit to bring that remorse. Show us, oh Lord, how we have hurt others. Show us how our sin has hurt You and dishonored you. Show us how our sin has hurt others, who perhaps we haven't even seen before as being hurt by what we've done. Show us, oh Lord, how we have dishonored You.

And Father, we just pray for the courage to suffer the consequences of what we have done. Help us, Lord, not to fear, but to know that if we will just receive the consequences Your grace will be there. Lord, help us not to care whether we are humiliated or punished; bring us to that place of just wanting to be clean and not caring who knows about it.

Lord, help us to confess when we need to confess. If we need to confess to a person we've offended, Lord, give us the grace to confess with grace, to not blame them, but just to say it's my fault. And Lord, if we need to confess to someone else, to have them pray for us, show us who that person is; if it's a sin against You that we need to confess to another person, show us who that person is. Show us if it needs to be confidential or public. Show us, Lord.

And finally, Lord, help us to be reconciled. Help us to reconcile with other people. And most of all, Lord, for those of us who have never been reconciled with You, we pray that You would bring those who haven't to that initial reconciliation, Lord, where they receive Your forgiveness that is only available by what You did.

And then, finally, Lord, we pray for the fruits of T'shuvah. We pray, oh Lord, that You would cause us to see if restitution needs to be made somewhere, and that we would not care what loss we have to suffer, but we would be willing to do all that is necessary to make it right. And then, Lord, we pray that You would give us the strength to rise above this failing that we are confessing. Give us the strength to change our behavior, oh Lord.

Finally, Lord, we ask that this would not just be a one-time occurrence, but because we do this yearly that this would carry through the rest of the year and we would have a contrite heart and that T'shuvah would be a way of life.

And Lord, we want to end up with joy because not only are we supposed to do T'shuvah on this day, but we are supposed to remember Your atonement and so we thank you for your atonement right now, Lord. We thank You. We thank You. We thank You, Lord for that greatest act of mercy that has ever happened. We thank You and praise You that we could receive it as a free gift and we rejoice that our names are written in the Lamb's Book of Life. In Yeshua's name. Amen.

Prayer of Salvation

If you've never received all Yeshua offers with His sacrifice for the sins of all people for all times, you can do that right now.

In studying all this, I'm sure that by now you understand the high standard of behavior and attitude God requires of us. I'm sure you see that like all of us, you have fallen short in serving Him only, honoring His name, keeping His Shabbat, honoring parents, not hating, lusting, lying, stealing or coveting. Ask God to reveal to you anything else in you not pleasing to Him. Then admit as I did more than thirty years ago that you are a sinner in need of an atoning sacrifice to deal with your sin.

So, bow your head right now and tell Him you are a sinner and you want to receive His atonement for your sins.

Take responsibility for your sin. Say, "My sin is not anyone else's fault."

Repent. Turn from sin and to God. Tell Him you are turning to Him.

Decide to follow Yeshua's direction for the rest of your life, and tell Him so.

Receive Yeshua's atoning sacrifice for yourself. Allow His blood to wash you clean.

Decide to do all you can to make restitution for any wrongs you've done.

Receive the power of Yeshua's atoning sacrifice to cleanse your conscience of guilt, shame, remorse, and sorrow.

Prayer of Repentance

Father, I confess I have broken Your commandments. In Yeshua's name forgive me for anything I've ever done that's been against Your will. I look to Yeshua's sacrifice of His life, the life of the Son of God, of You, God Himself, come as a man, to pay the price for my sin. I commit myself to follow Your direction for my life. Show me if I need to make restitution to someone. Wash my sin away from me by the power of Your Blood. I give you my load of guilt and shame. Fulfill Your promise to take away this burden and to set me free from it. Cleanse my conscience as I come to you, my Messiah. I receive Your atoning sacrifice for my sins and for cleansing my conscience. Fill me with Your Ruakh HaKodesh (Holy Spirit). Come and dwell in my heart. Connect me to other believers who will disciple me. Thank You. In Yeshua's Name I pray. Amen.

Now it's time to rejoice! This is the greatest thing that can happen to anyone! Allow His joy to flood your whole being. Lift your hands and begin thanking Him and praising Him.

This is why Yom Kippur is my favorite Jewish Holiday! I love to see people doing soul searching, repenting, and receiving His atonement!

Repenting for National Sins

Now let's turn to a prayer of repentance for our nation. In 2001, the fateful day of 9-11 happened just a couple weeks before Yom Kippur. That horrific event brought us all into an attitude of T'shuvah. We were all afflicted in our souls. It was a time of personal and national repentance for believers.

I had gone to a banquet the night before, which honored the person who did the most in our area for supporting the right to life. The words that just seemed to keep coming up at that banquet, as different people spoke, was, "It's been going on for so long, this struggle against abortion, that we've just grown to ignoring it. We're not zealous anymore. We're not standing up anymore." I realized that I too had fallen into that complacent attitude, and as I humbled my soul that evening of 9/11, my heart was aching for the sin of abortion in this nation.

The pro-death advocates demand that a woman have the right to abort her child, thus turning the abortion debate into a civil rights issue. But, all their arguments are based on the false premise that a yet to be born child in the womb is not a human being. Because if that unborn child was a human being, then the child's right to life would surely take priority over the mother's right to kill her child. In fact, because the child is innocent, defenseless, and vulnerable, it should be all the more protected by our laws.

The Bible clearly recognizes the child in the womb as a human being. A most dramatic instance of this recognition is the account of the pregnant mother of Yeshua, Miryam's visit to her pregnant cousin Elisheva (Elizabeth) in the first chapter of Luke.

Luke 1:41-44 *When Elisheva heard Miryam's greeting, the baby in her womb stirred. Elisheva was filled with the Ruach HaKodesh 42 and spoke up in a loud voice, "How blessed are you among women! And how blessed is the child in your womb! 43 "But who am I, that the mother of my Lord should come to me? 44 For as soon as the sound of your greeting reached my ears, the baby in my womb leaped for joy!*

The baby in Elisheva's womb was Yochanan the Immerser (John the Baptist). He recognized the presence of the Messiah in Miryam's womb nearby, and then leapt for joy inside his mother's womb. Obviously the yet to be born Yochanan was not only physically aware of Yeshua's presence but was spiritually aware enough to leap for joy that the long awaited Messiah had come.

So, what about the civil rights of that unborn human being? Our nation has not protected the ones in greatest need of protection and has instead protected the "rights" of those who seek to murder those unborn human beings. Tens of millions of innocent, defenseless, vulnerable unborn children have been slaughtered over the past fifty three years. Thus, as a nation, we need to repent for this great sin and for turning away from Him in other ways, too. So, let's pray according to these lines.

More Prayer

Lord, this is the time for repentance, for *T'shuvah*, for turning, and we come before you, Lord, as Your Word says, and we humble ourselves and we pray and we turn from our wicked ways, oh God. Personally, and as a nation, we ask Your forgiveness for what we haven't done, Lord. We haven't stood up strongly enough for the weak, for the oppressed, for the unborn. We ask Your forgiveness, Lord. We haven't stood up strongly enough to keep Your Name in this country. We ask Your forgiveness, Lord. We turn our hearts back to You, Lord. How often did Your Spirit prompt us to write a letter or make a phone call? And yet we were too busy. Too many things to do. Forgive us, Lord. We pray for forgiveness, Lord.

We pray for our families. We pray for our friends. We pray for the leaders of this country. We pray that You would raise up righteous leaders in this land, oh God. Men who would walk in Your ways. Women who would walk in Your ways. We pray for wisdom, Lord God, for this nation, for its leaders.

And, Father, we saw a great turning back to You in the weeks following 9-11, and we prayed so hard that it would not just be a temporary thing, but for so many, it was. We pray, Lord, that all those who turned toward prayer in those days, that they would come back; that it would be a long-lasting commitment this time, that they would turn their hearts totally to You. We pray that the tragedies these days—all the disasters, the shootings, the wars, and the terrorist atrocities—would turn more people to you. Help us, Lord. We desperately need Your help. Heal our world, oh God. Heal our land. Turn our nation back to You.

Open our hearts up, Lord. Open up our hearts to what You're saying, Lord. Help us to hear You and understand and obey. Help us to do our part that will help turn this country around. Help us to grasp the importance of the signs of our time and of what You are doing and what You want us to do in these last days.

We lift up to You those who are mourning the loss of loved ones from the shootings and wars, and the loss of lives and homes from other tragic events, Father. We lift them up to You, now, Lord, and we ask for Your comfort. Comfort them, Lord. We ask for Your healing for their wounded hearts. We ask for Your comfort and Your provision.

We pray for the President and all of his advisors, Lord, that You would give them wisdom. Give them wisdom from You. Help all those running this country to do what is right in Your eyes. Help them to do things that will turn the course of this country back to You.

We pray for the Peace of Jerusalem tonight, Father. As Your people are gathered in synagogues all across that land, doing T'shuvah, fasting, repenting, Lord, open up the heavens and reveal Yourself to them, we pray. Reveal Yourself. Reveal Your Truth, oh God. Protect Your people. Protect Your land. Give wisdom to the leaders there, too, Father. Thank you, Lord. Thank you, Father.

We thank You, Lord, that in these times of trouble we have You to turn to, that we can express these prayers to You, Lord. We thank You that You have given us a hope, and it's the hope of Your return, and we cling to that hope, oh God, in these times.

Come quickly. Come quickly, Lord Yeshua. Come quickly, Lord. Come quickly, and establish Your kingdom on this earth. Lord, we're coming up to Sukkot, the Appointed Time that speaks of Your Kingdom, and we pray that You would establish Your Kingdom in our days, oh God. Even in our days. In Yeshua's mighty Name. Amen.

Chapter 17

WHEAT AND WEEDS

A Religious Spirit

In this chapter we are going to look at the effects of a religious spirit. A religious spirit inspires people to hate and kill over what they believe about God.   It seems to be preposterous, but it has had incredible power over the centuries. It was not only behind Yeshua's murder, but also the first murder of the Bible was inspired by a religious spirit. Cain murdered Abel, and it was about whose offering was pleasing to God.

So it was a religious spirit that was behind the crusades, the inquisition, the pogroms and it's behind the conflict today between the Muslim world and the rest of the world. It's a religious spirit and basically it's the spirit that enters into the battle between the God of Israel and the gods of this world.

Why would anyone hate or kill someone over what they believe? It's crazy. But that's what this spiritual force does. We are going to get into this later.

Before we go on, let's pray.

Father we thank You for Your Word and we just declare today that Your Word will accomplish that which You purposed it to do. We open up our hearts and our minds and we stand against all the forces of the evil one that would try to keep us from all You have for us today, Father. And we thank You that it's Your great desire to give us fresh understanding and revelation of Your Word. In Yeshua's Name. Amen.

Our Scripture for this study on religious spirits is Leviticus chapters 14 and 15.

Chapter 14 deals with the leprosy and explains how to deal with molds and mildew. Chapter 15 is even more unpleasant. It describes how to deal with unclean discharges from the body— how to recognize them and how to get rid of them. The cure is quarantine.

This passage is actually the Torah Portion or Parasha called Mitzsorah - *afflicted with tsara-at* (Leprosy). It is a Torah Portion in the spring, but there is a wonderful message for Yom Kippur in it. During the week before the Shabbat that I was to teach on this, I began to seek the Lord. What shall I teach on? Where do I go with this? Is there something in the hafTorah? Or should I just go to something else?

I was just amazed that the Holy Spirit inspired me on two things that I consider really, really important in two areas of our life. First, the area of understanding and appreciating the power of the Holy Spirit in us. Doesn't seem related right now, right? Second, the area of how we, as followers of Yeshua, are to treat those who don't believe like we do.

That's what we are going to talk about in this chapter. Actually one of them is probably enough for you to chew on for a week. But the Lord gave them both to me so you're going to get them both.

Bodily Discharges

So first of all let's start out with this whole area of bodily discharges. This is like someone who has an infection that's oozing and obviously you don't want to get that on other people. I thought about this a little. What's a cold, when your nose is running? That's a bodily discharge. Or if you're coughing all over the place and spitting up stuff. I don't want to be too gross here, but that's also an applicable discharge. So these laws do apply to our physical lives, but I found that it has a more relevant application than I originally thought it had.

This passage shows how detailed and how difficult it would be to not touch something that is unclean.

Lev. 15:9-12 *Any saddle that the person with the discharge rides on will be unclean. 10 Whoever touches anything that was under him will be unclean until evening; he who carries those things is to wash his clothes and bathe himself in water; he will be unclean until evening. 11 If the person with the discharge fails to rinse his hands in water before touching someone, that person is to wash his clothes and bathe himself in water; he will be unclean until evening. 12 If the person with the discharge touches a clay pot, it must be broken; if he touches a wooden utensil, it must be rinsed in water.*

Later in chapter 15, this description of ways to become unclean goes on to include even if you touch an object that a woman touched during her menstrual period. I'm just picking out a few verses here, trying to get a point across at how extensive this is, of how many things there were that you were not allowed to touch because it could make you unclean.

First of all, on the medical side, this is absolutely astounding because this would have been a tremendous disease preventative. We only discovered how diseases were spread in the twentieth century. There were doctors that were infecting people up until the nineteenth century because they didn't wash their hands. This was God's command, without anybody knowing anything about germs, saying, you need to isolate these things.

Notice that this uncleanliness is a little bit different from other uncleanliness. If you touched something that an unclean person touched, you became unclean. It's like a second order uncleanness. You don't even have to touch the person. And this is very true scientifically! Look at how Ebola spreads so rapidly and easily!

Clean for God's Presence

Now, it's important to understand what "unclean" meant. It meant that you couldn't enter the Temple. You couldn't touch the holy things. But, God's presence was in the Temple so really what it meant—this is really key to our understanding—**you couldn't come into God's presence when you were unclean. You had to be cleansed to come into God's presence.** And a critical role of the cohanim was to separate the unclean from the clean because they had to keep them apart. They had to dwell separately.

Now understand as you read through these chapters that there were different levels of uncleanness for which there are different prescriptions of what's supposed to happen. For touching a person with a discharge, it was one day. Then that night, if you went and washed your clothes and yourself, you were clean again. But if you touched a corpse, it was a seven day cleansing. You had to wash a couple of times and immerse your whole body.

Understand that this is also a further understanding of uncleanness. There is a much more serious kind of uncleanness. Those who transgressed by worshiping other gods, believers in other gods, making idols, infidels, if you will, especially if they tried to spread that kind of uncleanness, that was dealt with much more severely than what we have in these verses here.

Deut. 16:6-11, 12-18 They had to be put to death and cities destroyed.

I hope you are getting the picture here, that this was not a small thing. This was a big thing in ancient Israel—all this dealing with physical uncleanness and spiritual uncleanness. It all had to do with coming to the Temple and worshiping God in the way that He had prescribed.

So how do these passages affect our understanding of God and of what He requires of us today? Well, many read these passages and say, "Well, God was just harsh back then and now He's changed." How many think God has changed? I don't. Others say, "Well, we see this change. God hasn't changed but His laws have changed. We don't have to keep His laws anymore." How many think that's the case? I don't.

Well, what we'll see is that there has been a huge change.

I would even call it a paradigm shift, our modern term when *everything* changes. But it isn't God who has changed and it isn't His laws that have changed. So what has changed? It's what God has done for us that has changed. Let me say that again. What has changed is what God has done for us.

A Purpose in These Laws

Now, let me explain what this is. Historically, and to give us perspective, God's laws for Israel were meant to set a nation apart for Him; to enable Israel to bring forth the Messiah. Everyone should be able to understand this because we see in history that soon after Israel brought forth the Messiah, what happened? Israel ceased to be a nation with a place. Right?

So there were all these laws in place to keep the nation clean enough, pure enough, to enable us to bring forth the Messiah. To do this, Israel was told when they went into the Promised Land, to do what? ... to drive out all the peoples in that land because their sin would infect Israel. And God was not unjust in driving out those people because those nations were already in deep sin and were deserving of judgment. Israel was the form of God's judgment upon those people.

But once Israel was established in the Land, these laws of the clean and unclean were God's method of keeping Israel as a pure nation to enable us to fulfill the purpose He had for us. Do you see that?

And we still see some of these laws in affect today. If you are familiar with Orthodox Judaism, you may know that Orthodox Jewish men will not allow a woman to touch them. They will not shake hands with a woman. Do you know why? We just read it. It might be her time of the month. She might be unclean. There's no way to tell, so they just will not touch any woman. So we need to understand that these laws had a great influence on the Jewish people. And once they were established in the Land, the laws affected the interaction of the Jewish people with the non-Jewish people.

Imagine if you're trying to keep all these laws and you're faced with the prospect of going into the home of someone who doesn't know anything about all these laws. You're afraid of everything you touch! Right? You might touch their clothing, their cooking utensils that were used to cook unclean animals. They're probably unclean all the time. And if you touch them, you would become unclean. So it made you not want to go into their homes.

Fences Around the Laws

This led to the creation of a fence around the laws, which is called the Oral Law. It was oral for a long time and then it was written down in what we call the Talmud. The Talmud has all the rules to prevent violation of the Torah. We have a reference to the Oral Law that is very important to understand in the New Covenant. It happened at a time when God sent Peter to the home of a Gentile for the first time. He's going to send Peter. And Peter's got all this in his mind—all these laws that he's been obeying all his life of not doing this.

Listen to what he says in Act 10:28 after God gives him the vision and tells him to go to the house of a Gentile. He's speaking to the Gentiles that he came to visit.

Acts 10:28 *He said to them, "You are well aware that for a man who is a Jew to have close association with someone who belongs to another people, or to come and visit him, is something that just isn't done. But God has shown me not to call any person common or unclean;"*

In that phrase "It just isn't done" Peter was summing up the oral law that says you can't do this. It wasn't the law of God, but it was based on the laws of God—helping you keep them.

So, as I studied this, here is how these two things came to me. It was like a revelation. I suddenly realized—maybe you've realized just sitting there reading —that you've come into contact with things touched by people with bodily discharges many, many times! How many times have you touched something that someone who has a cold has touched? Or maybe a woman in her menstrual cycle touched. Or someone who has an actual sore that's running. I believe that without even knowing it, everyone of you has touched something that has been made unclean according to this Biblical way. Do you agree? We all have.

Something Has Changed

So I began to ask God. "Lord, have these things separated me from You somehow? If I'm aware of that contact, do I need to go bathe and wash my clothes to come into Your presence? Would I be able to come closer if I had not touched that item?" Those were the kind of questions that were running through my mind that I was asking the Lord.

And immediately the Lord answered by speaking into my spirit, "Definitely not."

So then I got to this question, "Well, wait. Wait a minute. Have You changed?"

The answer I got was, "Definitely not."

Then I asked, "Well, have Your laws changed?"

And the answer again was, "Definitely not."

So my next question was, "Well, what has changed?"

I asked that because something has changed. Do you see that? And that's when the Holy Spirit showed me these two big changes or paradigm shifts that I believe are really important for us all to understand. I've been praying that I would be able to communicate this correctly, and that you would get it.

The first paradigm shift happened when Yeshua came on the scene—when He was in His time of ministry. We're going to read a familiar story from that time.

Matthew 9:20-22 *A woman who had had a hemorrhage for twelve years approached him from behind and touched the tzitzit on his robe. 21 For she said to herself, "If I can only touch his robe, I will be healed." 22 Yeshua turned, saw her and said, "Courage, daughter! Your trust has healed you." And she was instantly healed.*

Now understand this. In that culture, this woman would have had to be wearing something that identified her as an unclean person because she had this flow of blood. Twelve years she was like this. She was isolated. She was kept out of the community. And she touched Yeshua. What happened? Did He become unclean? No!

So here's the clear and critical insight that I began to understand. The rules of purification and uncleanliness dealt with people's ability to come into God's presence in the Temple. If you were unclean, you were not able to come into His presence. So did Yeshua violate the law by allowing someone unclean to touch Him?

No. The situation was different for Yeshua. In John 1 when Yeshua went into the water of the mikveh—of the immersion, this is what Yochanan (John) saw. He gave this testimony.

John 1:32 *"I saw the Spirit coming down from heaven like a dove, and remaining on him. 33 I myself did not know who he was, but the one who sent me to immerse in water said to me, 'The one on whom you see the Spirit descending and remaining, this is the one who immerses in the Ruach HaKodesh.'"*

This was the Messiah Yeshua being immersed. So how was the situation different for Yeshua? He didn't need to go into the Temple to be in the presence of God because the presence of God was where? IN HIM! The presence of God—the Holy Spirit was in Him. How long was the Holy Spirit going to be in Him according to this verse? "Remaining on Him." It didn't just light upon Him and then flitter away. So instead of Him having to go to the Temple to be in God's presence, He was always in God's presence.

So instead of being defiled or made unclean when an unclean person touched Him, what happened? She became clean! The bodily discharge, the uncleanness in her became healed. Why did this happen? The Scriptures tell us, Yeshua was filled with the Holy Spirit and the meaning of that is—it was overflowing—so when she touched Him, the Holy Spirit overflowed into her and healed her. So instead of Him becoming unclean because of her uncleanness, she became clean because of His cleanness and the Holy Spirit.

Whatever Touches Them Will Be Holy

There is a Torah law that gives us a clue about this. This is God's instructions for making the special oil for anointing the cohanim (priests) and all the things in the Temple to cleanse them.

Exodus 30:25-28 *It will be a holy anointing oil. 26 Use it to anoint the tent of meeting, the ark for the testimony, 27 the table and all its utensils, the menorah and all its utensils, the incense altar, 28 the altar for burnt offerings and all its utensils, and the basin with its base.*

So anointing these things with this oil made these things clean and holy. Now listen to what God says happens if something *unclean* touches them.

Exodus 30:29 *You are to consecrate them—they will be especially holy, and whatever touches them will be holy.*

So, if something unclean touches these things after they have been anointed, instead of the things become defiled and unclean, the unclean thing becomes holy.

Something Greater Than the Temple is Here

So what does this say about the woman becoming clean and healed when she touched Yeshua? Well, listen to what Yeshua said.

Matthew 12:6 *But I say to you that something greater than the temple is here.*

What is Yeshua saying? What is greater than the Temple? Yeshua! He is saying that He, Himself, is greater than the Temple. So, if the things in the Temple caused what touched them to become holy. How much more does everything and every*one* who touches Yeshua become holy and healed and whole?

This is the radical difference that is important for all of us to grasp between the two covenants. Do you see it? It's a paradigm shift that happened between the two covenants and I don't believe we have grasped it fully. It is so different.

In another place Yeshua explains this. He was talking with a woman from Samaria. She was questioning Him about where God was to be worshiped, in Jerusalem or where the Samaritans worshiped.

John 4:21 *Yeshua said, "Lady, believe me, the time is coming when you will worship the Father neither on this mountain nor in Yerushalayim.*

I thought He commanded us in the Torah to worship Him in Jerusalem? Right? But He just said here that we won't worship Him in Jerusalem....

John 4:21:22-24 *You people don't know what you are worshipping; we worship what we do know, because salvation comes from the Jews. 23 But the time is coming—indeed, it's here now—when the true worshippers will worship the Father spiritually and truly, for these are the kind of people the Father wants worshipping him. 24 God is spirit; and worshippers must worship him spiritually and truly."*
(NKJV) *You worship what you do not know; we know what we worship, for salvation is of the Jews. 23 But the hour is coming, and now is, when the true worshipers will worship the Father in spirit and truth; for the Father is seeking such to worship Him. 24 God is Spirit, and those who worship Him must worship in spirit and truth.*

In the Tenakh (the Old Testament), God commanded that He be worshiped only in one place. People were not allowed to sacrifice or make offerings anywhere else but on the Temple mount in Jerusalem where He had said it was to be done, a physical location. But here Yeshua says someday people will worship the Father, not in Jerusalem, but in the Spirit, meaning there will be no physical location for Him to be worshiped. People will worship Him by being in Spirit and in Truth in any physical location.

Actually, that's why we can worship Him in synagogues and churches. Right? But we don't appreciate that that was a paradigm shift, that we don't have to go to Jerusalem. I know you all want to go to Jerusalem. I do too. But, we don't have to go to Jerusalem to worship the Father. They had to go to Jerusalem to worship because that's where the manifestation of His presence was. Where is that manifestation now? It's in us.

History tells us the Gospel went to all the world and the Father is being worshiped in all the world, rather than just in Jerusalem. So what changed? God put His Spirit that was in the Temple and in Yeshua in us! Even though He's not here in the flesh, He's here in the Spirit, in us which means we can worship the Father where ever we are.

I Corinthians 3:16 *Don't you know that you people are God's temple and that God's Spirit lives in you?*

We don't have to go to the Temple in Jerusalem. This is what we find hard to grasp, we're always in His presence.

Hallelujah! Yes, Big Hallelujah!

The same Spirit that healed unclean people—where is that Spirit? It's in you and it's in me. Yeshua told us this at end of the Great Commission.

Matthew 28:20 "And remember! I will be with you always, yes, even until the end of the age."

It also says that the same Spirit—the same power of the same Spirit that raised Yeshua from the dead, that's how powerful it is, and it is the Spirit that is in you.

Ephesians 1:19-20 (NKJV) *what is the exceeding greatness of His power toward us who believe, according to the working of His mighty power 20 which He worked in Christ when He raised Him from the dead and seated Him at His right hand in the heavenly places,*

So, with that same mighty powerful Spirit that raises from the dead in us, if we touch someone who has had a discharge, will we become unclean? Will it drive that Spirit out of us? No! The Spirit will not leave because we touched something that is unclean. Instead, our touching that person will make them clean if they receive that touch as being from the Lord.

This is Huge!

How is this possible? We are mortal. We are flesh. We have a carnal nature. We have iniquity. How is this possible for the Spirit of the living God to dwell in flesh? This is another huge miracle that we just sort of take for granted. The Spirit of God dwells in me! That's miraculous! Maybe not for you, but for me! I know me! I know how much of the flesh there is there!

How can the HOLY Spirit dwell in unholy us? Because He made us Holy by His sacrifice. This is the great power of His atonement. The atonement was not just to cover our sins, but to bear away our iniquity—to carry it away. To remove our transgressions—our intentional sins—as far as the east is from the west! Not to cover them. Why was that greater atonement needed? So that His Spirit could dwell in us, permanently. The same Spirit. Do you agree with me? This is a huge change.

When someone asks you "What is the difference between the Old Covenant and the New Covenant?" This is it! It is huge! It is a huge difference. It's a huge change that we don't fully appreciate. You see, God didn't change. His laws didn't change. He gave us His Spirit. He put His Spirit in us. It's what He did for us— HE enabled He Himself in the form of the Holy Spirit to dwell within us. That is what has changed.

Touch the Unclean and They Shall Be Healed

What did that paradigm shift enable? What change in history did that enable? What change did Yeshua command his talmidim, His disciples to do as He was about to leave them? What did He command us to do? " Go into (where?)... all the nations. Amongst all the unclean people, heal, deliver, and don't be afraid of becoming unclean when you go. They understood that. They understood that it was the Holy Spirit dwelling in them that enabled them to touch the unclean and make them clean.

This is why Yeshua's followers have gone to the sick and unclean to help them, for centuries. And we go without fear that we would become unclean, that we would be separated from God because we are going amongst unclean people. The disciples accepted this. Yeshua told them, "Touch the sick, lay hands on them. " That's a radical thing right there. Touch the sick. We just saw that. You become unclean if you touch the sick if they have some kind of a discharge.

We see evidence of this in the book of Acts chapter 5. Crowds gathered from the towns around Yerushalayim (Jerusalem) bringing the sick and those afflicted with unclean spirits and everyone of them was healed. It became so much a part of what they were doing because they believed this and they walked in it! They had so much Holy Spirit power that crowds were coming to be healed. Peter prayed and touched the crippled man in Acts chapter 3. He had no problem with it.

Thought Gentiles Too Unclean

But there was a problem, and this is where we get back to that religious spirit. If you read through the book of Acts, you will notice it. It is unmistakable in chapters 1 through 9. All the unclean people that the disciples went to and were touching were Jewish. They didn't go to all the nations. They didn't obey what the Lord had told them to do in the Great Commission for perhaps thirty years. I was wondering why.

The answer, I believe, is that there was a level of uncleanness amongst the Gentiles that they didn't have the faith to get over. After all, it wasn't about if they had a running sore or had a cold. Amongst the Gentiles, it was because they were worshiping other gods. They were sacrificing animals to other gods. They were eating the food of those sacrifices. Acts talks about temple prostitutes in these places all around the Roman Empire. "We're supposed to go to *those* people?" Those were the people we were told to execute if we found them in Israel, not to just stay away from them. Do you see the difference there?

The oral law, by this time, had created such a big fence around this law of God about the uncleanness that it forbade Jews from even entering the house of a Gentile. That's what Peter is referring to when he said in Acts 10:28 "It's just isn't done." I believe that the fence was built because of this religious spirit. "Oh, no! We can't go. We just can't go into these places where there might be uncleanness" This kept the Gospel from going to the Gentiles for decades after Yeshua rose from the dead.

Then we see in Acts chapter 10, God had to give Peter a special vision and speak to him three times in that vision saying, "GO! It's time to GO." Then it became a big topic of debate amongst the leaders of the Messianic movement. In Acts 15 they were saying, "Well, okay, so after they become followers of Yeshua, don't they have to start keeping all these laws, these cleanliness laws like us Jews? Otherwise we can't touch them."

Finally they decided that the Gentiles could become followers of Yeshua, that we Jews could have fellowship with them. But I believe it was because they had this same revelation. "How could these unclean Gentiles worship the Father? They couldn't come to the Temple, but that's okay. They didn't have to come to the Temple. They didn't have to because the Holy Spirit was in them, just like the Holy Spirit is in us."

Do you remember in Acts chapter 10, what the sign was that convinced the Jewish believers that the Gentiles had received the Lord? They spoke in tongues! That was evidence that the Holy Spirit had come upon them and was in them. Therefore the Messianic Jewish believers said, "Oh, the Holy Spirit is in them. We have to welcome them into the family." That was an awesome change—a paradigm shift in their thinking. I could stop right here and let you chew on this for awhile. But there is more.

The Religious Spirit Changed Tactics

After this time when the Gospel started going to the Gentiles, that old religious spirit didn't just give up! He changed his tactics, using the laws in the Torah. For the next 250 years, the people of God's Kingdom, the followers of Yeshua were a persecuted minority, both in Israel and in Rome. We read in the history of the Roman Empire where many believers were fed to the lions, burnt at the stake, all these things because they were a persecuted minority.

But around the year 325, if you know your history, there was a big change. The Roman emperor Constantine became a believer, supposedly, and he decided that Christianity should be the state religion of the Roman Empire. This was a second paradigm shift—another huge shift. Now because of this shift the Messianic believers had to adjust. Instead of being the persecuted minority, they were now the majority. They were in charge.

The religious spirit now had fertile ground for a new tactic. Now that believers in Yeshua were in charge of the government, here's the big $64,000 question. How are they to treat those who are not followers of Yeshua? Certainly they are to reach out, spread the Word, heal the sick, drive out demons. That was clearly to be done. That is all through Scripture. But what about those who refused to receive the Good News? How were they to treat them?

We know that power corrupts. Let's go back into the Tenakh and see what the Israelites did when they were in charge. What did they do? What did God command them to do? He told them to give the foreigners and unbelievers a chance to change and become like us. If they refuse, throw them out! Expel them from the land because they are defiling the land of God's people. That makes sense, right? It says it in the Old Testament all the way through.

That religious spirit used these Tenakh passages to show that Israel did this to deal with the infidels among them. But, who were the infidels? Who were considered the unclean amongst the faithful after the year 300 into the 1500s and 1600s? Who were those who refused to believe? The Jews! There were also others, of course. There were many true Christians who refused to submit to the Pope's authority during these times. There were other sects of people who refused to submit to that authority and what did the leaders of the faith do with them? They threw them out. They persecuted them. They expelled them. The leaders that were in power followed the prompting of this religious spirit and expelled all those who were not believing like they were. After the year 700, it included Moslems, Jews, and true believers.

This is how these supposed followers of Yeshua treated those of other faiths. The religious spirit was speaking in their ear. Give them a chance to convert, but if they refuse, expel them. Wipe them out, just like I commanded Israel. It was a little bit merciful because they were given the chance to convert. We see much flight during these times, certainly during the Inquisition when the Jewish people were being expelled from Spain. You had to either convert or you were expelled. They were also expelled from England. The Pilgrims were among the non Jews who were leaving England because they couldn't abide by what the church was teaching at that time. There were the Puritans also. This is the history not of the Kingdom of God, but of the kingdom of the religious spirit that ruled in this world for a very long time.

The Parable of the Wheat and Weeds

That is history. But what was God's plan? Did God not know that at some point, His followers would be in a majority and be in the government? Did He have a prescription for those who did not agree with them? He did and we're going to read it now. Yeshua gives us this in a parable. It's so important that He actually interprets the parable Himself.

Matthew 13:24-30 *"The Kingdom of Heaven is like a man who sowed good seed in his field; 25 but while people were sleeping, his enemy came and sowed weeds among the wheat, then went away. 26 When the wheat sprouted and formed heads of grain, the weeds also appeared. 27 The owner's servants came to him and said, `Sir didn't you sow good seed in your field? Where have the weeds come from?' 28 He answered, `An enemy has done this.' The servants asked him, `Then do you want us to go and pull them up?' 29 But he said, `No, because if you pull up the weeds, you might uproot some of the wheat at the same time. 30 Let them both grow together until the harvest; and at harvesttime I will tell the reapers to collect the weeds first and tie them in bundles to be burned, but to gather the wheat into my barn."*

This is so important that a few verses later, Yeshua interprets it for us.

Matthew 13: 36-43 *"Then he left the crowds and went into the house. His talmidim approached him and said, "Explain to us the parable of the weeds in the field." 37 He answered, "The one who sows the good seed is the Son of Man; 38 the field is the world. As for the good seed, these are the people who belong to the Kingdom; and the weeds are the people who belong to the Evil One. 39 The enemy who sows them is the Adversary, the harvest is the end of the age, and the harvesters are angels. 40 Just as the weeds are collected and burned up in the fire, so will it be at the end of the age. 41 The Son of Man will send forth his angels, and they will collect out of his Kingdom all the things that cause people to sin and all the people who are far from Torah; 42 and they will throw them into the fiery furnace, where people will wail and grind their teeth. 43 Then the righteous will shine forth like the sun in the Kingdom of their Father. Whoever has ears, let him hear!"*

Let the Weeds Grow

The weeds are people who belong to the evil one. What's the message to Yeshua's followers when they are in a position of power? Let the weeds grow. Let them continue in their ungodliness. Let them have access to soil, water, air, and sunlight. Let them have all the privileges in our society that we have. If you study the history of the church like we just did and the church's interaction with Judaism and with others in other places, the question is raised in my mind. Did they ever read this? How could they have read this and do what they did? There was one nation—Poland—that read it. Many people that are Jewish are here today because in the Middle Ages, Poland was a refuge for us. It changed later, though.

We need to be thankful to America's founding fathers who understood the parable of the wheat and the weeds. Do you realize that? It became the underlying principal of our first amendment. "Congress shall make no law concerning the establishment of a religion or prohibiting the free exercise thereof or abridging the freedom of speech or the press or the right of the people to peaceably assemble and to petition the government for a redress of grievances." Do you see the connection here? We are here today because our founding fathers read the parable of the wheat and the weeds and understood that this is what religious freedom is all about. We need to praise God for that.

But, I'm going to be a little politically incorrect here now. The founding fathers understood that this freedom had some limitations. I believe in our culture today many people don't understand that this freedom doesn't mean complete license, that there are some limitations. Let's go back to thinking about how we classify God's laws. There are the spiritual laws – how we interact with God. "You shall worship only the Lord your God—love Him with all your heart." There are the moral laws – how we interact with each other. "You shall not murder, you shall not steal, you shall not commit adultery." Then there are the Jewish laws—keep these days, keep these foods. So, the weeds would be those people who choose not to obey the spiritual laws of the Bible. In other words, they want to worship God in some other way than God has said in the Bible.

What is the first constitutional amendment saying? What does the parable of the wheat and weeds say? We should let them do that. Right? Do you notice the reason? Because we might root up some of the wheat. What does that mean? Two things. First, it means there might be some people who change. If we kill them off or expel them, they're not going to change. We need to give them a chance to change. Second, it will harm the wheat to be involved in persecution of the weeds. God's people will be injured physically or spiritually by participating in the evil of persecution.

Everyone Must Obey the Moral Laws

The thing that our culture misses, and it is so important to grasp this, is that even though we are to let people live without obeying the spiritual laws of the Bible, they must obey the moral laws of the Bible, because those moral laws became the laws of the land. People of another religion—just because they are from another religion—cannot steal, murder, lie, or commit adultery. That would be ridiculous. Also, they cannot sacrifice their children. They cannot torture animals. They cannot make noise at night and keep their neighbors awake. They can't have multiple wives. They can't keep slaves. Those are the moral laws of the land. These are the laws that govern how we interact as human beings.

However, everyone is free to worship God in any way they choose, even if it violates how we worship God. As long as they obey the moral laws, they can practice their religion. What if it gets even a little dicier than that? What about people who actually oppose what this Book teaches? Who should get up and say, "This is wrong." Who should get up and say, "This was not inspired by God. It's the work of men." There are all kinds of things like that. There is the spreading of heretical teachings. Are we to even allow that? What do you think? That's freedom of religion. That's the rest of that amendment. Freedom of Speech! Even if they are saying the wrong things!

Those Opposed to the Wheat and Weeds

But again, there are some limitations. We miss that sometimes. What if the person who is speaking and opposing the Bible speaks against the parable of the wheat and the weeds? What then? What if he says, "I want to get into power and I'm not going to let there be religious freedom." Do we just let him do that? No, of course not. There are some limitations. We have to oppose that, not in an unlawful way, but we have to oppose doing that. If they have a philosophy or a religious mandate to restrict religious freedom or freedom of the press, or freedom of speech once they get into power, we're not supposed to just let that happen. That's not according to what Yeshua was saying. That would be contradictory. That's ridiculous.

Who would do that? Can you think of any group that, if they got into power, would want to overturn the parable of the wheat and the weeds and the first amendment? In Israel there's a group called "Yad L'Achim." It's the Orthodox organization in Israel that persecutes and opposes Messianic Jews. There is a video on the internet—a documentary—titled, "What is behind Yad L'Achim?" They are inspired by a religious spirit, trying to keep Israel pure of Messianic Judaism which they view as an insidious, contaminating enemy. They see us as weeds. So, their way of getting rid of weeds is to "cut them down and get rid of them" which is just the opposite of what Yeshua is saying. This group is inspired by a religious spirit.

Can you think of any group in the United States that would want to overturn our freedoms? I was thinking of Islam. This is public knowledge that Islam's purpose is world domination. They want the whole world to be part of the Islamic Caliphate. The Caliphate means it would be an Islamic government. This is what is being set up in Iraq by the ISIS terrorist group. It is mixing religion with the government. This had already existed in Iran, in Pakistan, and a few other Middle Eastern countries.

Now if you were a good Koran believing Muslim, who would you think were the weeds? Followers of Yeshua would be. We are the infidels. How does Islam treat the infidels? They are slaughtered as ISIS has been doing. Or they are treated as second class citizens in terms of their rights before the law. They can be accused by another Muslim—one person—one witness. This is happening all the time in Pakistan and Iran and many other countries where speaking against Islam is punishable by death.

So, when the Caliphate exists over all the world, which is their goal, what will the situation be like? Will the first amendment be in place? Obviously not. So are we to just let that happen because we don't want to upset the weeds? No. Of course not. To summarize, we are directed to be tolerant of people who violate the spiritual laws of the Bible, but we must resist their attacks on religious freedom or the law of the wheat and the weeds. If their religion is teaching against the principle of the wheat and the weeds, they must be opposed. There is good reason behind the laws against hate speech—sometimes we oppose that because sometimes they are used to stop believers from speaking out about the laws of God. The original intent of the first amendment was to stop people from promoting religious intolerance. That opposition should involve any legal means necessary to prevent them from taking our religious freedom from us.

We Must Stand Firm

This also arises with other people from other belief systems and philosophies, when they're not just speaking out against religious freedom or against what the Bible teaches, but when they disagree with our moral laws and they make it difficult for us to live in a way that we're obeying our moral laws. For example, we are opposed to pornography. We don't want to see any pornography around, but those who disagree with our stand on pornography, who disagree with what God says about pornography, make it difficult for us by fighting in court to allow pornography to be in public places. They are claiming freedom of speech to do this. We must oppose those things because they are destroying the moral fabric, the moral teachings of the Bible. We allow them to practice freedom of religion, but not to destroy the Bible's moral teachings that we must obey. The problem is most Americans don't understand these principles, but you do now. It doesn't just apply to Muslims, and to religious groups, it also applies to pro-abortion groups who are trying to undermine what we believe is morally right to not murder innocent babies. It also applies to pro-homosexual groups. They are all pushing to have their moral laws, what they believe, to become the moral laws for our society.

Even in the light of the wheat and the weeds, we are not supposed to just sit back and let them take that over. We are supposed to oppose them because they are attempting to change, or have already changed, the basic moral code by which we live, which is the Bible. Yes, it also says we are allowed to have them live among us, but we have to stop them from trying to change and control us.

Let's pray

Father we thank You that You are kadosh, holy, separate from evil, and that way back in the time of Moses You taught Your people to separate themselves from evil and made a way for us to do that. You gave us the laws of ritual purity to enable Your presence to dwell among us in the Holy Temple in Jerusalem. Thank You for being willing to come and dwell in the midst of Your people. Thank You for also giving us Yom Kippur, the day when atonement was made for the entire nation to enable You to dwell in that Temple because even with the laws of ritual purity there would surely have been much un-cleanness in Israel. Help us to understand the special atonement that was made on Yom Kippur by the scapegoat, atonement for our iniquity that was not made at any other time.

We thank You that You are a God of paradigm shifts. Help us to see the great change You made when You gave us the New Covenant. We thank You that in the New Covenant You promised that You would dwell inside the hearts of Your followers, that You sent Your Ruakh HaKodesh to enable that miracle. Help us to see how amazing it is that You would dwell in the heart of a sinful human being. Help us to understand that a greater atonement had to be made to enable You to dwell in our hearts, than was made to enable You to dwell in the Temple. Thank

You for revealing that Yeshua fulfilled the scapegoat sacrifice, as predicted by the prophet Isaiah, by being bruised and dying for our iniquity so that You could dwell in our hearts. Give us a greater appreciation of the price Yeshua had to pay to atone for our iniquity, of the way He had to suffer.

Thank You that because You dwell in us we can worship You in Spirit and in Truth anywhere and anytime. Thank You that we can touch the unclean and not become unclean because of the power of Your Ruakh within us. Thank You for the power to heal the sick by the laying on of hands. Thank You that the ability to lay our hands on the sick without becoming unclean was a paradigm shift.

Thank You for moving upon Your Jewish disciples to cause them not to fear touching the unclean and not to fear forming relationships with Gentiles. Thank You that they brought the Good News to the Gentiles who received it with open hearts. Thank You that you directed Your Jewish disciples to welcome these believing Gentiles into the Body of Messiah without them having to live as Torah observant Jews.

Thank You for instructing us through the Parable of the Wheat and the Weeds on how to treat those who didn't receive the Good News. We repent for the many, many times Your people ignored the teaching of this parable and persecuted those who did not believe in Messiah, especially Your own Jewish people. We stand against the power of the religious spirit that caused this persecution in the past and is still trying to cause it today. Thank You that the Founding Fathers of America understood the parable. Give our leaders wisdom to apply this parable according to Your will. Preserve religious freedom in our land and prevent the abuse of the privilege of having religious freedom. In Yeshua's name.

Chapter 18

YOVEL

Before we learn what "Yovel" is, let's have a little humor. A wealthy man named Moishe died. At the reading of his will, everyone was waiting eagerly to see what they were going to get. The will said, "To my wife I give my house and 50 acres of land and a million dollars." It went on giving his children and siblings lots of wonderful things. Lastly it read, "And to my brother who always said health is better than wealth, I leave my sunlamp."

Well, the things we are learning about Yom Kippur are definitely better than wealth. In this chapter, we are going to learn about an amazing, beyond genius command from God. It is connected to Yom Kippur. It is the command to pronounce a Sabbath year on every seventh Yom Kippur, and a Yovel on every fiftieth Yom Kippur.

Leviticus 25 is about Yovel. You may not recognize that word. It's Hebrew for Jubilee. They got two of the letters right when they transliterated it into English. In Hebrew we pronounce it Yo-VEL.

This chapter in Leviticus has a very strong connection to the tenth commandment, which is "you shall not covet." It deals with God's way of dealing with human greed and covetousness.

I'm going to summarize a lot of the verses, but we will go into depth in some of them.

In verse 4, we have the command that every seventh year is a Shabbat, not for the people, but for the land, that there would be no planting and no reaping of crops during that whole seventh year until the eighth year.

Sabbath years are also called Shemitah years (pronounced Sh'meeta). It means "release" because on the last day all debts are supposed to be released (Deut. 15:1-2, 7-10). This is for monetary debts, not land debt. 2014-2015 was a Shemitah year. [Perhaps you have read Rabbi Jonathan Cahn's book, *The Mystery of the Shemitah.*] Remember that the seven-year cycle ends on the 49th year, the year before the Yovel or Jubilee year.

Leviticus 25:8-9 *You are to count seven Shabbats of years, seven times seven years, that is, forty-nine years. 9 Then, on the tenth day of the seventh month, on Yom-Kippur, you are to sound a blast on the shofar; you are to sound the shofar all through your land.*

Now, it's interesting to try to calculate which year is the year of Yovel. There is much disagreement on it, even among the sages. But it poses no problem in Israel today because Yovel has not been observed since the second Temple was destroyed. However, some people still try to calculate it. If it is based on Israeli events, you would think the year when Israel became a nation in 1948 would be a Jubilee year. Or should it be, as some say, the year Israel got control of Jerusalem and the Temple in 1967? Whatever year is actually the year of Yovel, we know that It starts on Yom Kippur.

Leviticus 25:10 *and you are to consecrate the fiftieth year, proclaiming freedom throughout the land to all its inhabitants. It will be a yovel for you; you will return everyone to the land he owns, and everyone is to return to his family.*

327

Do you know where that verse is written? Yes, on the Liberty Bell, "proclaim freedom throughout the land." We'll see the reason for this proclamation of freedom in a minute, but Yovel, the fiftieth year was to be in addition to the Shabbat years. So it was like a double Shabbat year those two years.

In verse 15-16, it speaks about returning to the land here. There really was never any sale of the ancestral lands. So, if you owned the lands that the people were given when they first conquered Israel, you never really sold them. You leased them to somebody for the number of years that were left up to the Yovel, the Jubilee, and then they came back to you.

Then in verses 20-22, the Lord promises to bless the sixth year so that the crop from the sixth year will last until the eighth year crop comes in. If you think about that for a minute, that means that in the sixth year, you are going to get enough crops to last for eighteen months because you're missing a whole year until the next year's crops come in. When you add in the Yovel, the Jubilee year—you have the Shabbat year on the 49th year and then the Jubilee on the 50th year. That crop from the 48th year actually has to last thirty months—almost three years! And that's exactly what God says in verse 21. He says He will bless the harvest from the 48th year for it to provide for three years.

Now, I just want you to grasp this. I know that there are many among us who struggle with taking a Shabbat once a week because they find it hard to say, "I'm not going to do anything. I'm just going to rest and to worship the Lord." They feel like they have to do something. They have to work at something. Can you imagine what it would be like to take a whole year off? You're a farmer. You've got to take the whole year off. And then every fifty years you have to take two years off. That would be tough! And it would take tremendous trust in the Lord—tremendous trust—to be able to do this.

Is the Sabbath Year Kept Today?

So, what has happened with this commandment? Well, here's how the seventh year is kept in Israel today. At the beginning of the seventh year, the Jewish farmer sells his land to a Gentile for a year. The Gentile farms the land with Gentile workers and the Jewish farmer gets paid! So, that's how it is in Israel.

And you can see their way of getting around the law. But you should also be aware that there is a significant movement called Sh'mittah. That's the way they spell the word. This movement in Israel today is encouraging taking the sabbatical year because of the belief that if they did, God would bless them—that there would be plenty. But, once again, not quite trusting in God, the organizers of the Sh'mittah movement come to Jewish people all around the world, especially the rich ones here in America, to try to raise funds to support the farmers during the seventh year when they don't farm. They're not trusting that God will provide in the sixth year for the farmers to do it.

Now some farmers have started to obey this command of God, and He is rewarding them. One vineyard's wine from the year after the sabbatical year won the European award for the best wine! So, that's where the plans are now for the sabbatical year. Someday I believe it's going to come back and actually going to be practiced.

Land Never Sold

Leviticus 25:23 *The land is not to be sold in perpetuity, because the land belongs to me—you are only foreigners and temporary residents with me*

This is an amazing verse in light of what's going on in Israel right now. There's talk about dividing up the land and about who owns the land. The Palestinians claim they own the land. Who owns the land? God!! He says right here He owns the land. This is the most powerful deed you could ever imagine to a piece of land. God Himself says, "I own the land and I am renting it—giving it—to the people Israel to take care of it."

So, because God owns the land, it never can be sold and it reverts back to the original owner in the 50th year.

Kinsman Redeemer

Leviticus 25:25 *That is, if one of you becomes poor and sells some of his property, his next-of-kin can come and buy back what his relative sold.*

So, even if it's not the fiftieth year, if I had to sell my land and my brother saw that I had to sell it because I was in dire straits financially, he could come in and without the new owner's permission, the new owner would have to sell back the land to him. He would redeem the land. This is where the whole idea of the kinsman redeemer came from that is discussed in the book of Ruth. The kinsman redeemer would come in and actually pay an amount for the land that varied according to how much time was left until Yovel, until Jubilee. If it was only two years you wouldn't pay much for it. But if it was 48 years, you would pay a lot for it. Essentially, God says you're paying for the number of crops you can grow on the land because the land is still Mine. You're just renting it.

Do Not Charge Interest

Leviticus 25:35-37   *If a member of your people has become poor, so that he can't support himself among you, you are to assist him as you would a foreigner or a temporary resident, so that he can continue living with you. 36 Do not charge him interest or otherwise profit from him, but fear your God, so that your brother can continue living with you. 37 Do not take interest when you loan him money or take a profit when you sell him food.*

This is another verse in this chapter that has had an enormous impact. I don't know if anybody can see it yet, but this instruction to have compassion on a brother going through hard times and specifically not to charge interest to your brethren had a huge impact on the church, on western civilization, and on Jewish history. What happened was that the church decided that people needed to obey this law and therefore a Christian could not loan money to another Christian. As you are aware, in Medieval times everybody was a member of the church, except the Jewish people, of course. So this meant that nobody could loan money to anybody else with interest. Well, if you don't allow anyone to earn interest on their money, people aren't going to want to loan money. So no one could get a loan. Then somebody realized, "Well, the Jewish people are not our brothers. They can't loan money to each other at interest, but they could loan money to us at interest." So, the history of this is that Jewish people were forced to become bankers for society. This was a mixed blessing. Many of our people greatly prospered in the banking industry. They didn't have any competition. That was great. But, if you are aware of Jewish history, you know that when things turned bad and the economy went into a tailspin, who got blamed? The bankers! So, it was a mixed blessing.

Slave to Lender

The thing to understand about all this is that it was different from our time. There were no such things as bankruptcy laws. Now, if you can't pay your debts, you just declare bankruptcy and the debt just goes away. They take what property you have, but they leave you some things. But in those days there was no such thing as that. So, if a person couldn't pay his debt, his property was taken. And if that didn't pay his debt, the person became a slave of the lender and he worked off what he owed.

So, in verses 39-41 there are commands to treat humanely fellow Israelites who get into that situation where they have to sell themselves into slavery. Then in verses 44-46, it's very interesting that the Torah actually allows Israelites to have foreign slaves. I've questioned God many times. "Lord, why didn't you just ban slavery at this time?" But the time was not right. And yet, this passage had a powerful impact on the thinking of our Judeo-Christian culture that eventually led to the abolition of slavery. When the Gospel went out to the Gentiles, what happened? They became grafted into Israel. And now, who could you take as a slave? The people in the nations were your brothers so you couldn't take them as slaves anymore. And so this eventually worked itself out, I believe, and had its effect on eliminating slavery in the world.

Redeeming a Slave

Verses 47-49 are instructions for redemption of Jewish slaves, those who had to sell themselves as slaves. If a person had to sell himself into slavery, his kinsmen, a brother, had a right to redeem him by paying the amount that his labor would be worth for the remaining number of years. And, of course, this is where the whole concept of Yeshua as our redeemer comes from, that idea of someone paying the price for someone else to be set free from slavery.

But if an Israelite sold himself into slavery, in the year of Yovel or Jubilee, he would go free even without someone paying the redemption price (Leviticus 25:40, 54).

Modern Economic Crises

So, now I would like to look at this chapter with a modern lens and ask the question of how this relates to us today. And I think you'll see after I share about it, that this chapter is incredibly timely for what the world is going through right now. Also, I think you will be able to see the wisdom of God. The wisdom that is in here is absolutely amazing.

When we study the history of the world, we find that the world has gone through a series of economic crises. In our own lifetime, we know of two of them. The ones that happened in 2008 and, of course, the Great Depression. But if you go back in history, you find that there were many, many of these that happened. Crashes and crises. Why did they happen? Well, back in 1929 people were allowed to buy stocks on credit. Then when the stock market began to go down, they couldn't cover the loans that they had taken and everything crashed.

What happened in 2008? People bought homes they couldn't afford on credit without any money down. They call it today toxic debt. And everything crashed. But this happened many more times throughout history. What's the cause?

The cause is always greed. Borrowing more than can be repaid. The motivation always comes out of a violation of the tenth commandment—covetousness. I want more. I want what someone else has. The symptom of this greed is taking risks. Taking financial risks that should not be taken.

Now I want you to realize that when you buy a stock or you invest in something, essentially you are loaning money to that institution. If I buy a stock, I'm loaning money to that company. If I put my money in a bank, I am loaning that money to the bank to use to invest in other things and they pay me some interest for it. So, when we do that, what is the risk? The risky part of it is always lending the money without there being sufficient collateral.

Collateral

Collateral is something you would get if the person isn't able to pay back their loan. So today what kinds of loans do we have that have collateral? Mortgages! There's another one. Car loans. There's a hard, physical object there, the land, the house, the car. If you default on being able to pay, the lender gets that back. So there's a lower level of risk. But we also have in our society loans that are made totally without collateral. What are they? Credit cards!! There's no collateral at all. And they're all over the place!

God's Financial System

Now, God knows the danger of greediness and He knows that we as human beings—it's so amazing how He knows us—that we can't resist the temptation to get in, as we say, over our heads—to get into debt more than we can afford. We think, "Oh, I can pay on this." And then something happens and some other expense comes up and then we realize, "Oh, I can't make that payment anymore." So, God knows this. And He has a financial system that is in this chapter that caused Israel in Biblical times to avoid financial crisis. When you read all through the history of Israel during Biblical times—you don't find anything about there being great financial crises. Let me show you why. There are three pieces of wisdom in this chapter concerning finances. The first Biblical wisdom—it's almost like it's assumed in here—you never lend money without collateral. It's just all through the Bible. There's always something that's given. If you lend somebody money, you take his coat as collateral. Or it's himself. He's going to pay it back by working.

Do you know what caused the 2008 crisis? They were called subprime mortgages. Lenders were lending money out at below the interest prime rate. The home was the collateral, but then the value of the homes started to drop and they no longer had the collateral when people couldn't make their payments. The whole bottom dropped out on this. And of course, it was the same with the credit cards. When people couldn't make their payments, banks lost millions of dollars. And many of them as we've seen had to go bankrupt which is our way of getting out of debt.

God's Mortgage System

Second amazing wisdom in here is that at the Yovel, the Jubilee, all the land reverted back to the original owning family. So land was able to be bought only for a period of time. So what did this do? This kept the land in the hands of the children of Israel. This was God's intent. He wanted Israel to be a nation before Him. And He knew that if he left them on their own, they'd sell off their land and buy other things, and pretty soon they would be dissipated among the nations. Instead every fifty years the land went back to the original owners and everyone came back to the land.

God's Debt Limit

The third one is this. Through the Yovel instructions, God limited the amount of debt that people could run up. Let me show you how this works. If I was the owner of some ancestral property that came to me because my ancestors fought with Joshua and conquered the land, and I decided that I would sell my land. Well, the amount I could sell it for would depend on how many years were left until the year of Jubilee. So, I couldn't get a very high price for it if the year of Jubilee was near.

Now, suppose I wanted to buy land. I see that my friend, Mark, has some land to sell. So I go to the bank and I ask for a mortgage. The bank says well, the Jubilee year is near when that land will go back to Mark no matter what. So we're only going to give you a mortgage that will be paid off by the time Mark gets the land back. So, we're not going to give you a real big mortgage. The amount of money that you could borrow would be limited.

If I borrowed money and didn't have the land anymore and couldn't repay, I'd have to work as a slave to pay that lender off. That's how the system worked. But once again, because everybody was set free on Jubilee, how much I was worth as a slave would only be according to how many years were left until Jubilee. So, it wouldn't be that much if, let's say, there were only four years left until Jubilee. So, it would be four years of your labor. I'll only give you that much money and no more.

Debts Cleared

So, what happened was every fifty years, all the land debts would be paid off. Everyone knew everything was going to go back to the way it was fifty years ago, every fifty years. The whole society would start all over again and would be debt free. Can you imagine how different that would be from what it is today? Every fifty years all mortgages would be cleared. Every seven years all other debts were released. It wasn't that lenders would lose money because they knew that was going to happen so they structured all loans so they would be paid off in seven or fifty years. When the fiftieth year came all debts and mortgages would be paid up. There would be no more debts!

So, here's what's going to happen. I'm going to start a political party that's going to nominate a candidate that's going to run on this platform. We're going to start having the Jubilee year. Want to join me? I think it would be amazing. It would solve the world's economic problems because the run away debt which causes all the economic problems: inflation, bankruptcy, poverty, recessions, turmoil, and wars would be gone. All those things wouldn't happen because everything gets reset every fifty years. Everybody goes back to no debt. Amazing wisdom of God! Do you see the wisdom in there? It's also amazing how well He knows us! I mean, He knows that we get into this kind of trouble, so He designed this wonderful system.

The Spiritual Application of Yovel

So, that's the financial application of this. Now, let's look at the spiritual application of Jubilee. We don't have to really search to find the application because Yeshua Himself made an application of what Yovel is all about. We find it in Luke when He was in His own home synagogue in Nazareth and He was called forth to read from the book of Isaiah and He opened up to chapter 61. Some of this is very familiar, but this is what He read.

Luke 4:18-19 *"The Spirit of ADONAI is upon me; therefore he has anointed me to announce Good News to the poor; he has sent me to proclaim freedom for the imprisoned and renewed sight for the blind, to release those who have been crushed, 19 to proclaim a year of the favor of ADONAI."*

Isaiah 61: 1-2 *The Spirit of Adonai ELOHIM is upon me, because ADONAI has anointed me to announce good news to the poor. He has sent me to heal the brokenhearted; to proclaim freedom to the captives, to let out into light those bound in the dark; 2 to proclaim the year of the favor of ADONAI*

Now that phrase "the year of the favor of ADONAI" means the Jubilee. So Yeshua was saying, "I am proclaiming to you that there is now coming a year of Jubilee. And then He says this.

Luke 4:20-21 *After closing the scroll and returning it to the shammash, he sat down; and the eyes of everyone in the synagogue were fixed on him. 21 He started to speak to them: "Today, as you heard it read, this passage of the Tanakh was fulfilled!"*

And, of course, if you remember the story, they got upset with Him about this. But what His application was, was this: That the Kingdom of God—of the New Covenant—that Yeshua was bringing, it brings Jubilee. It brings the Yovel. It IS a Yovel. Here's what I felt led to do by the Spirit. We really can't appreciate what that means unless we grasp in our feelings and our emotions of what it would've been like to live in a culture like I just described—every fifty years having Yovel.

The Yovel Experience

So, I want to just kind of tell a story here and I want you to use your imagination. Try to be this person and imagine what it would've been like to experience the Yovel. The point is, Yeshua is saying that's what it's like to enter the Kingdom of God. It's like the year of Jubilee. Are you following me? So, here's the story.

Imagine that your grandfather fought with Joshua. He was one of those soldiers that came in and took the land of Canaan. And he was given a piece of that conquered land—a large tract—a large piece of land. He built a house and farmed that land. Understand that in those days, land meant everything. There weren't any factories. There weren't any offices. There was just land! Everybody farmed the land or they raised sheep. That was it. Well, there were other people that did other trades, but everything was based on the farming. They were an agricultural society.

Now, this grandfather of yours passed that land down when he died to your father and your uncles who were your father's brothers. They divided it up. And, if you understand the way it was in the Bible, the eldest got a double portion, but the others also got a portion, too. So, they each got their part of the land and it still would've been a big chunk of land. Each of your father's brothers and your father built a house on their portion and they farmed that land. And you, whether you're a man or a woman, you grew up in that culture. You grew up on that piece of land.

And what did you have? You had a piece of land, but more than that. You had an extended family that lived right around you. And you grew up playing with your cousins. You were taught by your uncles and aunts. You rejoiced together at births and bar mitzvahs, and weddings. And you mourned together at funerals. And you always had help. Can you imagine that? Anything that went wrong, you always had someone who could help because you had family all around. If you needed help caring for the kids; if you needed help to build on the house; if you needed help bringing in the harvest; if someone was sick, there were always cousins, aunts and uncles, nieces and nephews—everybody around to come and help you.

So, you grew up in this culture. It sounds pretty good, doesn't it? So, you grew up and then the land was passed down to you! It was divided up a little more, but there was still plenty enough for each family. You built and you farmed and you all remained close. All your cousins had their own farms around you and they had their children. You all helped each other. So, another generation was growing up in this culture. The word in Hebrew is "mishpokhah" which means "clan." It means more than "family." It means "extended family."

So, that's great! This is where you're living. This is wonderful, but you had a little taste for the extravagant and you made some purchases that were a little bit beyond your means and you got into some financial trouble. You had a couple years where the harvest wasn't so great while you were trying to live a lifestyle beyond your means. So, you had to go into debt. And that was okay. You made the payments. But your land was the collateral. The piece of land you inherited was the collateral. And then you found you couldn't make the payments anymore. So, what happened? You had to give up the land. You had to sell it to someone to pay your debt. You had to move. It seems like there wasn't anybody in your family who could redeem the land for you. There just wasn't anybody. They were living beyond their means, too, so they didn't have any extra. So nobody did that for you. Some of them—your brothers and cousins and uncles— they had the same thing happen. They had to sell their land, too.

So, you moved to a far off city, got a job working for some- body else and lived in a rented house. Not only didn't you have your house and land, but just imagine, you no longer had that mishpokhah. You no longer had that extended family. In fact, you didn't even know what was happening with your family because you were working so hard. You know transportation costs a lot of money. You couldn't go back and visit. They didn't have cell phones or Facebook. They didn't have any way of knowing what was going on.

So, you continued to have these financial problems. You got into more debt. Without the land as collateral, you, yourself, were the collateral now. Then you couldn't pay your debts, so you had to sell yourself into slavery. Now, not only you but this includes your wife and your children. You are all slaves. And you're slaves to the person who loaned you the money. And he treats you like a slave! This is not so great. Now, you will never get to see your extended family for sure. You're now living a very different life from the way you were brought up. And you live like this for many years. There's no way out. You're a slave! You're not even making any money! What you're doing is you are working off your debt. So, whatever you make in labor goes to pay the debt off.

Then the year of Jubilee comes—the year of Yovel. The shofar is sounded on Yom Kippur and here is what happens. You, your family, every other Israelite that's a slave gets up, walks out, goes back to that ancestral property—that mansion—that land and it's yours again—totally free and clear!! No mortgage! No debt! Nothing! All your debts have gone to zero.

Now, more than that, you get there. You are just rejoicing. I've got my house back! I've got my land again! Then you start seeing other people returning. Your brothers! Your cousins! Your uncles! Your aunts! They're coming back, too! They lost their land and sold themselves into slavery, too! And they're all coming back now. Can you imagine what that would be like? Can you imagine the reunion? The catching up?! The hugs?! The JOY?!!! You see what I'm saying? We really don't grasp what Yovel is until we think about what that would've been like. It would've been the most wonderful experience. I mean, I would almost go into slavery just to experience that joy! This is why it was the year of the Lord's favor!

Now, here's the other side of this. Nobody lost money in this deal! The lenders didn't lose any money because when they made a business deal, they made that deal based on the fact that this was going to happen. So, everybody won! There were no people saying, "Oh, that's great for you, but I just lost my shirt." Everybody won. Everybody had joy!

Yeshua Fulfilled Yovel

And Yeshua says that when He came, this was fulfilled. See, you don't grasp it until you realize what it is. But what is it? How is it fulfilled? Well, first of all, when we enter the Kingdom of God—when we enter by the New Covenant, by receiving Yeshua as Messiah, receiving His atoning sacrifice and we make Him Lord of our lives—He becomes what? Our Redeemer! So, He is our kinsman redeemer. He pays the price and He takes us out of slavery. Slavery to what? To sin and to ha-satan! All the ways that ha-satan can manipulate us and torment us! Our debt, though, our debt to God for our sins, that's paid! It's totally wiped out. It's as if Jubilee had come because He came.

In addition to that, as many of us have experienced, as we walk with the Lord and as we appropriate the power of the Spirit, we begin to break those bondages that the enemy has put on us, those ha-satanic things that have held us back. Sometimes we don't even know they're there, but over time God reveals them and helps us break those bondages.

So, that's the first, awesome part of why it's like Yovel. But it's more than that. Here's what I think many of us miss. When we get grafted in, when we come into the Kingdom, here's what happens. We get grafted into the olive tree which is Israel. If we are Jewish, we get grafted back in. If we're Gentile, we get grafted in for the first time. So, we're grafted into this olive tree which is the faithful Israel—God's people. It's the Kingdom of God, Jews and Gentiles who are trusting in Yeshua together. We get grafted into that. And we become children of God. Yeshua says this. We become part of God's extended family! We're like adopted children in this extended family with all the rights and all the privileges and responsibilities of family members. We have the responsibility to care for each other and the property. We have the rights of His Name and of the power that He gives us. All of those things become ours when we are adopted into the family.

Our Inheritance

And we receive an inheritance! What's our inheritance? Well, I know when I came into the Kingdom, everything that I owned became part of the Kingdom of God. "It was mine, but now it's yours, Lord." It's now God's. But we also have a joint inheritance. What's our joint inheritance? Your congregation's building is. It's something that's part of this family. It's a part of the physical inheritance and we take care of it. It's all part of the fulfilling of the Yovel. And then there is the inheritance promised us in heaven. The Lord told us we all have mansions waiting for us.

The most important part of the Yovel, let's appreciate it, is that we become part of an extended family a mishpokhah, part of a clan. Now, some of us had extended family. We grew up that way as children, with siblings and aunts and uncles. How many of you had a good extended family as children? How many had a bad extended family? How about in between? Mine was kind of in between. Sometimes our extended families are so messed up that it's more a curse than a blessing. But it's supposed to be a blessing.

Now, my family was somewhere in between. Sometimes it was a blessing. Sometimes I could do without it. It was enough of a dysfunctional family, that I remember before I found Yeshua, I searched for that loving extended family. I joined clubs. I joined a fraternity in college. I joined political parties. I joined athletic teams. All of those seemingly for a purpose, but now I know it was really because I wanted that friendship that comes when you're doing something together, when you're part of a group like that. I don't know about you, but every one of those groups disappointed me. Every one of those things let me down.

There were times when I didn't experience the acceptance I was looking for, when I didn't experience the forgiveness or the love I wanted. The biggest thing was, there were times when my values didn't agree with the rest of the group's values. And my goals didn't agree with the rest of the group's goals. So, there was always this conflict. And I remember when I found the Lord, immediately I was brought into a khavarah group (small group) meeting in a home next door to us. We met there once a week and it became my spiritual family. I remember, I sat there the first few times thinking this is what I've been looking for! This is what I've been searching for—this kind of extended family fellowship. This is what I've longed for all my life! It's so good! So, really, I experienced Yovel right in that first week that I came into the Kingdom! And I began to seek out that fellowship wherever we went, when we moved or went to a different congregation, etc. We always sought that out. For the past 30 years, this congregation, Shema Yisrael in Rochester, has been my mishpokhah— my extended family! That's part of the Yovel.

And I've come to realize more and more in the last few years how significance this is. I think part of it is that we've had life cycle events—many of them in the last few years. We've had eight births. Each one is such a joy. We've also had seven weddings. But we've also had seven deaths. Those are sad, but they are still family. We're still in it together.

My biological family is very small. I'm an only child and my cousins are scattered. Most of my aunts and uncles are deceased. So, this family has become so much more to me. I know many of you have experienced that Yovel benefit of mishpokhah. But I know that for some of you it sounds weird because you've never realized that the Kingdom of God isn't about just a relationship between you and the Lord. It's also about you being plugged in and being part of the family. They are both very important. Being in relationship with the Lord is absolutely necessary, but being part of the family is also very, very important. I think many of you don't realize that this is part of the Kingdom of God. You've entered into the New Covenant, but you haven't seen how much that involves being part of the family.

Let me just clarify a little bit because the analogy of the Yovel breaks down a little bit. When you come into the Kingdom of God, it's really not a reunion because you don't know all the folks. It's more like, if you go back to that story that I told, imagine that you were a young child when that happened. So, you grew up in slavery. You didn't know any of that extended family. Then, when the year of Jubilee came and the whole family went back, you came back to this place and there are all these uncles and aunts and cousins. You're meeting them all for the first time. I mean it could be a little scary if you're not used to this. But the thing is, though it takes time, eventually you become part of that family. It's not instantaneous. It's a slow process. You've got to get to know people. People have to get to know you. That's why we gather together.

I'm always so thrilled with my Messianic Judaism class. I get such a kick out of it. The class basically ends at 9 pm. We don't get out until 10 pm, and even then I have to kind of push people out the door because they are all talking to each other, not just to me, but to each other. That's the thrill about it. They have grown close enough to see each other as mishpokhah and they don't want to leave! We also have khavarah groups. "khavarah" means "fellowship." That's the purpose of those groups. You can't stay in my Messianic Judaism class forever. Some people have tried! We hope to create that same atmosphere in the khavarah groups, so that people will feel welcome and at home.

Why does this work in congregations and not in political parties, companies and teams and so forth? Well, it's very simple. We have the Spirit of God here and we have the Love of God. And the Spirit and Love of God say this is what we are supposed to be doing. And we have shared values and goals. So, those conflicts don't happen because we are all heading in the same direction. We are all seeking the Lord for what we are supposed to be doing. We're all here because we're called to what God has called this congregation to do. And so this extended family lasts and doesn't disappoint like other organizations can. So, are there dysfunctional parts to our mishpokhah here? Yes, there are!! I know in the last several months we've had several disputes amongst people. We've prayed and I've tried to help settle them. But that's just like family! It really is. What happened in your family when brother and sister started to fight each other? You know, Dad had to step in and settle it. So, I try to settle those things. I'm not always successful, but I try to do what I can to get people reconciled.

There's also another thing that happens in a family. The mom gets pregnant and a new baby is born. The other kids ages range up to eight years old and suddenly there's this new baby. All the attention goes to this new baby. And what do the older kids do? They get jealous! Yea! So, there's also this tendency with people in a congregation to say, you know, I don't know if I want more people. Things are fine the way they are. Of course, we have to fight that because the Kingdom of God is an ever-expanding Kingdom. Part of what we're called to do by the Lord is to welcome new people in. So, I just exhort you to do that. We need to be welcoming new people into the Kingdom. We need to help the people get welcomed in—not just by saying hi, how are you, but by making good friends and helping them find the place where they can be plugged in, where they can serve, where they can do their part, where they can feel fulfilled and bear fruit—all those things. Those things are hard to do, so we need to pray and do our part.

That's the application Yeshua was making. The Kingdom of God is a Yovel. And we should be expecting that. If you haven't experienced that, you're missing your inheritance. It's what God intended for you.

So, let's pray

We'll start by praying about the financial side.

Father, I know that there are many people who are struggling financially because they have gotten themselves over their heads in debt. We pray right now, Father, for You to do a miracle to set them free from debt, to show them a way to pay it off, and to clear all of those debts. Father, we also pray for all of us for the wisdom for us to not get in over our heads; to know how to live within our means and to not take those risks. And Lord, we're also amazed at the level of trust that You expected from Your people to take a whole year off for Shabbat and then every fifty years to take two years off. So, we pray, Lord, that You would increase our trust in You, even to take Shabbat off and to bring it to you as Yours.

We see also in this passage, Lord, that the land is Yours. And we pray, for our president, that that understanding would come to his mind. The Land of Israel is Yours, O God, and You have given it to a certain people, not because we are any better than anybody other people, but just because it was in Your purpose to do this—not for any other reason.

And Father, we pray for our nation, and for the world financial situation right now. We see what incredible wisdom You had for people, and we pray that You bring that wisdom to this world, O God.

Then Lord, we thank You for being our kinsman Redeemer. We thank You that You redeemed us from our debt of sin. You paid the price with Your tremendous suffering to make that atonement. We also thank You that the power of Your Spirit promises us that every bondage can be broken. Every way in which the enemy has a hold on us can be broken.

Finally, Lord, we ask that each of us would receive that promise of mishpokhah, of extended family. Father, we are Your mishpokhah. You created us. You called us to be Your children. We are Your extended family. We pray that each one that hasn't been fully connected into the family, that You would do a miracle and draw them into a good, faithful group. We pray also that each of us that does feel connected, that we would be able to welcome others in, that our hearts would be enlarged to do that, O Lord. And we pray, Father, that we would be family for each other, that we would be helpers, that we would stand with each other, that we would pray for each other, that we would do all that is needed to help each other.

We commit all these things to you in the mighty Name of Yeshua.

Aaronic Blessing:

יְבָרֶכְךָ יְהוָה וְיִשְׁמְרֶךָ׃

יָאֵר יְהוָה פָּנָיו אֵלֶיךָ וִיחֻנֶּךָּ׃

יִשָּׂא יְהוָה פָּנָיו אֵלֶיךָ

וְיָשֵׂם לְךָ שָׁלוֹם׃

Yee-va-re-kh'-kha Adonai v'-yish-m'-re-kha;
ya-er Adonai pa-nav a-le-kha vi-khu-ne-ka;
yee-sa Adonai pa-nav a-lekha.
v'ya-sem-lekha Shalom.

May the Lord bless you and keep you
May the Lord lift up His face unto you,
and be gracious unto you.
May the Lord lift up His countenance upon you
and give you Shalom.
In the Name of Yeshua our Messiah.
Amen.

Pronunciation Key

' (an apostrophe) - a very short vowel called a guttural stop

ai - pronounced like "igh" in light.

ei - pronounced between "eh" and "ay"

i - "ee"

kh - a guttural sound pronounced like the "ch" in Bach
    (Spelled "ch" in most sources.)

Glossary

[Key: term (Strong's number) - *actual meaning;* English equivalent]
(All terms are Hebrew unless otherwise noted.)
[Some spellings are different from the Complete Jewish Bible (CJB) for pronunciation clarity.]
(In Hebrew, adjectives are placed *after* the nouns they modify.)
(Plural Hebrew words end in -im or -ot, not in -s or -es.)
(Page numbers indicate where the term is introduced or explained or important, not every place it is used.)

avodah (pronounced ah-voh-DAH) *work*
avone (H5771) - *inclination to evil;* iniquity (p. 58, 235)
Al Chet - *for sin;* short for: "for the sin which we have committed"; the list of sins read as confession on Yom Kippur (Pronounced "Ahl Khet") (pp. 14, 17, 41)
anah (H6031) - *to afflict, to chasten* [or] ... *to humble one's self* (p. 263)
Aseret Yemei T'shuvah - *Ten Days of Repentance;* what the ten days between Rosh Hashanah and Yom Kippur are sometimes called (p. 40, 283)
Avraham - *father of a multitude;* Abraham

Barukh Haba B'Shem, Adonai - *Blessed is He who comes in the name of the Lord* (p. 157)
BCE - Before the Common Era (same as B.C.)
b'rit - *covenant*
B'rit Hadashah - *New Covenant;* New Testament
b'rit milah - *covenant of circumcision*

CE - Common Era (same as A.D.)
chet (pronounced "khet") (H2399) - *sin*
cohane - *priest* (singular noun) (spelled "cohen" in CJB)
Cohane HaGadol - *The High Priest*
cohanim - *priests* (plural of "cohane")

Diaspora - (Greek) *dispersion;* referring to the history of the Jewish people being banished from Israel and scattered

348

among the nations (p. 18)

Elul (Aramaic) - *search;* the Hebrew month before Feast of Trumpets and Yom Kippur (p. 40)

erev - *evening or eve* (as in New Year's *eve)*

ezkhar - *I will remember* (p. 93) (Modern: ez-eh-khehr)

Ger - A Gentile who has chosen to live among the Children of Israel like Ruth did.

Ger Mishikhi - *Anointed Ger* (singular noun and adjective); A Messianic Gentile who has chosen to worship and fellowship with Messianic Jewish people.

Gerim - (plural of Ger) Gentiles who have chosen to live among the Children of Israel.

Gerim Mishikhim - *Anointed Gerim* (plural of Ger Mishikhi); Messianic Gentiles who have chosen to live and worship among the Messianic Jewish people. (This term solves the problem of wondering what to call Gentiles who join the Messianic Movement aside from calling them "Ruths.") (p. 20-21, 74)

Goy - *nation;* Gentile

Goyim - *nations* (plural of Goy); Gentiles

ha - *the*

hamartia (Greek, G266) - *sin* (p. 64)

HaMashiakh - *The Anointed One;* The Messiah

ha satan - *the adversary;* satan

Henani - Here I am (pronounced: hee-nay-nee)

kadosh – *holy, separate*

kippa - *covering;* cap worn by Jewish men

khatahah - *missing the mark;* unintentional sin (p. 36-37, 58, 293)

khavarah - *fellowship, friend* (p. 342-3)

khet (or chet) (H2399) - *sin*

kol (H3605, H6963) - *all; the whole; voice*

L'shanah Tovah Tikkah Tevu - *May your name be inscribed to a good year;* Rosh Hashanah greeting (p. 40)

L'shanah Tovah Tikkah Tevu v'Tikkah Temu - *May your name be inscribed and sealed for a good year;* Yom Kippur greeting (p. 40)

L'vi'im - Levites

lev - *heart*

lo - *no*

Lo ezkhar od - remember no more (p. 92)
Mashiakh (H4899) - *anointed one;* Messiah
mitzvah - *commandment*
mitzvot - *commandments* (plural of mitzvah)
Moad (H4150) - *Appointed Time* (p. 16)
Moadim - *Appointed Times* (plural of Moad) (p. 15)
mikveh - ritual bath place (p. 312)
Mishikhi - *anointed* (singular adjective) Messianic
Mishikhim - *anointed* (plural of adjective Mishikhi) Messianic
Mishna - the collections of the Jewish oral traditions (p. 40)
Moshe - Moses

od - *more*

Parasha - weekly readings from the Torah
Parush - Pharisee
Pesakh (H6453) - *Passover* (p. 15)
P'rushim - Pharisees (plural of Parush)
pasha - *to transgress or rebel* (verb form of pesha)
pesha (H6588) - *intentional sin* (noun); transgression
                      (pp. 36, 58, 235)

Rabbi Sha'ul - Rabbi - *honored one;* Sha'ul (H7586) *desired;*
      asked for. Rabbi or Apostle Paul [Jewish Believers in his
      day would have addressed him as Rabbi. Paul is the Greek
      translation of Sha'ul (Saul).]
rhema (Greek) - *an utterance; thing said;* the spoken Word of
      God; a personal Word from God (p. 167)
Rosh Hashanah - *Head of the Year;* Biblical holiday: Feast of
      Trumpets
Ruakh HaKodesh (H7307, H6944) - *The Holy Spirit*

Shavuot (H7620) - *weeks, Feast of Weeks;* Biblical holiday,
      Pentecost (p. 15)
Slikhot - *forgivenesses;* (also spelled selichot); repentant
      prayers traditionally recited during the days preceding Rosh
      Hashanah and the Ten Days of Awe (p. 14,17,41)
Shabbat (H7676, from H7673) - *to cease, to rest;* Sabbath
Shabbaton (H7677) - *Sabbath; a day of rest* (p. 16)
shabbaton zih-kh'ron teru'ah - a Sabbath of remembrance with
      the blowing of the Shofar and shouting for joy (The Biblical
      description of Rosh Hashanah/Feast of Trumpets) (p. 16)

350

Shalom (H7965) - *completeness, wholeness, well being, peace,* (and much more*)*
Shalu - *pray*
Shalu Shalom Yerushalayim - *Pray for the peace (wholeness) of Jerusalem;* (also the title of a song) (p.157)
Sha'ul (H7586) - *desired; asked for,* Saul [Paul is the Greek translation of Sha'ul (Saul).]
Shofar (H7782) - *ram's horn trumpet* (detailed explanation in the book, *Yom Teruah,)*
Shofarot - (plural of Shofar)
S'udat Adonai -*The Lord's Supper;* Communion (p. 129)
sukkah - *booth; tent; tabernacle*
Sukkot (also spelled Sukkoth) (plural of sukkah) - Biblical holiday, Feast of Tabernacles (p.15)

Talmid - *study;* the name of the traditional Jewish Commentary on Scripture
talmidim - *students, disciples* (p. 144)
Tanakh - Old Testament (also called the Old Covenant) or sometimes refers to the whole Bible.
Tashlikh (imperfect tense of H7993) - *casting off;* the tradition of casting bread on flowing water on Rosh Hashanah (pp. 82-83)
Teruah (H8643) - *sounding the Shofar and shouting for joy*
Torah (H3384) - *instruction, law;* what God gave on Mt. Sinai; refers to the Five Books of Moses, sometimes to the whole Old Testament
T'shuvah (a form of H7725) - *to return, turn back, restore;* repentance (introduced on p.)
Tikkah Tevu - *may your name be inscribed* (p. 40)
Tikkah Temu - *may your name be sealed* (p. 40)
Tishri - *beginning;* seventh month in the Jewish calendar in which Rosh Hashanah and Yom Kippur occur

v' - *and*

Ya'akov - Jacob, James
Yarden - Jordan
Yericho - Jericho
Yerushalayim - Jerusalem
Yeshua - *He will save;* Jesus
Yeshua Ha Mashiakh - *Yeshua, the Anointed One;* Jesus, the

Messiah

Yetzer Ra - evil inclination (p. 59)

Y'hoshua - Joshua

Y'hudah - *God praiser;* Judah

Y'hudi - *a God praiser* (noun); Jew

Y'hudim - *God praisers* (plural of Y'hudi); Jews

Y'hudi Mishikhi - *Anointed God Praiser* (singular noun and adjective); Messianic Jewish person, called this because of embracing Yeshua (Jesus) as the Messiah

Y'hudim Mishikhim - *Anointed God Praisers* (plural of Yehudi Mishikhi); Messianic Jewish people, called this because of embracing Yeshua (Jesus) as the Messiah (p. 20, 22)

Yitz'khak - Isaac (also spelled Yitz'chak)

yom - *day*

Yom HaShoah - *Day of Calamity;* Holocaust Remembrance Day

Yom Kippur - *Day of Atonement*

Yomim Nora'im - *Days of Awe* (also spelled Yomim Norim)

Yonah - Jonah

Yovel - Jubilee (pronounced Yo-VEL) (p. 326)

yud - *"y"* the smallest letter of the Hebrew alphabet (pp. 18, 254)

za-khar - remember (root word)

zih-kh'ron - *memorial* (pronounced zee-khrone)

Zih-kh'ron Teruah - *Memorial for sounding of the Shofar and shouting for joy* (pp. 16, 283)

Thank you for reading this *Yom Kippur* devotional study. If it has blessed you in any way, I would appreciate your taking a moment to write a review on Amazon, as well as on other sites like Barnes and Noble, Christian Book, and in social media. This will greatly help me in getting the exposure this book needs. For example, at this writing Amazon has the policy that if I get 50 reviews on my book's Amazon page, then when a customer buys a similar book, Amazon will say, "Customers who bought this item also bought..." and will include *Yom Kippur* in the list.

If you send the links to your reviews (just copy and paste the addresses from the browser) to my publisher (olivepressbooks@gmail.com), we would like to thank you with a free gift (perhaps some bonus material or perhaps a special discount).

I am grateful to have you join me in encouraging others to dig deep into God's Moadim (Appointed Times) to find out the personal depth of meaning for their lives.

– Rabbi Jim

YOM KIPPUR

is available at:

olivepresspublisher.com

amazon.com

barnesandnoble.com

christianbook.com

deepershopping.com

and other online stores

Store managers:

Order wholesale through:

Ingram Book Company or

Spring Arbor

or by emailing:

olivepressbooks@gmail.com

www.ingramcontent.com/pod-product-compliance
Lightning Source LLC
Chambersburg PA
CBHW060039100426
42742CB00014B/2637